D1488711

Other books by Lenn E. Goodman:

Islamic Humanism, Oxford University Press, 2003

In Defense of Truth: A Pluralistic Approach, Humanity Press, 2001

Jewish and Islamic Philosophy: Crosspollinations in the Classic Age, Edinburgh University Press and Rutgers University Press, 1999

Judaism, Human Rights and Human Values, Oxford University Press, 1998

God of Abraham, Oxford University Press, 1996

Avicenna, Routledge, 1992

On Justice: An Essay in Jewish Philosophy, Yale University Press, 1991

Saadiah's Book of Theodicy, Commentary on the book of Job, translated with commentary, Yale University Press, 1988

edited volumes:

Jewish Themes in Spinoza's Philosophy, co-edited with Heidi Ravven, SUNY Press, 2002

Neoplatonism and Jewish Thought, SUNY Press, 1992

and classic texts available from Gee Tee Bee:

The Case of the Animals versus Man Before the King of the Jinn, a tenth century ecological fable from the Epistles of the Ikhwan al-Safa

Rambam: Readings in the Philosophy of Moses Maimonides, selected and translated from the Arabic and Hebrew texts, with commentary

Ibn Tufayl's
Hayy ibn Yaqzān

Ibn Tufayl's
Hayy Ibn Yaqzān

a philosophical tale
translated with introduction and notes
By Lenn Evan Goodman

gee tee bee
11901 Sunset Boulevard, 102
Los Angeles, CA 90049

The figure shown on the cover:
A Thoughtful Man
Mohammad 'Ali, Mughal, ca.1610
Watercolor on paper, 12.2 x 10.3cm
Francis Bartlet Donation of 1912 and
    Picture Fund.
Courtesy, Museum of Fine Arts, Boston.

Ibn Tufayl, Abu Bakr (ca. 1110-1185/6)
Goodman, Lenn Evan (1944-)
Hayy ibn Yaqzan
1. Philosophy, Islamic. 2. Literature, Arabic
    3. Mysticism, Sufi

I. author II. translator/commentator III. title

Manufactured in Canada
Printed on acid-free recycled paper

To my parents,
Calvin Jerome Goodman
Florence Jeanne Goodman
Los Angeles, California

Preface to the Fifth Edition

It is now nearly forty years since my friend and teacher Ilse Lichtenstadter first suggested that I translate Ibn Tufayl's *Hayy Ibn Yaqzān*. The book that grew from that suggestion appeared as the first volume in her Library of Classical Arabic Literature. Ilse is gone now. She died at 89 in 1991 and is warmly remembered by her many students and friends. A pioneer in Arabic and Islamic studies, she was the daughter of a progressive rabbi in Frankfurt am Main and a student of the great orientalist Josef Horovitz. She came to the study of pre-Islamic Arabic love poetry while still a teenager, inspired in part by the poetry of Goethe. She earned two doctorates, the first in Germany and the second in England after the Nazis came to power. Her studies ranged from classical Arabic literature to modern Islamic thought and culture. She published widely and became one of only two tenured women faculty members at Harvard–although, in the deep discriminatory climate that endured in academe even into the 1960s, she was never accorded professorial rank. Like many Jewish Arabists, Ilse was motivated in her studies by intellectual interest and kinship, critical sympathy, and a deep commitment to cross-cultural understanding. Her friendships touched four continents and included many of the most thoughtful and open minded leaders and intellectuals of Egypt and Pakistan but also the Egyptian villagers among whom she lived as a Fulbright scholar. She lived to see the establishment of the State of Israel, and she welcomed the Camp David accords as the first flowering of her lifelong hopes of peace for Israel with her neighbors. As I send this fifth edition to press, I persist in the belief that genuine scholarship can contribute, through understanding, to mutual recognition and the peace that so many others, like Ilse, have longed for and labored to achieve.

The first edition of this book, prepared in that spirit and well received in this country and abroad, was out of print for several years. But demand for the work has been sustained, and it is now in its fifth edition, ornamented with a Mughal watercolor that beautifully captures the meditative spirit of Ibn Tufayl's rational mysticism.

The Muslim philosopher's limpid faith in reason as the guide to and through the highest apprehensions of the soul strikingly contrasts with his darker view of all human activities that do not aim toward our perfection, the realization of our deep inner affinity with God. In the clarity and sobriety of his spiritual vision and the roundness of his dismissal of all that is cheap and tawdry in religion and its many surrogates, Ibn Tufayl has as much to say to our age as he had to say to his own. For this reason I have left unaltered the language of my translation and notes, designed to welcome the modern reader into a world not so very foreign to our own.

The ebullient juxtapositions I made in my introduction, inviting comparison of Ibn Tufayl's premises and their outcomes with those of some of our own intellectual folk heroes and anti-heroes, still stand. I remain convinced that Skinner was misguided in his attempt to lead humanity beyond freedom and dignity. I remain convinced as well by what I called the point zero argument: Those who would dismiss our human power to initiate actions have denied many of the very actions and effects to which they appeal when seeking to lay individual responsibility at the feet of others. They both assume and deny personal agency.

Cancer has taken the wife of my young manhood, who was beside me when I completed this first book of mine and the translation that forms its core. Our two daughters have grown to young womanhood and are parents now themselves. The clarity of their love and ardor of their minds as they pursue the visions of science and truths of art give substance to Hayy Ibn Yaqzān's loftiest dreams, but with an unmistakable codicil as to their mother and her nurturance and wisdom, which they in turn, along with their brilliant young husbands, are now imparting to their children. Beyond the bourne of thought experiments, children do not grow like weeds. The sunlight that opens up the mind and heart is focused most clearly in the care and love that parents give.

Friends know that I left Hawaii in 1994, after twenty five years in that magical place–a place made magical by its people. I teach and write now at Vanderbilt University, continuing the philosophical quest I began as a student and still convinced that comparative work is a critical component of philosophical exploration, testing and discovery. Since my Ibn Tufayl was published, other writings of mine have honored teachers, colleagues, and friends. My philosophical defense of truth was fittingly dedicated to my new bride, whose insight and integrity are a model and a beacon to the many who know her work. But this first book mine, the one now in your hands, remains the property of my parents. I join Ibn Tufayl in the wish that it may help you along the road that his philosophy traversed and that you may reach and surpass the limits set by his understanding or my own.

L. E. Goodman
Nashville, Spring 2003

Preface

When Descartes pronounced his *cogito ergo sum,* he was not disburdening himself of an insight that had sprung full-blown from the pregnant vacuum of methodical doubt. He was responding to a challenge thrown down centuries before by Avicenna. Building on Plato's equation of thought with being, Avicenna had framed a powerful argument for the substantiality of the soul, based neither on the evidence of the senses nor on *a priori* deduction but on an introspective test that anyone (so he advises) might successfully perform.

Anyone who doubts the substantiality of the soul has only to conceive of himself as spontaneously created, fully formed but perceptually isolated from all external objects, out of touch, as it were, even with his own body, radically deprived of input from the senses. The fact that even in such a state consciousness can be conceived proves, Avicenna argues, that the soul is real and distinct from all things physical. For it is conceptually independent of them.

To philosophers in whom the passion to believe burned strong, Avicenna's argument seemed definitive. To many it would still seem so today. For if epistemology is to draw up the standards of ontology, what firmer resting place than self-consciousness can be found? Kant, of course, will rebut such claims, as he finds them in the Cartesian recension. He labels the approach "problematic idealism" and argues that we cannot take consciousness to be somehow logically prior to the fact of our embodiment. For even the self-consciousness that Avicenna posits would involve an awareness of the passing of time, and that in turn presupposes some physical object, as substrate of the processes which set the rhythm of that temporal flow.

Committed followers of Avicenna might reply that Kant has merely psychologized an old argument of Aristotle's which makes time the unmistakable marker of the presence of bodies. In Avicenna's terms the Kantian riposte is suppositious: Intentionality and a history are enough to render consciousness real, and individuality inviolable.

My own response would build on the fact that the mind can intend even what it cannot experience, as when we comprehend the pure and timeless concepts of mathematics, logic, and the sciences–or, for that matter, the pure idea of God. Here intentionality does not seem to presuppose any reference to a body, even if the actual, always temporal instantiation of our intentionality cannot be achieved without body. But I am not as invested as Avicenna is in the project of philosophically protecting personal immortality. My larger concern is with human freedom and agency–and our access to the thought of God.

vii

Preface

To those who lived in closer range of Avicenna's thought and writing, his thought experiment was exciting, but also a goad. For it suggested problems of its own: What would a human soul be like in isolation? What would one know? What practices would such a soul pursue? What accidents or miracles would be necessary to promote so strange and radical a form of self-sufficiency, and what would the life of such a soul tell us about human nature, culture, society, and tradition? For these too, and not just the body, are wombs within the womb of nature from which man never seems to be delivered. If the soul is a substance, what sort of substance is it, and what sort of content, in isolation from the senses and society, could be posited as the content of its consciousness? What discoveries would be made by the soul freed from prejudice, untutored in language, and unimpeded by dogma and tradition?

Hayy Ibn Yaqzān, the story of a man growing up alone on an equatorial island and passing gradually to that other, less metaphorical stage of self-sufficiency and distance from which the truth itself would be visible, is Ibn Tufayl's attempt to answer these questions.

The present translation, the first complete English version since Simon Ockley's of 1710, was begun at the suggestion of Ilse Lichtenstadter while I was still an undergraduate at Harvard. It was she who first introduced me to Ibn Tufayl. She was my teacher for all of my four years at Harvard and remained a friend and ally through her remaining years. This book would not have existed without her kind and constant encouragement. Nicholas Heer was my guide in preparing the honors thesis that forms the nucleus of this book's Introductory Essay. Samuel Stern, with whom I spent many a pleasant Sunday morning reading Arabic texts at Oxford, aided my steps in the still halting translation. Richard Walzer, my doctoral supervisor, bemused that I would contemplate readying a book for publication even as I was writing my doctoral dissertation on Ghazālī, was enormously supportive in every way. I have fond memories of the many hours we spent at tutorials in his home, working through philosophical ideas, Islamic, Greek, Jewish or European, surrounded by the priceless heritage of impressionist and post-impressionist art that Sophie Walzer had inherited from her father, Bruno Cassirer. With Albert Hourani too I met weekly, to read modern Arabic political thinkers. I gained immensely from his seminars. Then there were meetings with Urmson, Ryle, Berlin, Prior–a rich environment and a rich time. This book and all my later work owes much to all of them. But the errors that remain are my own, and I can only hope that the merits of Ibn Tufayl's story will help make up for them.

Table of Contents

Introduction

I

The Life of Ibn Tufayl

It was considered unseemly for Muslim authors in the
middle ages to discuss personal matters in writings intended
for the public. Sons were an achievement, and of these we
know Ibn Tufayl had three, but whether he had as many
daughters, whether he was happily married, widowed, or
divorced is no longer known. He wrote once, quoting words
attributed to Muhammad, that to make one wife happy is to
make the other miserable, but even here it is not known
whether his choice of adage is based on bitter experience,
contented monogamy, or merely the exigencies of the argument. Those searching for a figure into which they may
breathe again the colors of sentiment and passion had best
be warned to find another. Ibn Tufayl will not respond to
their efforts at resuscitation. Yet he lived and his life was
an important one.

Abū Bakr Ibn Tufayl was born shortly after the beginning
of the twelfth century in the little Spanish town of Guadix,
about 50 miles northeast of Granada. He was born a Muslim in a Muslim country and he remained a Muslim all his
life. He was well educated and taught medicine as well as
practicing it. He was minister to the governor of Granada
and served several members of the Almohad dynasty in the
same capacity. His highest post was that of minister and
chief physician to the Almohad Sultan Abū Ya'qūb Yūsuf.

The Sultan, Ibn Tufayl's patron, was himself a learned
man deeply involved in the intellectual movements of his
time. The historian, 'Abdu-l-Wāhid of Marrakesh, writes:
"He continually gathered books from all corners of Spain and
North Africa and sought out knowledgeable men, especially
thinkers, until he had gathered more than any previous king

3

in the west. Among the intellectuals that were his friends
was Abū Bakr Ibn Tufayl, a Muslim philosopher, expert in
all branches of philosophy, who had studied the work of
many of the truest philosophers including Ibn Bājja. I
have seen works of Ibn Tufayl's on both natural and metaphysical philosophy, to name only two areas of his philosophical competence. One of his natural books is called
Hayy Ibn Yaqzān. Its object is to explain the meaning of
human existence according to philosophical ideas. The
book, written in the form of a letter, is slim but of tremendous benefit in this study. Among his metaphysical or theological writings is an essay on the soul which I have seen in
his own hand (God rest his soul). In his last days Ibn Tufayl
devoted all his energies to metaphysics and renounced everything else. He was eager to reconcile religion and philosophy and gave great weight to revelation, not only at the
literal, but also at the more profound level. Besides this he
was tremendously learned in Islamic studies. I understand
that he used to line up for his pay with all the regular em-
ployees, medics, engineers, secretaries, poets, archers, sol-
diers, etc. He said 'If they're in the market for musical
theory, I can supply it.' The Commander of the Faithful
Abū Ya'qūb loved him so well that he stayed with him in the
palace, night and day, not coming out for days at a time."

Ibn Tufayl's duties presumably included giving advice on
political questions as well as medical ones; and whether
formally or informally, he seems to have performed the role
of a minister of culture. Marrākushī writes: "Ibn Tufayl
made it his practice to gather scholars from all over the
world and saw to it that they obtained the interest and favor
of the ruler. It was he who recommended, to the Sultan,
Ibn Rushd who first became known and appreciated as a
result."

Ibn Rushd (or Averroës, as he is known to the West) himself confirms this, according to one of his students whose
words were taken down by the same historian: "I often
heard Ibn Rushd relate the following story: 'When I went
in to the Sultan Abū Ya'qūb, I found him alone with Abū
Bakr Ibn Tufayl. Ibn Tufayl began praising me and speaking of my family and my background, very kindly adding
many good things which I really did not deserve. Having

inquired as to my name and origins, the first thing the Commander of the Faithful asked me was "What do they (he meant the philosophers) believe about the heavens? Are they eternal or created?" I was seized with consternation and did not know what to say. I tried to excuse myself by denying that I had studied philosophy. I had no idea how far his prior discussions with Ibn Tufayl had gone. His Excellency saw that I was frightened and confused. He turned to Ibn Tufayl and began to discuss the question with him, referring to the positions of Aristotle and Plato and all the other philosophers, and citing the arguments of the Muslims against them. I soon realized that he was more learned than I would have expected a full time specialist to be. He put me so well at ease that I myself spoke up and he soon saw that I was not as ignorant as I had seemed. When I had gone he sent me a gift of money, and a splendid robe of honor, and a horse.' "

Despite the disappointing performance of the great champion of philosophy, Averroes, at his first interview with the Sultan, it was Ibn Tufayl's evaluation of the man that prevailed at court, and it was through Ibn Tufayl that Ibn Rushd was commissioned to write his monumental commentary on the works of Aristotle. Marrākushī writes: "The same student reports the following words of Ibn Rushd: 'Ibn Tufayl sent for me one day and said, "The Khalif was complaining today about the difficulty of Aristotle's language—or perhaps that of his translators—and the resultant difficulty in understanding his ideas. He suggested that if these books could be furnished with a good interpreter who could explain them after he had thoroughly mastered them himself, then people might grasp them more readily." Ibn Tufayl then said "If you have the energy for such an undertaking, go ahead. I believe you can do it because I see that you are sincere and I know how brilliant and dedicated you are. Only my age and the responsibilities of my office, (and the fact that I must devote myself to something thát seems to me to be more important) keep me from doing it myself." It was this that determined me to write my first outlines of the works of Aristotle.' "

When Ibn Tufayl retired as court physician in 1182, Ibn Rushd was asked to serve as his successor.

Abū Ya'qūb Yūsuf died in 1184 of wounds received at the siege of Santarem in Portugal.   His son Abū Yūsuf Ya'qūb succeeded him and continued his father's patronage of the elderly Ibn Tufayl and deference to his advice.   In 1185 Ibn Tufayl died at Marrakesh.   The Sultan himself officiated at the funeral.   Behind him Ibn Tufayl left his disciples, his children, and his books.

The books include poetry and textbooks on medicine and astronomy—some of which are in verse.   One philosophical work survives, *Hayy Ibn Yaqzān*.   About the progress of the inner life, as distinct from the private life, Muslims were not reticent.   It is through this book that we know Ibn Tufayl.[1]*

---

* Notes to the Introduction begin on p. 239.

Educational Philosophy

The story of Hayy Ibn Yaqzān is a history of the progressive development, alone, on an equatorial island of an individual human soul. What is the purpose of telling such a story? Close to the surface as subject-problems posed by the premiss of Ibn Tufayl's book are the problems of educational philosophy: 'What is education?' 'What is personal development?' 'How does human growth take place?' 'How can a man attain fulfillment?'

An examination of the form and matter of Hayy's education —the successive phases in the dialectic of his growth and the substantive achievements within each of them may reveal what sort of philosophy gave rise to Ibn Tufayl's attempt to deal with these problems, and perhaps it will expose the coloration of the answers he hoped would solve them.

Hayy's development is schematized in seven stages of seven years each, heptads or septenaries, which may seem, when first observed, the products of an overly neat mind eager to designate "a time for everything." Yet we may come to see these phases, like the ages of man, as a symbolic device, a mirror set against the flux of human growth, portraying the impact of irreversible change: each phase has its own character, in each the soul has a way of life, a method of inquiry, and a level of achievement distinct from what went before and in some sense higher.

Hayy's first phase is childhood. He is nursed by his doe foster-mother; and, when he gets his first teeth and learns to walk, he is weaned. But his weaning is no more than a nominal diminution of his dependence. Now he must follow the doe: she finds him fruit and cracks the shells, warms and shades him and protects him. He relies on her, and she answers his call: his feeling toward her is more trust than love.[2] His identity, at this stage, like that of any infant, is easily lost in the needs beneath which it is submerged and by which, at times, it seems to be subsumed.

His imitation of the animals[3] is intuitive. The infant's first cries for help are directed to the environment at large; gradually they become more specific, are addressed to particular sectors when particular sorts of help are needed,[4] but there is not yet the flash of understanding[5] that means what is "asked for" is planned and expected. There is not yet, behind these cries, a reasoned sense of purpose.

Slowly Hayy develops a sense of the world and the things in it, a taste for some and an aversion for others,[6] but his likes and dislikes are not yet actively expressed, they are passive, ineffectual "affections"; they accomplish nothing. Likewise, his jealousy of the horns the fawns begin to grow and his shame at his own nakedness[7] are emotions of frustration. Childhood is dependence, helplessness: ends without means, wants without grasp and childish aversions that cannot be enforced. Hayy's childhood begins to end at age seven, when he first tries to *do something* to help himself.

From seven to twenty-one, Hayy lives the life of practical reason, the kind that finds means to ends: he is developing an executive capacity. No longer content to be annoyed by his nakedness, he decides "to do something about it"; he starts to make his own clothes. He grows impatient with waiting for horns to sprout on his head and tired of fighting a losing battle against the animals. So he makes himself a weapon.[8] The doe weakens with age, and he finds the love that once meant dependence turning to concern and care for another being: now it is he who must, somehow, provide. Even when she dies, his grief turns to a desire to do something, to bring her back.[9]

Sparsely at first, then more steadily, as if marking the approach of puberty, signs of a spiritualization appear in Hayy's practical concern. The soul is discovered in his search for the vital part which failed his mother-doe, a momentous discovery for Hayy: *action* in the natural world remains the basis of his life, as is indicated by his first glimpse of the soul as a hot, gaseous, governing "spirit"—but the plane of action has been elevated. Hayy's involvement now is with souls.[10] He soon learns to dissociate the soul, which he honors as master, from the body, which it abandoned and which is subject to corruption.[11] Like the Stoic *hegemonikon*, the soul as Hayy knows it at this stage, though material, is a principle of rule; so he trains himself in mastery, by learning to ride.[12] His approach to life remains action oriented: he no longer helplessly wishes for a being like himself, but actively seeks one.[13] By the time he discovers fire he finds it to mean more to him than the utilitarian functions of warmth, light, and cookery; his practical concern is so deeply tinged with the spiritual that he associates fire's universal power, as did the pagan Stoics, with the powers of the soul, and its light, as did the pagan Platonists, with the beauty of the stars. He is infatuated with fire and virtually ready to worship it.[14]

The subtle way in which Ibn Tufayl makes Hayy's ontogeny recapitulate human phylogeny must convince us, if nothing else can, that the figure of Hayy represents something more than himself. His Adam-like position alone on an island, his Promethean role as discoverer of fire, his progress and backsliding, brilliantly experimenting with fire and rashly trying to grasp "a piece of it," show that he is intended to symbolize mankind, for he, like the first man, and like mankind, must discover everything newly for himself. And, if he is man, the incipient spiritualization of his practical reason, even at this primitive stage when he knows no more of the soul than its vital, animal aspect and conceives of its work in terms of the motor functions and of its nature as a crudely material vaporous spirit seated in the heart—is still a momentous step. It marks the entry of *man* into a world at least quasi-spiritual.

Hayy has gone through three ages: the frustrations of childhood, the ascent to practical reason, where he learns what he can do with his hands and his brain, and the far side of practical understanding where love for the spirit, if only the animal, animating spirit, makes him prone to see spirit everywhere. At twenty-one[15] he begins to think seriously about metaphysics.

All the world lies before him, the stars, like limbs of some great dissected animal symmetrically displayed for his examination.[16] Every being is unique—yet in species, genus, Kingdom, all are one. Pervading Hayy's thought is that strange Platonic logic which identifies souls with forms and, in the unity of forms and functions shared by all living and even non-living things, finds a higher unity of which all objects participate like parts of the same body; and all forms and souls, like scattered drops from a single bowl of water.[17]

This is the age of wonder. The soul seeks questions it cannot answer and struggles with their meanings; the heart seeks a window for itself on the Universe. Hayy's discovery of forms is his first experience of the intellectual, that is, the truly spiritual world.[18] He cannot maintain this attitude; he soon tires of abstractions like forms and prime matter and longs to return to the simplest things.[19] But like the Arab horsemen, for whom *farr* and *karr*, mock flight and wheeling charge were one maneuver, Hayy seems to gain more ground in his recovery than he lost in his retreat;[20] for, stopping to consider the changing forms of the elements, he discovers God, the necessary producer of actual change. Again, not knowing whether God is one or many, Hayy recapitulates human history.

The age of wonder cannot last: reason is all too prepared to satisfy the spirit's hunger. Hayy looks and wonders at the stars: are the heavens finite or infinite? But by now he is twenty-eight and reason will not leave him wondering. Elaborate proof is given, *a priori*, of the finiteness of the heavens, a *reductio ad absurdum* that seems at once to mimic and epitomize the process of pure reason.[21] Reason does answer questions: to the paradoxical unity and diversity of the world it sets the figure of a great animal with stars for eyes, spheres for limbs, and the corruptible world as wastes and fluids in its giant belly:[22] Man can now visualize with ease his place in the universe. And yet, somehow, there seems a certain taint of the unreasonable in this ultra-rational reason. When Hayy sets out to prove the eternity of the world or its creation in time, Ibn Tufayl lets the diaphanous persona slip for a moment, and behind it we may glimpse a face annoyed at the wrangling of divines: the proofs conflict; and either way, Ibn Tufayl says, God exists.[23] Perhaps there is, in reason itself, a certain room for growth, room to seek beyond abstraction and air-tight proof, in the tangles of whose impeccable logic all is solid but conviction. It is no repudiation of reason to detect in it a sophism or a sophomoric self-certainty that is at once the mask and mark of ignorance. Given room for further growth, reason might mature to wisdom.

Wonder discovers God in a beautiful, unexpected moment and sees Him in the working of the world. Reason proves Him as Designer of the Universe, perfect Cause of Himself and Creator of all. But wisdom awakens when the soul begins to seek deeper. Knowledge itself is a passive affair: is belief any more than willingness, if asked, to affirm a proposition? Conviction is perhaps a state of mind, but like a family sword it is dragged out rarely, only on special occasions, as if it had no more use than for fighting the formal duels that may arise with scholars. For lovers it is not enough to be convinced beyond refutation of one another's existence. Wisdom seeks more than knowledge: it seeks an active relationship of love with the beloved, and with God.

Hayy's wisdom begins as he approaches thirty-five,[24] when he begins to relate to God not merely by knowledge, but by love. God becomes a passion for him that absorbs all his attention and distracts him from everything else.[25] The soul recognizes itself as non-material and comes to see its task as the active seeking of God. Hayy is ready to enter a final pair of seven-year phases. He finds in himself resemblances to the animals, to the stars, and to God Himself. He realizes that his well-being, his happiness and self-fulfillment lie in promoting those resemblances.[26] The physical needs of his animal soul are necessary encumbrances. Beyond them, he must heighten his resemblance to the stars: he must be clean and kindly, graceful in his movements, and ascetic in his habits. But just as the spiritualization of practical reason marked the two-stage transition from adolescence to young manhood, so the spiritualization of his wisdom, its rise from exercise to experience, marks the end of tutelage and beginning of maturity, the fulfillment of self-awareness in the realization that all that has gone before is a "ladder of love" to union with God; for, at the end of his seventh set of seven years,[27] Hayy attains the beatific experience.

From the intimations we have of his symbolic role, we can say that the summit of Hayy's achievement is meant to represent the highest point man can attain, a point he reaches not by aid of institutions and instruction, but seemingly by being simply let alone. What sort of educational philosophy permits belief in such a possibility: that a child left alone and exposed will develop into a fulfilled human being?

The followers of Dewey hoped to relax the rigors of traumatic childhood by freeing the atmosphere in which learning took place. School was opened to the imagination of the child. From primary schools, where subjects were hand-tailored and cut to fit a child's span of interest, to colleges, where "cafeteria-style" offerings allowed students to gratify their tastes and interests by sampling from Western culture *ad libitum*, efforts to motivate, to broaden interests and to plant the seeds for new avenues of expression and experience were anathema—they were considered to be misguided urges "to run another person's life." And yet, if these reformers' attempts to be progressive made education suffer on the side of the permissive, what can be said of Ibn Tufayl? The progressivists may have lacked a clear sense of the value of some form in upbringing; they may have lacked a devotion to past literature and arts which made them prone to try to raise a generation of "well-adjusted" happy philistines—but they still had, with Dewey at their head, a vital concern for the establishment in the public schools of a mutually reenforcing relationship between education and the state: the promulgation of "good-citizenship-attitudes" and "socially useful behavior" and the regeneration of public institutions by a populace socially articulated and technologically informed. They saw in education a conscious endeavor toward the moral molding of human beings who would in turn renew the state.[28] But of all this Hayy is lacking. His education has no seeds in public policy, nor is the advantage of it thought to accrue to anyone but himself; his development, alone in nature, makes permissive "progressivism" seem like thought-control and programmatic molly-coddling.

In compensation for the stifled atmosphere of the old schoolroom and under the subdued influence of Hegel, Dewey developed a firm belief in the integration of action and thought, practical and intellectual experience in education.[29] But the field-trips, visual aids, and take-home projects that grew out of his approach pale in comparison with the head-on confrontation of Hayy's wit with nature. Dewey seeks a balanced, reciprocating interchange between thought and action, to prevent stuffiness by discounting the mind-body distinction,[30] but Hayy finds a spiral upward progress, rising from his interchange with nature toward perfection, even though he accepts the distinction! How is it possible for Ibn Tufayl to expect what Dewey could not and would not dare to ask? What premises does Ibn Tufayl hold and Dewey lack that make it possible for the Arab to give a child the run of a tropical island while the Vermonter can only pretend to give him the run of a school, for Ibn Tufayl to set his boy alone in nature on a course toward fulfillment, while Dewey, who asks no more than normalcy and social concern, must create artificial situations to simulate the practical world?

The extra premise seems to be Hayy's natural endowment of capacities. Dewey seeks the level of the lowest common intellectual denominator, for fear of setting his norms over the heads of the dullest. But Ibn Tufayl postulates in Hayy natural capacities for brilliance, boldness, curiosity, and goodness.[31] The very name 'Hayy Ibn Yaqzān', the standard patronymic which translates 'Life Awareson', should indicate what Hayy stands for; he is wide-awake, ready to learn, unrivaled in sensitivity, receptivity, openness to experience. The Arabs called the sum of a man's natural capacities his '*fitra*'; we might say his nature or his talents. In the case of Hayy, the *fitra* rapidly comes to mean his genius. Perhaps the super-abundant strength of his abilities[32] contributes to the independence of Hayy's self-development. But is genius enough?

Rousseau, like Dewey, fears trammels on the growing soul and one may suspect that his fears lie closer to the root of liberalism than Dewey's, for his concern is not the molding of socially acceptable members of the public by society itself, but the cultivation of an individual human soul. And Rousseau with Ibn Tufayl, goes beyond Dewey, hoping to make it conceivable to free the child not just in word and wish, but in fact: he too postulates a natural human endowment. He writes of conformity, "Are there not habits formed under compulsion, habits which never stifle nature? Such, for example, are the habits of plants trained horizontally. The plant keeps its artificial shape, but the sap has not changed its course, and any new growth the plant may make will be vertical. It is the same with a man's disposition; while the conditions remain the same, habits, even the least natural of them, hold good; but change the conditions, habits vanish, nature reasserts herself."[33] The whole might of society cannot destroy human nature, for the root of human nature is God-given. "God makes all things good; man meddles with them and they become evil", thus Rousseau begins his *Emile*.[34] He proceeds to describe the uncurling of the natural capacities along a Lockian framework from primitive sensation to human concern and complex emotion. There is a plain resemblance between his eager anticipation of the colors of a new phase of human life[35] and Ibn Tufayl's natural expectation of the character-growth of higher stages. For human development at least, both are firm believers in orthogeny. Education must have a base to grow from and it does have a goal. But never does Rousseau leave Emile to his own devices, and never does he dare nature, as Ibn Tufayl seems to do, to produce a natural man and show what he will be: "Under existing conditions a man left to himself would be more of a monster than the rest . . ." Society would trample nature in him[36] and how could he possibly survive outside society? Rousseau must "remove this young tree from the highway and shield it from the crushing force of social conventions";[37] if there are capacities for growth in the nature of the young soul, he must foster them and tease them out. He begins an unceasing dialectic with his student, trusting his own knowledge of human nature to tell him what is a shoot and what a weed, what a natural growth of the soul, and what a social deflection. If we see in Rousseau's admittedly pedantic teaching the practical meaning of Platonic "reminiscence", the active use of

Socratic mid-wife methods, we still must ask what sort of faith made Ibn Tufayl able to wager with nature that a child, even granted optimum endowments of potentiality, and seclusion from "the highway", could realize his potential without a preceptor and utterly alone.

The answer is, of course, that Hayy never is alone. Not only is the *fitra* he is endowed with the gift of God, but the realization of its potential is not a tutor's work, but God's; for the philosophy that makes possible Hayy Ibn Yaqzān's remarkable story is *radical monotheism*, the belief in a Deity so great that His presence pervades the Universe, and Who is the *place* of the Universe, Whose unity is so absolute that it is polytheism to claim there is any power but in Him.

How can it be, asks the radical monotheist, that a world of diversity arose out of the supremely simple God? Spinoza's theory of modes and Hegel's dialectic, which sees one world spirit proliferating in historical reality toward the perfection of the ideal are cognate efforts to come to terms with the paradox of plurality in unity. A third effort of the same family is the Plotinian theory of emanation, which Hayy Ibn Yaqzān himself accepts.

The theory of emanation saves the unity of God for radical monotheism by refusing either to distinguish or to identify the being of the world and that of God. Thus Hayy, in his great, ecstatic vision,[38] beholds the mind of each sphere and sees that it is neither the same as nor different from the essence of the Most High, for each lower sphere's intelligence is an emanation of the one above, and their diversity forms no plurality. Like object and image—or more exactly, object and idea or a man and his soul—the two are somehow at once the same and different. And the Active Intellect at the base of the hierarchy of sphere-minds is the source of all the world's diversity, at once the world-soul and the form of forms. Thus neo-Platonism solves the knotty problem of God's relationship to the world not by calling Him its creator *ex nihilo*, but by seeing in Him the ontological fountain from which all creation springs; and in concrete being, ripples in the ocean of God's mind. To the Platonist-radical monotheist, whatever exists, inasmuch as it does exist, is an emanation of the divine. All being can reflect, to one degree or another, the splendor of God. The more brilliantly He shows up in it, the higher its ontological status, and accordingly its value. Evil is ontological weakness, a lack, non-being. To the extent that a thing is whole or good or sound or fulfilled, it is a mode of the divine Being. And thus it is that Hayy's soul itself is "breathed" into him by God, that is to say the endowment of his *fitra* is a mode of the divine, and man is made "in the image of God."[39]

But further, the hierarchical ranking of being according to degree of participation in the divine and the origin of forms and souls in the divine make it impossible to confine the reach of divine emanation to the grant of existential status 'it is,' 'he is': it becomes necessary for the pervading World-Spirit that is God's to be called the bestower of essential status 'it is that ', 'he is that man'. It is no longer possible to be content with 'inasmuch as he *is*, he is of God'; we must say 'inasmuch as he is himself, he is of God'—which is to say, for Hayy, that God does not merely found his *fitra*, but continues on with him as the active energizer of his capacities, for wherever ontological hierarchy becomes the basis of value, the concept of more perfect essence must be fused with that of superior rank in the chain of existence. So it is that Hayy first knows God as the necessary Activator of forms, without Whom no development would take place.[40] Thus, too, he knows that if God did not "teach" the animals to use their limbs, they would not know how to use them.[41] And most importantly, *we* know that had not God activated the *fitra* he emplanted in Hayy's soul, allowed it to perfect itself to such degree as it can, had not the Active Intellect, identified with the angel Gabriel, the messenger and muse of God to men, inspired him, taught him, and awakened his reason, Hayy's fulfillment would have been inconceivable. If prophets can express the existential dependence of man on God by saying that man is created in the image of God, then surely the essential dependence of man on God can be put symbolically as providence.[42] God does not "depart" from man once man has been created, does not "detach" man, as in the splendid, frightening image on the ceiling of the Sistine Chapel, but "answers" a mother's prayer for mercy and protection, as He answers Hayy's real mother's prayer in the story—by infusion of His essence into the soul of man.

Thus Hayy's education is just that, the leading out of tendrils from seeds that have been planted in his soul not by a human teacher, but by God. But this brings us face to face with the old, old problem of free-will. If Hayy—and with him the whole species he represents—is granted faculties that are no less, but still no more, than emanations of the Godhead, and if those faculties are activated by the spirit of God himself, surely there is no room for human freedom. Can radical monotheism answer such a question? It might be valuable to see how it can.

Strange as it may seem at first, radical monotheism does not demand rejection of free will. The same determinism which we associate perhaps with "middle eastern fatalism and lassitude" may equally have been the spark that powered the industrial revolution. What makes the difference between fatalism and the kind of determinism that inspired the Puritan work ethic is the extent to which subjective identification is achieved with the divine purpose. Islam may be interpreted to mean resignation to the will of God; but if that will remains no longer other, but is accepted by the consciousness as self, then the I can expect of itself the ability to move mountains. In place of the confinement of the infinitesimal, beneath the weight of the Infinite is found the limitlessness or a humanly bearable share in the limitlessness which is the freedom of God. For Ibn Tufayl, at least, this was the meaning of Islam: the progressive assimilation of self to God (so far as lies in human power). This entails acceptance of the divine will, but not as something alien. The transmuting of selfish purpose to the will of God need not imply a surrender of will because the assimilation of self to God does not imply a surrender of self. On the contrary, as Plato and Ibn Tufayl are agreed, this assimilation is the meaning of man's fulfillment *qua* man, the substance of Plato's answer to the cryptic challenge of the oracle, "Know thyself!"

For Ibn Tufayl, as for the Platonist, to know oneself was to see in oneself affinities to the divine and to accept the obligation implied by such recognition to develop these affinities—to become, in as much as was in human power, like God.[43]

Given the assimilation of individual personality and individual purpose to the person and purpose of God, freedom remains no longer a problem. The free and joyous execution of God's will comes naturally. That the power to achieve such assimilation is a given has never been denied by the radical monotheist. Such power may be given less generously than might have been wished, but it would defeat the purpose of proposing radical monotheism as an image of the world to omit from the deterministic world some glimmer of this golden key by which freedom is attained.

Thus, in interpreting the meaning of Islam Platonically, Ibn Tufayl cannot have been untrue to the spirit of Muhammadan tradition. Muhammad was keenly aware of the presence of God as a motive force in every human action and event. But for Muhammad God infused the moral sphere as well, and the felt weight of moral responsibility imposed by God's constant presence was too great to allow Muhammad to ignore the special burden of freedom imposed by the very fact that man is a moral agent. Muhammad was no more a fatalist than Ibn Tufayl, for Muhammad was no less a participant of that extraordinary transference of purpose that marks the life of the ecstatic radical monotheist. As Tor Andrae writes in his keenly perceptive study of Muhammad:

> It seems as though the certainty that God by an unchangeable decree has destined us in advance either to bliss or to damnation would cripple all desire and power of initiative, and would deprive men of any inclination to struggle on in the way of salvation, or would at least cripple all enthusiasm for the religious training of men, or for the preaching of reform and conversion. But as a matter of fact, belief in foreordination has really the opposite effect. For it gives the human will new energy, and makes all earthly obstacles seem negligible and unimportant, and this gives man the courage to hope and to dare what is apparently impossible.[44]

To be sure, the key of grace, transference of man's human purpose to the transcendent purpose of the divine, was to be obtained, in Muhammad's radical monotheism, only from the hand of God. But that key at least, if no other, opened the door to freedom. Grace, if nothing else, could bring recognition of the necessity of moral choice, and with it the necessity of freedom. This it must do, for the same radical monotheism which had demanded of man that he see God in everything had specifically demanded recognition of the moral alternatives imposed by awareness of God and had done so since the God of Israel first confronted His people with the drama of the human situation: "Behold I set before you this day a blessing and a curse."[45]

Is it inconsistent that such words should be spoken by an omnipresent God? By no means. An infusion of God's essence into the soul of man carries no imputation of passivity or impotence. Quite the reverse, if human fulfillment is assimilation to God and if the drives that bring a man to fulfillment are implanted by God, then the fostering by God of those drives and the realization of the potentials they represent will make a man more perfect, more himself. This is the meaning, Ibn Tufayl tells us, of the dictum accepted by Muslim, Christian, and Jew that man is created in the image of God.

Free will is autonomy, self-rule, a capacity to choose among the limited opportunities life provides in accordance with internal motives, self-generated criteria. Without free will, the individual would be reduced to nothing. Impressions and sensations would pass through him like light through a point in a vacuum, or bounce off him like an echo. He would be changed, but change nothing. For all his influence on the world, he might as well not exist. He is a null point. Yet surely it is no part of the radical monotheist program to deny the existence of the individual or affirm that for all the being God gave him he'd as well not exist. On the contrary, the purpose of theories of creation and emanation is to explain the fullness of a world bursting with God's presence in terms of a relation of ontological dependence between that world and God. That purpose is defeated if ontological dependence is equated with existential identity—or for that matter with the nonentity of either member. Unless things have being, a being of their own, enough in man's case to allow moral freedom, God's gift is empty, meaningless. Even an asymmetrical relation must have more than one member.

For the doctrinaire determinist, of course, the notion of self-determination is specious, useful perhaps, and phenomenologically impeccable, but objectively an illusion. All behavior is externally determined, he argues, since behavior itself is no more than the pattern of conditioned response. Of course it is absurd to allow reduction of the subject to point zero. Obviously an organism relates with its environment. It does not merely absorb input and spew it out unchanged. It modifies, reacts, selects. We are not marionettes. But the self that does what we call choosing is itself the product of powerful forces (whether natural, or if you prefer, supernatural) which are not only alien but external, not only insurmountable, but out of reach in the past long before their victim can come to grips with them, before he constitutes a conscious identity.

The only possible reply to this line is to reject its categories. Man is more than mechanism, and human action is more than behavior. If the crude determinism that invariably pleads (with ever diminishing plausibility) "I was shoved" reduces man to a point in space, does not this more cautious model of "pre-programming" reduce him to a semiconductor, modifying input in a predetermined way? A pinball machine can give stereotyped responses to the stimuli it receives. The remarkable thing about human beings at their most human is not how consistently and uniformly they react, but the fact that they can create their own values. Human beings do not just weigh and measure, accept and reject, but assess and decide, and can decide for themselves what matters, what is worthwhile. There is no machine and no mechanical process that can decide for itself what counts, what is worth considering, what values are to be invoked in considering a course of action. It is precisely the fact that human beings do not always just react, but judge, and choose, and consider, select their own criteria and their own values that makes their troubles worth more pains than, say, pinball games.

Of course the reason ideas have a history is that one man's

reductio ad absurdum is another man's philosophy. There are those who suppose they have accomplished a great deal when they have described human lives as games—war games, role-playing games. A concerted effort is made to reduce action to behavior and behavior to standardized, mechanical response. Often we oblige by living the weak analogy, acting the part of machines and treating each other the same way. But is this really how we act at our most human, when we consider? Is this what we mean by choosing? Granted the past is out of reach; for us at least, who have become, the question at issue is the future. If we feel a tug of aesthetic or moral revulsion at the reduction of human hopes and dreams to automatic responses in the dialectic of some unseen game or excrescences of long suppressed, perhaps pre-natal traumas, then it may be worthwhile to find in Ibn Tufayl a non-Pavlovian alternative.

Ibn Tufayl admits the vital influence of environment on Hayy; if he did not, he would not so concentrate his attention on the bountifully accommodating island where Hayy grows up. And indeed, the formative influence goes much further, for as we have seen, the commodious island, as answer to Hayy's mother's prayer, is no more than the material shadow-symbol of the outflowing immanence in Hayy of God—and yet it is not the case that the endowment of Hayy's *fitra* and the actualization of its forms constitute a predestination that renders freedom impossible. For what is it, after all, that is actualized? Not programs of behavior surely, but capacities to act with reason and self-awareness as a human being.

To observe human development is to see that there comes a point of "moral take-off" when the individual becomes morally self-sufficient and can choose for himself. For some time beyond that point the soul can choose its values; with good fortune it can, to some extent, determine the course of its future life. But most importantly, once past that point, a man who stands in a moral situation can choose, and no analysis of "input", regardless how complete the data, will be of value in predicting what he will choose to do. A knowledge of his character and actions in the past may help us form an educated guess—but he will always be able to surprise us, to change his mind; even to shock himself; for to say he is a moral adult implies that his soul is in his own hands.

Education is, for Ibn Tufayl, a process of molding? Perhaps. But the molder is God Himself, the being molded is filled with God's being, and the mold is no determinate pattern but the cast of humanity: to use human choice, to invoke human values, to be, at times, surprising.

III

Religious Philosophy

Theoretically the possibilities of religious belief and unbelief are infinite; and the variety of forms actually taken on by religious expression and experience from nation to nation and from age to age seems almost to have tried to exhaust the possibilities. There can scarcely be found two people, even of the most orthodox, whose thought-out religious beliefs—and notions of what is meant by those beliefs—will correspond in every point. In confronting the diversity apparently inherent in religion the mind may be led to seek an underlying unity by which, in conception if not in manifestation, the seemingly disparate phenomena are bound together. If generously conducted, such a confrontation will grow into toleration, the realization that men's approaches to God differ but are motivated by the same drive towards a certain kind of higher truth; this is intellectual toleration, not merely living and letting live, but active seeking to understand the beliefs of others and a principled refusal to attribute these to prejudice, superstition or moral laxity—refusal to treat the religion of others as a heresy of one's own. For the citizen toleration is sufficient. But for the thinker, the analytical and synthetic activity of the mind refuses to confine itself to differentiating among historically defined sects and discovering a unity in their outlook, but seeks deeper, for unities that transcend cultural categories and divisions that cut across historical continuities. Here begins the philosophy of religion. Theology deals with God: 'Does He exist?', 'Is He good?', 'What are His powers and attributes?'. The philosophy of religion does not deal with God, but with religion *per se*: 'What is religion?', 'How did it arise?', 'Why is there religion?', 'For whom does it exist?',

'What is a characteristically religious experience or activity?', 'How is it possible to know God?'. As the last question in particular should indicate, there is some overlap between theology and the philosophy of religion. It would be simple to say the former deals with God and the latter with man; more truthfully, the former deals with God's relation to man and the latter with man's relation to God. As a tool, to pry apart the concepts of theology and philosophy of religion, it may be useful to say that an atheist can contribute to philosophy of religion, the explanation of religion as a phenomenon in human experience, although he cannot without hypocrisy participate in theology. One must proceed with caution however: the assertion that atheists *can* participate in the philosophy of religion should be taken more as an invitation than as a history of their past efforts; few atheists in the past have had a catholicity of sympathy like Weber's which would allow them to participate in philosophy of religion without descending into anti-theological polemics like Freud's in *The Future of an Illusion*. Let us be content, then, to say that theology is the public record of religion, man's groping toward God, while philosophy of religion is the intellectual confrontation of that groping itself.

Up to now we have discussed only the educational philosophy of Ibn Tufayl wrapped within the tale of Hayy Ibn Yaqzān's personal evolution, yet the reference to theology in the explanation of that philosophy has been essential. Moreover, the subject matter of Hayy's education, the ultimate Truth that Hayy comes to know, is God, manifest in His works and concealed in His mysteries, but known to those who seek Him. Is it any surprise that *Hayy Ibn Yaqzān* expresses a definite philosophy of religion? No thinker can let himself be carried to a level of ecstatic experience "beyond description,"[46] surrender himself to God, and come to see all in terms of God without attempting to generate a philosophical understanding of religion itself, the phenomenon by which he has been entranced. In order to understand Ibn Tufayl's philosophical confrontation of religion, it will be necessary to distinguish among three types of religion: rational religion, mass religion, and mystical religion. In each case we must discover what answers are given to the fundamental questions about religion: 'How is it possible for men to know God?', 'For the sake of whom does religion exist?', 'What is the most fitting expression of religious involvement?' Since religious philosophy attempts to define religion as an aspect of experience and a branch of human concern the answers will differ according to what religion is conceived to be.

The essential characteristic of rational religion is its simple and direct answer to the question 'How can God be known?': God can be known by human reason; and, of the human faculties, reason is the only one by which God can be known. The varieties of rational religion are multiplied by philosophical diversity as to the nature of our knowledge of God, 'How well can He be known?' Some, like Aquinas, maintain that we can know Him, but not comprehend Him; others, like Plotinus, that we can know him only in negative terms but can attribute no definite positive description to him; others, again like Aquinas, hold that when we delineate His attributes, our words are systematically transformed into homonyms of themselves. The motivation behind these attempts to hedge and qualify our conception of the extent of theological knowledge is, of course, a pious fear of making God merely a product of human conception, on one hand, or anthropomorphism on the other: To the rational-religionist no less than any other, God is a reality, anything but a construct of human thought or imagination. Qualified and hedged about as these pious notions may be, they have in common with the most unbounded faith in human capacities, the belief that human reason is the necessary *and sufficient* condition of our knowledge of God.

The rationalist wants to come to terms with the Universe and with God. To achieve this end, he knows only one way: the use of his mind. He sees himself as a sentient, conscious being and would have great difficulty finding any other label for himself. It is a fact of his personality, for example, that he does not initially conceive of himself as a creature of God; he would, were that identity proposed to him, as likely as not dismiss it as begging the question: for him there is always a question. To answer the questions that naturally arise before his mind, he has only his own

reason. He would look at you quizzically were you to propose he tried a standard other than reason: "Do you want
me to guess?" Even those who do not feel reason is sufficient to establish the truths of theology, who feel that some
"higher" faculty is needed to make religion possible, if possible it is, ought to confront the rational religionist with
sympathy, for they should be able to understand at least
intellectually that the identity of the rational religionist is
constituted in his self-awareness as a conscious, reasonable
being; it is this identity that demands of him that he reduce
all other standards, whether pragmatic, aesthetic or moral
to reason: if a claim does not ultimately appeal to reason,
on what grounds can it be accepted?

Such sympathy has been conspicuously lacking in critical
confrontations of rational religion. Thus W. D. Ross[47] dis-
misses the conception of God presented in Book Lambda of
Aristotle's *Metaphysics* as "certainly an unsatisfactory one."
Aristotle's conception is, of course, that of the Unmoved
Mover who knows Himself alone, the first and final cause of
all becoming, a supremely elegant synthesis of the human
mind, designed to account for the origin of motion and order
in the universe; and, at the same time, to locate in one great
Source all which is worthy of worship and emulation: supreme intellectual beauty, perfect contemplation of truth,
and epitome of value, toward Whom all beings strive. Yet
Ross finds Aristotle's Deity, "a God so remote from popular
religious ideas that no element of accommodation to the
intelligence or the prejudices of his audience is to be suspected . . .", "unsatisfactory" because "Aristotle has no
theory either of divine creation or of divine providence."
Likewise "he has no serious belief in divine rewards and
punishments." Ross' disappointment with Aristotle seems
at first blush to be directed at some form of emotional sterility in rational religion. And it must be admitted that somehow a table of the precessions of the spheres does not seem
satisfactory as a system of theology. Yet a defense for the
emotional fecundity of Book Lambda and of many another
set of rationally based theological beliefs may be suggested
by pointing out that they by no means lack the potential for
poetic and artistic elaboration that would render them

equivalent, if not superior, to the emotional expressions of the other types of religion. Lucretius can make atomism blossom into a garden. T. S. Eliot achieves the same emotional impact from the metaphysics of Heraclitus in *Burnt Norton* as from the Christian image of the martyr in *The Cocktail Party* or *Murder in the Cathedral*.

Presumably Ross would admit that the poetic development of any religious idea can render it emotionally satisfying, yet he would argue that the emotional impact achieved in the poetic elaboration of rational religion is sophistical, that man has needs from which he may be diverted by verses but which cannot be satisfied by any form of rational religion. We see now that the suggested imputation of emotional aridity was merely the veil behind which lies the real charge against rational religion: that it does not answer to man's deep-seated religious needs. What these needs are is indicated by the substance of Ross' charge: that God is not seen by Aristotle as Creator, Providence, or Judge. What man needs, apparently, is a Providence to watch over him; wickedness needs an avenger; and the soul, inadequately recompensed for this life, needs some great Power to bless it with another.

The precise nature of the needs that have been slighted is made a good deal more explicit in Walter Lippmann's attack[48] on Whitehead in particular and in general the advocates of rational religion, "those thin argumentative rationalists who find so much satisfaction in disproving what other men hold sacred." What is the great fault of rational religion? "Plainly the modernist churchman does not believe in the God of Genesis who walked in the garden in the cool of the evening . . ." so he has set up for himself another God, a God "remote from the God men have worshipped." Whitehead, for example, had said "God is not concrete, but He is the ground for concrete actuality." The statement might have seemed eminently satisfactory to Plotinus, whose God transcended even being. But it did not satisfy Lippmann. What precisely is wrong with it? First, setting up some new being under the "misleading" name of God has made faith difficult for the peasant, who now will be at a loss to choose among rival gods. Second, Mr. Lippmann does not understand the

concept, "because it was too deep for me"; but third, and
most important, Whitehead has fallen into the same fault
which he himself recognizes in Aristotle's theology which
does "not lead him very far toward the production of a God
available for religious purposes."[49]   Whitehead's God fails
because "he does not satisfy the passions of the believer.
This God does not govern the world like a king nor watch
over his children like a father.   He offers them no purposes
to which they can consecrate themselves; he exhibits no image of holiness they can imitate.   He does not chastise them
in sin nor console them in sorrow.   He is a principle with
which to explain the facts, if you can understand the explanation.   He is not himself a personality who deals with the
facts.   For the purposes of religion he is no God at all; his
universe remains stonily unaware of man."[50]

Not all the charges made in this outburst are true of every
God conceived by reason.   Nothing prevents a rational religionist from accepting a dynamic God, and the God sought
out and discovered by the human mind may well be more
than an explanatory hypothesis; nor is there any reason why
the God discovered by reason cannot become a ground of
values, as did the God of Aristotle, and more recently the
God of Copleston.[51]   Thus the accusations of Lippmann
against Whitehead seem to lose some of their force when
applied to rational religion in general, but airing them may
still serve a purpose: at least now we have a fairly concrete
notion of just what religious "needs" Ross found unfulfilled
in Aristotle and Lippmann found unfulfilled by Whitehead:
man's need is for a father in the sky.   The guilt-ridden soul
needs an all-powerful big brother to put everything right.
The frightened creature needs an ally and defender.   Yet
somehow these notions seem inadequate.   The religious
mind seeks a more elevated conception of God.

Thought comes alive in religion with the realization that
anthropomorphism is idolatry: when the first glimmer
crosses the soul that meaningful religion is possible without
giving God a long white beard or stationing angels on His
right hand and grandmother on His left, rational religion has
begun.   The mind has gone into the service of religion and
soon forgets that any other path of approach to God was

possible, as it tries to conceive a Being worthy of worship and not an image of itself. This is not creating a new God, but an attempt to synthesize a new concept. To be sure, disagreements will arise, but are they really caused by rational theologians' being more argumentative than other sorts of people or their enjoyment of "disproving what other men hold sacred"? On the contrary. The rational religionist conceives of theology as the struggle to derive a concept which fittingly describes a holy Being. It would be foolish to say that such a concept will not grow and change with the growth of the human mind. Just as all who engage in philosophy must be prepared for the accusation that their accounts of reality are inadequate or subjective, so all who engage in good faith in theological discussion must be prepared to face the accusation that what they have described is not in fact a holy Being, but is no more than a veiled image of themselves, or their fathers. Nor should the poser of such an accusation need to face charges of intolerance, for argument is not persecution and may even lead to truth, as Mill hoped, unless from the constant conjunction of the heat of debate with the light of understanding nothing can be inferred. A philosophy of religion which sees theological knowledge as inherently rational, thus takes on the role of guardian of theology's chastity: it will never allow the defilement or corrupting of the concept of God by mingling it with crude wish-fulfillments; for it was in the role of theology's guardian and purifier that reason first entered theology, and as such it remains.

What of the intellectual difficulty? We should perhaps train our minds. The universe is difficult to understand. What of those human needs? Perhaps we shall learn to conquer our insecurities and supply our wants from our own resources: we know at least that guilt and fear will not be overcome by treating sin as the inevitable human condition. D. H. Lawrence knew well enough that no love of a heavenly surrogate could replace the father he could not love as a child. This is a beginning. It is not theology but ethics, which teaches the art of living our lives, by which our "needs" can be supplied. Ethics is a difficult art, but it seems of small advantage to evade learning it while debasing theology with projections of our own needs. Rational religion is not the sterility but the chastity of the mind; it seeks to satisfy no needs and allay no passions but only to know the truth about God.

The philosopher who holds a theory of rational religion considers religion to be basically the activity of the human mind imaginatively seeking to articulate a conception of the divine without idolatry. For whom does he believe such a religion exists? Considering the complexity of the concepts generated and their high degree of abstraction from the workaday world (although not from the underlying unity of reality) it might seem that the appeal would be to a small, specially trained intellectual elite. And, to an extent, such is the case, for the numbers of participants in rational religion have not been large enough to contradict what the "difficulty" of the subject matter leads us to suspect. Nevertheless, in a more real sense, rational religion is universal. To conceive of religious truth as open to the imaginative, inquiring mind is to propose, by suggestion, that reason should try to discover that truth. Such an endeavor is open, in theory at least, to every human being. If it happens to be the case that a certain intellectual agility is requisite, if it happens to be a fact that some knowledge of the culs-de-sac and through passages of past thought is helpful, it still remains possible for any human being, regardless of his background (to the degree that he informs himself of history and masters the give-and-take of dialectic) to participate in the rational search for God. And every human being is invited to do so by the universal claim of rational religion: it seeks a truth for all.

How does rational religion express itself? What form of activity would characterize one man's religious involvement as rational, in opposition to that of another? Contemplation, of course, is the key. The contemplative man spends his mornings studying the world of fact and tracing, from the tips of its experiential roots to the divergence of its twigs, the branchings of logical possibility, in search of truth; in the evening, he rests his eyes on the little truths he has won, seeks out their worth and enjoys them in quiet: rational religion seeks God in its active phase and rests in peaceful contemplation of Him. It was the peace achieved in contemplation that led Aristotle to consider a contemplative life the highest good for man: what human life could be more self-sufficient, what man could be more godlike than one whose needs from the world and involvement in its commotion are modest and whose only great desires are supplied by the mind itself? What life could be better, asks the rationalist, than the constant use of man's highest faculty directed upward towards the highest Truth?

The activity reason has chosen for man's religious expression is not reflexive, it is not mere introspection, not navel-gazing, for the contemplation is of God, not of the mind itself, and the obligation of self-knowledge implies, as we have seen, an obligation to become like God. Reason itself must recognize the dullness of a life of only one activity, even directed to the Highest. Such an existence has none of life's vitality. It does not show the creative outpouring characteristic of the life of God, but would be called, more aptly, stultification.

> . . . always a strange resemblance is
> Between the idiot smile and bliss-drenched faces
> Suffering the beatific vision.
> There is a way of knowing
> Whose peaks achieve, almost,
> That vacant vastness of the mindless mind,
> Where evil fades into ineffable good,
> And good itself diminishes to spotless nullity.[52]

Reason must either discover the necessity of an active human involvement with the world's life from which it sought to free itself, towards which its only relation was dispassionate contemplation, or else risk sinking into the deep, sweet, dull slumber of self-satisfaction that bears no resemblance to the active seeking and subduing that is the vitality of reason, and out of which a terrified scream from the human world will awaken it too late. Thus the religious activity of reason, while it remains reasonable, is not confined to contemplation. The search, by reason, for a purely contempla-

tive life is condemned to futility. For just as action without
thought is directionless and inept, thought without active
involvement soon loses its content and its meaning. For the
thorough rationalist, man is above all the rational creature
and contemplation is the obvious and archetypical religious
activity, assimilation of self to God. For us, reason itself
warns against confusing what might be man's "highest" activity with the integrated summation of a good life,[53] as it
warns the rationalist against the subtler anthropomorphism
of creating God in his own image—an intellectual. Nonetheless the fact remains that a life of constant harassment,
without a moment of contemplation to balance the moment
of involvement—to weigh it, in fact—and yield a meaningful
synthesis, will hardly be a true, rich, or human life. All of
us who believe that reason should guide the progress of religion therefore hope that it will lead the religious impulse
not merely to social action but also to contemplation and
fuller understanding of the truth.

Is reason really capable of achieving knowledge of God?
Mass religion begins by denying the first premiss of rational
religion. Thus Reinhold Niebuhr writes of the adherents of
rational religion, among whom he justly numbers Thomas
Aquinas, that they usually "claim to know too much" "about"
the eternal mystery:

> Sometimes they sharply define the limits of reason, and the
> further limits of faith beyond reason, and claim to know
> exactly how far reason penetrates into the eternal mystery
> and how much further faith reaches. Yet though they
> make a distinction between faith and reason, they straight-
> way so mix and confuse reason and faith that they pretend
> to be able to give a rational and sharply defined account
> of the character of God and of the eternal ground of exist-
> ence. They define the power and knowledge of God pre-
> cisely, and explain the exact extent of His control and fore-
> knowledge of events. They dissect the mysterious relation
> between man's intellectual faculties and his vital capacities,
> and claim to know the exact limits of *physis, psyche* and
> *nous*, of body, soul, and spirit. They know that man is im-
> mortal and why; and just what portion and part of him is
> mortal and what part immortal. Thus they banish the mys-

tery of the unity of man's spiritual and physical existence. They have no sense of mystery about the problem of immortality. They know the geography of heaven and of hell, and the furniture of the one and the temperature of the other.[54]

Reason cannot teach us all these things, and Niebuhr's point in this regard is well taken by any thoughtful adherent of rational religion, nor does rationalism always find a sense of mystery out of place. Niebuhr takes as his text I *Corinthians* xiii 12, "For now we see as through a glass darkly . . ."—let this be admitted by the rational religionist—we certainly don't know everything. Niebuhr replies: but don't you see *faith* is needed. He writes "there is a light which shineth in darkness; and the darkness is not able to comprehend it. Reason does not light that light; but faith is able to pierce the darkness and apprehend it." Rational religion confuses reason and faith as well as demarcating them too clearly. But the rational religionist, strange as it seems, recognizes the need for faith: he must have faith in his premises, and above all a Cartesian faith that his mind will not betray him.

This, patently, is not what Niebuhr meant at all: Now the issue between Niebuhr and rational religion is clearly "Faith *in what?*" Niebuhr's answer, "The Christian faith, at least, is a faith in revelation," readily betrays how rapidly what was taken as a friendly suggestion of modesty in describing reason's achievements in religion has grown into a full scale attempt to replace reason with revelation as a source of religious knowledge. Yet may not anyone receive a revelation? Is not reason itself a divine revelation vouchsafed to man—as we have seen to be the belief of the radical monotheist? Niebuhr recognizes the danger, in allowing just any revelation, of new life being pumped into the veins of the *bête noire* he has just vanquished. Were he to say with the Torah that the ultimate test of a true prophet is whether he speaks the truth, he would only restore reason as the ultimate criterion of choice. Niebuhr sees that he must particularize, and particularize he does: only certain revelations, made at certain times and in certain ways, are legitimate, only those available to us in certain chains of

manuscripts verified by their accompanying traditions: "The
Christian faith . . . believes that God has made Himself
known. It believes that He has spoken through the prophets
and finally in His Son. It accepts the revelation in Christ
as the ultimate clue to the mystery of God's nature and purpose in the world . . ." Thus revelation and tradition, in-
dissolubly linked, have replaced reason as answers to the
questions, 'How is religious knowledge attainable? By what
faculty can we know God?' A new variety of religion has
been generated.

It is the particularization of revelation by confining its
legitimacy to a historically specific set of traditions that
yields a second answer to the philosopher's question 'For
whom does religion exist?' The new form of religion, since
it has decried the activity of reason in religion and elevated
the role of revelation is forced to become evangelical in its
appeal: an evangel is the good news, the true report of a
revelation. It addresses the multitude, the crowd in the
market place, for its message is too charged with excitement
to be phrased in the measured tones of the lectern. It may
seem a strange juxtaposition, but there is a deep community
of spirit between the learned Reinhold Niebuhr who puts
revelation in place of reason and Billy Graham, who says 'I
can't prove there's a God; you've just got to believe . . .'
This is mass religion. It depends on reason only as far as
the minimal requirements of communication demand; for
the rest, it relies on emotion.

Now mass religion, like rational religion, claims universality; and doesn't the claim seem more justified, for mass religion preaches to high and low, rich and poor, wise and
foolish? There is no intellectual élite here, no ignoring of
the needs and passions of the people. The evangelist brings
his tidings to all men of good will. Yet because allowing
choice among revelations will only restore rational religion,
tradition has been introduced, and precisely because the
"needs" and passions of the people are not ignored but fed
by the emotional appeals of the evangelist that tradition will
be particular, not universal. Through a sense of ethnic identity, through common bonds of history, through common
needs and common passions, and even through the religious

tradition itself, *the* people will become *this* people, the Chosen People, God's children, the People of the Only true Way, the Children of Light. If a prophet discovers the force behind the drive to peoplehood, how can he avoid calling that force to the service of God? Just as traditions help single-out peoples, evangelists have a way of particularizing traditions, popularizing them. It seems hardly necessary to cite Gerald L. K. Smith, Stokeley Carmichael, or Adolf Hitler to demonstrate the tremendous forces particularism can unleash in behalf of its Cause. Muhammad brings a Qur'ān *for the Arabs*, Moses brings a Torah *for Israel*. And even Mr. Niebuhr, catholic though his Protestantism may be, writes "The Christian faith, at least. . . ." Rational religion will reason with anyone who can think. It claims validity for all. Mass religions appeal to common stores of tradition. They each appeal to all who can hear, but will be heard by no more than some.

The particularism of mass religion expresses itself clearly in the distinctive answer it gives the question 'What is the characteristically religious form of activity?' The dismissal of reason from its office of handmaid has shifted the general emphasis of religious attention: the focal problem is not now 'How can we know God', but 'How can we serve Him?' Each tradition that bears the news of a particular revelation bears with it its own conception of holy service, to which the metaphor of agricultural labor is applied—*avodah* in Hebrew, *'ibādah* in Arabic, *cultus* for the Romans: the *summum bonum* has become a life of labor in the service of God. Sacrifice is the first service, but soon it is followed by the observance of a vast, codified, positive law, the law of God. Observance of the Law becomes an end in itself, for such a Law is the concrete expression of the divine will. Special restrictions of cleanliness, and of its "sublimated" cognate, purity, are put on the people to signify their sanctification to the service of God. Prayer is introduced and drives out sacrifice by its higher level of spirituality—but prayer too is service. Fasts, vigils, and even works of kindness come to be seen as service. Groups worship in the sacred language of the common revelation, common laws, common feasts and pilgrimages—the particularisms of time and place—common rituals—the elaborate panoply of "organized religion" is built into a great edifice that all but obscures the original kinship chalk-line above which it rose—the cult has grown into a culture. The original ethnic appeal has come full circle, now it is peoplehood that is seen in terms of religion.

Rational religion and mass religion have in common the assumption that there is somehow a problem regarding man's knowledge of God. Reason and revelation are introduced as opposing solutions to this problem; but mystic religion stands apart from both. To the mystic, reason and revelation both seem irrelevant. The mystic sees no problem in knowing God: God is manifest. 'Do you need a candle to see the sun?' he asks. The mystic has come within sight of the God-head. From his heights anything in the finite world of men looks ant-like; and even human reason, even the law itself may seem petty and laughable. He scorns reason and looks down on the weak efforts of those who put their faith in it. After his direct confrontation with reality, the processes of reasoning and even the service of obedience seem wasted ingenuity, wasted devotion. Their results are veils, illusions that keep the mystic from contact with his God. He not only rejects the truths of reason and the duties of obedience, but toys with their opposites: he becomes a lover of paradox and rebellion and may even utter the ultimate paradox, *credo quia absurdum,* or commit the ultimate disobedience, antinomianism. The rationalist knows God as a study; the believer serves Him as a master; but for the mystic, God is a friend, a lover.

Here already, is seen the answer to the question 'What is a religious activity? What is a religious experience?' If rational religion tries to know God and mass religions want to serve Him, the mystic finds his highest religious expression and his deepest religious experience in the love of God. Knowledge is an easy first step, the spirit simply plunges through the diaphanous veil of otherness and God is known. The service of fasts, vigils, and prayer is an exercise of spiritual purification ultimately perhaps to be dispensed with. But the moment of life and beauty in which the meaning of all religion becomes clear is *unio mystica,* not an intellectual apprehension nor a rendering of service, but an all-consuming emotional experience, contact with God, absorption in His being.

For whom does such a religion exist? The ecstatic union of God and man, lover and beloved, blots out all the rest of the world. Only the lover remains, aware only of his Beloved. And in that awareness, his own identity may be absorbed. This union is as intimate as the other holy form of love in which poetry has found its symbol, and like its analogue, it asks solitude. Rational religion is cosmopolitan; it makes public a truth of universal validity. Mass religions are social and congregationalized by dogma and ritual. But when the mystic seeks God, he seeks Him alone. Mystic religion is for *one*.

The categories of religion before us, rational, popular, and mystic, are derived from experience, and one therefore feels hesitant about attributing any special logical status to them: it may well be the case that they are not jointly exhaustive of the possibilities of religion, which has a strange way of deceiving predictions. Yet these three classes do seem to have some logical structure. Thus rational religion says man *can* know God; atheism says he *cannot*; mass religion says we *should* know God; mystic religion says we *must* know Him, for He is manifest. Rational religion opens religious truth to *all*, atheism, to *none*; mass religion offers the service of God to *some*; mystic religion seeks the love of God for *one*.

If we are hesitant to say the three members of this scheme are jointly exhaustive of the potentialities of religious diversity, we should not be hesitant to recognize that these members taken as units are by no means mutually exclusive. Indeed it seems there has never been a world religion that did not to some extent partake of all three. Thus Judaism has had its Karaites and Rabbinites, its Hasidim and Mitnagdim; Islam has had its Sūfīs and Mu'tazilites; Catholicism has had its Thomists and Jansenists. When concretely embodied the three ideal types are in far less vivid contrast. Few religious movements that might be chosen as exemplars of one type or another are so willing to put all their eggs in one basket as to shun any hybridization among the three. Yet, no matter how much mixture we admit to exist, the three types still seem to represent genuine differences of religious outlook.

Empirically, the reality of the contrasts among them can be realized no better than by observation of the changes from one type to the next. Rational religion has a way of stagnating, for example, into mass religion. Contemplation degenerates into study, and the open, free-wheeling discussion which invited all becomes the academic debate of the study-group, a closed circle, protected by jargon from the intrusions of the critical and inquisitive world. The group may be erudite and elevated but the erudition is confined within a tradition of literary culture or academic values, and the elevation is no more than the *esprit* that arises from acceptance of a common intellectual authority. Such men are no longer thinkers, but followers; their religion, refined and arcane as it may be, is no more a religion of reason than that of the masses. Contemplation may equally take a turn toward the ecstatic and become mystical. Mass religion, because of the inertia of traditionalism, seems not to "bear within itself the seeds of its destruction"; it changes only in spite of itself, as, for example, when a rational or mystic mind, out of ennui or anger, attacks its dogmas and formalities. On such occasions new religions are born out of the ruins of the old. Mystic religion, on the other hand, may seed-out in many different ways. Its fervor may calm into the tranquility of rational religion; grafted to its old scion by nostalgic discussions of "mystic theory"; or it may turn in the direction of mass religion, towards what Weber called routinization, the institutionalization of charisma. It will seek to regulate and regularize the fleeting beatific glimpses through forms characteristic of mass religion, fasting, vigils, wine bouts, hypnosis, *dhikr* rites like those of the dervishes, considered no longer as "exercises" but as stimulants to "bring on a mystic state." The disappointed mystic may resort, in the extreme, to "psychedelics", whether in the form of cannabis, peyote, LSD, or soma. The true mystic, insisting on the existential reality of a living God, is, of course, not satisfied by phenomenological mimicry of the religious experience. He labels all of these ersatz.

Rational, mass and mystic religion may be neither jointly exhaustive nor mutually exclusive, but no one who has witnessed the change of one of these types to another can deny the reality of the differences among them. We must now discover how Ibn Tufayl's philosophy of religion relates to these three categories.

The climax of Hayy's development, the heart of his religious experience, is a beatific vision of cosmic proportions. Ibn Tufayl falters before the task of relating what it is that Hayy has experienced, but after warning us not to take his words literally, not to interpret him superficially, but to seek the inner meaning,[55] he attempts to convey figuratively the beauty and sanctity of Hayy's experience.[56] Hayy reaches the highest plateau of human experience. He gazes out at the immaterial essences of each of the spheres, from the highest to the lowest. He sees the essence of the world with its seventy thousand faces, each face with seventy thousand mouths, and each mouth with seventy thousand tongues all praising, glorifying and extolling God. Hayy sees himself— as it were—among these faces; he achieves union with the Godhead.

We may ignore Ibn Tufayl's warning against taking his words literally, but then we would have no means of explaining the sudden appearance of this many-headed hydra in the usually austere world of radical, rational monotheism. If we hope to make a serious evaluation of Ibn Tufayl's thought, it must be admitted that his sudden descent from sublime abstraction to a concrete, if colorful world, is inspired not by a passion to mythologize but by a feeling that no ordinary use of language can convey the awe of Hayy's paradoxical discovery that he is simultaneously at one with, yet distinct from God Himself. Hayy's first moment of beatific awareness is the climax of a lifetime of ascent; all that Ibn Tufayl can write after that moment has been described is anti-climax, no more than "the rest of the story."[57] What actually happens in that great moment of union with God, we must be left to ponder for ourselves.

Ibn Tufayl's placement of the beatific experience as dénouement and the reverent periphrasis with which that experience is described seem to leave no doubt as to how he

answered the questions of religious philosophy. Clearly, he
was a mystic, plain and simple. It is for the sake of the
climactic union with God that all the rest takes place. But
is it really so simple?

Where is the mystic's willingness to render to God the ultimate and greatest sacrifice, the sacrifice of reason? Odin
gave up an eye for wisdom, he cast into a well the organ of
lower knowledge and in return was given a higher, mystic
form of knowledge. Oedipus too is brought by fate, against
his will and reason, to tear out his eyes to reach the inner
irrational wisdom of the blind seer Tiresias, "the peace that
passeth understanding." Yet no such sacrifice is recommended by Ibn Tufayl. For a perfect mystic, paradox is the
ultimate test of courage, the heart of the mystery is to love
God enough to cry *"Credo quia absurdum"*—to bear the cross
of self-contradiction. Yet Ibn Tufayl says explicitly that
nothing revealed in a beatific experience can contradict the
truths we learn through the use of reason.[58] What required
him to make this reassuring qualification? There seems to
be some as yet un-dormant critical urge in him that needs
to be reassured. A pure mystic would long ago have suppressed such promptings of reason—What is it to him if God
does contradict human reason! The most peculiar feature
of Ibn Tufayl's mysticism, if we can call it that without
qualification, is the consistent refusal of reason to abdicate
its role. What is the role of reason in Ibn Tufayl's mystic
religion?

First, reason must precede direct intuition of God. We
have already noted the evolutionary character of personal
development as conceived by Ibn Tufayl. Growth and education are the successive unfolding of hierarchically ranked
natural capacities. Each prior capacity and each primitive
state of awareness to which that capacity gives rise is more
elemental and less important, more basic and less subtle,
more pragmatically vital and less spiritually vitalizing than
the next higher capacity and the next more perfect state.
Just as a man with sight is more perfectly developed than
a blind man,[59] a man with divine intuition is more perfectly
developed than one who depends on reason. His evolutionary concept of human development allows Ibn Tufayl to

consider each new stage of a man's development not as a personal cataclysm, but as an increment added to what has gone before.

When the blind man gains sight he is not asked to give up his other senses; the knowledge he has acquired through them has been substantial. Ostensive definitions and report[60] can teach him, for example, that a camel and a mud-brick wall have roughly the same color, even though he lacks the clarity and pleasure of a more perfect level of awareness. His non-visual senses have not merely preserved him until he attained sight, they have prepared him for it. Dropping the analogy, reason is not merely a less perfect way of knowing God than intuition; it is and—except in the case of rare prophetic individuals—must be our first means of knowing Him. Reason does not merely precede intuition, but prepares the way for it. Thus, it is by the use of reason that Hayy, Ibn Tufayl's paradigm of mankind, reaches his first knowledge of God's nature; he would remain ignorant even of God's existence were it not for reason.

Ibn Tufayl does not adopt the attitude characteristic of mysticism, that rational proofs of God's existence are futile or irrelevant and that it is vain to try to seek God intellectually. Apparently he does not feel with the pure mystic that God is manifest or he would not devote two of Hayy's septenaries and the largest single portion of his own text to reasoned discovery of God's existence and rational comprehension of His nature.[61] There seems to be some disparity between the mystic's belief that no candle is needed to see the sun and Ibn Tufayl's admonition[62] that a desire to know the truth implies genuine hard work.

Often, as Ibn Tufayl observes,[63] a mystic may feel so exalted by the joy and wonder of his experience, or may feel the immanence of God so intensely that he will utter blasphemous ejaculations like Hallaj's famous ecstatic cry "I am the Truth!" Such exclamations, Ibn Tufayl believes, would be impossible given adequate training in intellectual pursuits. Ghazālī, the brilliant scholar, known to the Muslims as the "Proof of Islam", was protected from such lapses by the refinement of his mind through education. At the opposite extreme, the mystic, overwhelmed by the vastness of

God and his own insignificance has often sought self-annihilation, a submerging of the ego in the great Totality.
This *fanā'*, or dissolving of the soul, is carefully qualified in
the passage dealing with it quoted with approval from
Avicenna: "The soul loses consciousness of itself and beholds only God; only to the extent that it beholds God does
it regard itself at all."[64] Apparently, the danger of spiritual
or even physical self-destruction threatened by many forms
of mystic self-effacement has been observed and an intricate
intellectual hedge has been constructed to prevent excessive
zeal in pursuit of *fanā'*. It is reason, the seeker of middle
ground, that has carefully protected the mystic experience
from the extremes of self-aggrandizement and self-annihilation. And it is reason that safeguards against the dangers
of mystic antinomianism by recognizing the moral worth and
civic necessity of the revealed law.[65] Nor is the role of reason confined to preparing, preceding and protecting.

For even when the mystic experience is fully achieved,
and the initiate soul has attained a high level in the ranks
of mystic perfection, intuition is not alone, but reason seems
always to be at its side; at times, in fact, it seems hard to
differentiate Ibn Tufayl's conception of the phenomenological reality of beatitude from contemplation. Hayy decides
that he must imitate the animals, the heavenly bodies, and
God.[66] To imitate animals he must satisfy his physical
needs; to imitate the stars he keeps clean, acts kindly, moves
gracefully—and in circles—and contemplates God; to imitate
God, he must contemplate God, and nothing but God. Consistently, Hayy's highest self-imposed religious obligations
are contemplative. It is in contemplation that he spends
most of his time. Does Hayy contemplate through reason
or intuition? No doctrinaire answer will suffice; of course
the joy and clarity of direct divine intuition often overwhelm
him, yet his mind is at work, and surely no mere analysis of
the focal point of his mind could reveal accurately whether
intuition or reason were at any given moment the window
through which his vision was perceived.

Reason and the mystical experience seem to have formed
a symbiotic union in Ibn Tufayl's thought. Reason is never
discarded by him as by a pure mystic. It is given the role

of precursor of the mystic experience, but it also defines the
content of religion and provides the first elements of religious knowledge and the first impetus to religious endeavor; its inherent caution protects against the passionate
excesses of purely mystical religion; and it often seems to
moderate the fervor of mystic union into contemplation.

Ibn Tufayl's express purpose[67] in telling the story of Hayy
Ibn Yaqzān is to reveal, as best he can, some of the secrets
of the "oriental philosophy" or "eastern wisdom" in which
Avicenna had engaged. It was to demonstrate his intention
to participate in that tradition that Ibn Tufayl chose names
for his principal three characters which had already been
used by Avicenna in allegorical stories of his own.[68]

"Oriental philosophy" for Ibn Tufayl has initially a cultural and geographical significance. The expression is *al-
hikmat-ul-mashriqiyya*. *Hikma*, the Semitic word for wisdom or philosophy, is consciously used in place of *falsafa*,
which is of course a Greek borrowing. The hope is that an
indigenous, non-Western philosophy can be developed to
replace unsatisfactory Greek transplants. Ibn Tufayl, living
in the Maghrib, is himself, of course, a Westerner; he is pain-
fully conscious of the lack of vital books by such authors as
Ghazālī.[69] The philosophy he hopes to engage in is as rare
as the philosopher's stone, "especially in our part of the
world."[70] He hopes his efforts will bring some of this eastern
type of wisdom to the West. Avicenna is thus taken to mean
the adjective in contrast to 'Peripatetic', indicating a departure from the Greek school of the West to which he himself
devoted the bulk of his work.[71]

The meaning of *mashriqiyya* does not however seem inclined to confine itself to the purely geographical. The
triliteral root *SH-R-Q* will gradually reassert the basic meaning of *orient*, and a school of *illuminationist, mushriqiyya*,
philosophy will arise. Gauthier even went so far as to read
mushriqiyya for *mashriqiyya*,[72] a perfectly credible change,
since Arabic gives no orthographic indication of vocaliza-
tion, but premature in Avicenna and unjustified in Ibn
Tufayl, whose intention to convey a geographical contrast
by the use of this term is explicit in the text and seems to be
attested by his contemporary, Ibn Rushd.[73] Nevertheless,

even before the rise of Illuminationist "theosophy" had
shifted the points of reference, elevating the east to a sideral
realm of lights and demoting the west, by a pun, to the land
of exile, reference to 'Eastern philosophy' would still have
had vague connotations of divine light, on the old assumption *ex oriente lux*. To be sure Ibn Tufayl gives the term a
geographical *reference*, but the *sense* is of a difference in
cultural perspective. The sun does rise in the east, and since
Plato, Aristotle, and Plotinus, the sun had been paradigmatic
not only of what gives things their forms, and so makes them
apprehensible, but also of what gives man that special form
which makes him apprehending. The sun, as vehicle of
emanation and visible symbol of the divine generosity, was
adopted from the pagans by the Sūfīs and Ghazālī; and the
neo-Platonist theory of sunlight as model of emanation was
copied from Avicenna by Ibn Tufayl to set the tone of his
opening pages. Ibn Tufayl can scarcely have been unaware
of the associations 'eastern philosophy' would suggest to
those who troubled to find an "inner meaning" in his words.
As Suhrawardī (1153-91), the real founder of Islamic illumi-
nism, put it, "Woe unto thee, if by thy country thou meanest
Damascus, Baghdad, or any other city of this world!"[74]

What did Ibn Tufayl expect this oriental philosophy to
achieve?

What Eastern wisdom could achieve that had been so rare
in Andalusia and in Peripatetic thought was a philosophical
approach to God and the mystic experience. Ibn Tufayl's
complaint is that, up to his own time, almost all the intelligence in his part of the world had been devoted to logic and
mathematics. The possible objects of intellectual endeavor
seemed to be divided, as one of his predecessors put it, between unattainable truths and readily available trivia.[75]
Such a position cannot destroy religion if there is a dominant
tradition of faith to oppose it; but it suffocates rational religion by isolating the religious sphere from the intellectual.
It was an escape from the stifling positivism of these rigid
dichotomies—fact and tautology, reason and religion—that
Ibn Tufayl sought in his oriental philosophy. His own philosophical predecessor, Ibn Bājja,[76] the Avempace of the West,
had hoped that metaphysics, the science that transcends sci-

ence, might furnish means of reaching a higher truth; but he had missed the clarity, the joy, and certainly the experience of ecstasy. Oriental philosophy goes beyond Ibn Bājja's metaphysics, and rejects positivism, which does not allow for the budding of the soul's potentialities. Oriental philosophy is a reasoned approach to the mystic experience.

Corbin has classified Avicenna's oriental wisdom as mystic-gnosis;[77] and to the extent that Hayy's ultimate knowledge comes from a faculty that "surpasseth understanding" it is valid to label his version of Avicenna's enterprise mysticism. And yet it is a very strange variety of mysticism: it seems to be "rational-mysticism."

Reason, as we have seen, is reluctant to be left behind or outgrown. Is it not annoying to a young man off on his grand tour to have a family servant who is not content to plan his trip and make his arrangements, but wants to come along as guide and protector and set up house with him when he reaches his ultimate destination? What possible use is reason in the mystic adventure? Yet Ibn Tufayl does keep reason on. What is his motivation? It seems that a philosopher's sense of identity as thinker is harder to change than even the character of his substantive beliefs.

For the whole project of giving an account of the ineffable, the composition of *Hayy Ibn Yaqzān* itself, is a rationalist's affair. To convey directly the substance of what becomes known in a mystic experience is impossible, but to give a rational introduction to the nature of that experience and what it teaches is possible and is precisely the task of oriental philosophy.[78] A faculty that "surpasseth understanding" is one that knows more than can be learned by the simple-minded use of simple minds, not one that knows what cannot be understood. Of course, Ibn Tufayl must resort to "hints and guesses", symbols, ultimately to angelology and constantly to allegory, but this itself is a reasoned process. Fitting words into sentences and incidents into a plot, assigning symbols to meanings and making sure the symbols convey the right meaning, these are tasks for the mind. A real mystic stays in his cave, keeps his eye on his navel and concentrates on the sacred syllable "OM." The truth, he will tell you, if he speaks at all, is ineffable. For a man to

begin the hard work of trying to express a mystic truth in
any form, he must have in him some demand for communication, a desire to make things as clear for others as they are
for himself, a desire to make himself and what he knows
transmissible, acceptable and understood—an element of the
rationalist.

The religion of Ibn Tufayl is a hybrid, a synthesis of mystical and rational religion. God is known first and most safely by reason, ultimately and most intensely by intuition, but
calmly and constantly by a philosophical mind that seems to
find no phenomenological distinction between the two. The
relationship of man to God, in which the "oriental philosopher" wraps himself, *wilāya*, combines the intimate, intuitive
understanding of friendship with the passion and immediacy
of love; this uniting of reason and emotion marks the union
of rational and mystic religion.

For whom does this rational-mystic oriental philosophy
exist? Ibn Tufayl tries hard to resist the temptation (to
which Ghazālī had succumbed) of preaching to the crowd[79]
and the urge to lecture like an untempered rationalist at the
cosmos. But if he speaks softly he does not keep silent like
a mystic. He addresses his own dear friend[80] whom he
hopes will become his disciple. Unlike a pure mystic, he
believes he can convey what he knows; unlike a pure rationalist, he does not think he can "convince everyone"; not
everyone is capable of sound reasoning,[81] not to mention a
beatific relation with God.[82] He must find a disciple whom
he can guide. Avicenna's Hayy was his Vergil through the
spiritual world; this role of guide, Ibn Tufayl adopts toward
his disciple. Oriental philosophy is passed from one individual to the next,[83] it exists not for some, all, or one, but for
two: it is a quiet dialogue between master and disciple.

Ibn Tufayl faces squarely the inevitable charge that he
has abandoned reason.[84] He answers that what his opponents call reason is hardly worthy of the name; it is no more
than the logical ability of abstracting general concepts from
particular data. With Gestalt psychology he recognizes that
there is more to perceptual experience than sensory data;
he sees, with Frege, that there is more to the *a priori* than
tautology; and with Tolstoy he faces the reality that there

is far more to life itself than perception and conception; yet this is not an abandonment of reason; the idea seems rather that reason should "rise to the occasion", should prepare itself to guide the soul upward through the intricate manifold of life's experiences and even to the most sacred experience. It may be that reason had been confined to classifying data, or to unweaving and reweaving the webs of logic; this must end: reason must discover its own unopened capacities. As 'Abdul-Hamīd Khwāja put it,[85] reason is "untrue to itself" if it does not lead to the ecstatic union. The demand is not that reason abdicate, but that it transcend itself.

George Hourani[86] has emphasized that Ibn Tufayl's basic purpose in writing Hayy's story was the exposition of oriental philosophy and the depiction of the highest truth as conceived by that philosophy; he has emphatically pointed out the error of Gauthier and others who thought the book written to show 'the-harmony-of-philosophy-and-revelation.' His argument, based on Ibn Tufayl's explicitly stated purpose and on calling attention to the sheer quantitative distribution of focus, treats the book's final incidents involving Absāl and Salāmān as an aesthetic release of tension, inspired, on the model developed by Leo Strauss in *Persecution and the Art of Writing*, by the necessity for any post-Ghazāli philosopher to make a bow in the direction of religion, especially in the "conservative Maghrib." This seems certainly to be a valid analysis. Having indicated the character of oriental philosophy, Ibn Tufayl feels obliged to show its relationship to traditional Islam. He does, in fact, press the correspondence of reason and revelation. Absāl's awakening comes when he recognizes the congruence of the two,[87] and Ibn Tufayl even goes so far as to allow Hayy to apply to the revealed tradition one of the formulae he applies to reason: it bore not the slightest contradiction to what was revealed in his mystic experience.[88] But his remark that the "true religion" is one cause of the rarity of any plain, un-veiled statement of Eastern philosophy[89] is worthy of Strauss himself and goes a good way toward confirming the hypothesis that the "harmony" is meant as a bow in the direction of the divines.

The fact is that such obeisances as do occur seem formal,

or formularized—the brief, shallow type of bow, rather than
full length prostrations. Organized religion, as viewed by
Hayy on his first exposure to civilization, seems a fine and
necessary thing, for the masses; but surely much of it is far
too literal for the superlative mind, and most of its restrictions are unneeded by him. How can Ibn Tufayl express
such a view? An explanation, perhaps, will be found in the
fact that the "conservative Maghrib" of Ibn Tufayl's day was
an image on the official façade, rather than the reality of
the inner chamber. The political power of Ibn Tufayl's protector, Abū Ya'qūb Yūsuf, the "Khalifa" of Spain, whose
family he served for thirty years as physician-counsellor,
rested solidly on the rigid-line religion of the Almohad
dynasty.[90] But in his private garden, with his friend the
philosopher, Abū Ya'qūb was apparently quite an independent thinker.[91]

No Muslim writing on religion could fail to confront the
overwhelmingly powerful Islamic tradition into which he
was born. Yet apparently deference to political realities demanded no more obliqueness in the encounter between rational-mysticism and traditional Islam than some show of
respect for the value of law and myth in their proper place.
The picture of traditional Islam presented by *Hayy Ibn
Yaqzān*, is simply that of mass religion, as seen from the
heights of rational mysticism.

Hayy recognizes[92] Islamic religious concepts to be products of the Islamic tradition of prophetic revelation. He
feels no scruple in admitting the truth of that revelation,
but how can anyone who has a direct knowledge of the pure
truth be satisfied with a traditional report? Ghazālī himself
urges his disciples to leave behind the truths of tradition
and seek direct intuition, personal revelation of God's manifest presence, in which tradition is eclipsed:

> Forget what you've heard and grasp what you see;
> At sunrise what use is Saturn to thee?[93]

How can anyone who has seen the realities remain content
with the symbols? Hayy cannot help but wonder why God's

messenger brought his truth in the veiled form of concrete representation.

Likewise with the law: traditional service of God seems strange to a rational-mystic. Ibn Tufayl takes on a tone of amusement when he first introduces Hayy to Absāl. Hayy has, assuredly, not the least idea what to make of the anchorite, shrouded, despite the perfect climate, in his heavy black wool robes which are taken at first for fur, weeping, praying and beating his breast.[94] When Hayy learns to speak, he can understand neither law nor ritual, and asks Absāl why they are needed.[95] Once he has seen for himself the weakness of human nature Hayy is ready to accept positive law as a necessary concession. Ritual he accepts out of respect for a prophet who spoke the Truth. Ibn Tufayl is chary of any appearance of assigning prophetic inspiration to the imagination of the prophet.[96] But all these matters, law, ritual and the symbolic reification of divine truth are sticking points: the intimacy and understanding of ecstatic experience would seem to obviate the need of laws to prop up moral weakness and regulations to stiffen the spiritual discipline, just as they obviate the need for myths and conceptual crutches to support intellectual deficiency.

Hayy's inability, when first informed by Absāl of the existence of society, to understand the role of mass religion in conveying knowledge by tradition, and purity by service—observance of ritual and obedience to law—stems from the fact that since his brilliant mind and hearty soul have always found him ready access to truth and right, he has no more conception of sin than of error. His inability to understand mass religion's answer to the problem of religious knowledge and his inability to follow its conception of the characteristically religious expression both stem from his unfamiliarity with the people for whom mass religion is intended. Once he is informed by Absāl[97] that not everyone has a mind as capable of reaching the truth as his or a soul as willing to cleave to it, that "men would devour each other"[98] if they had no law to keep them apart, he is ready at least for an intellectual rapprochement with the prevalent religion. Myth is needed because the very concretization Hayy finds

offensive makes religious doctrine available to the people.
Ritual is needed to modulate the spiritual and physical
spectra of asceticism and sensuality. Law is needed to as-
sure the continued existence and functioning of society.

But precisely because of the inherently social nature of
these great elements of mass religion, they exhibit the particularism to which mass religion is prone; and it is because
of this particularism that mass religion and rational-mysticism can coëxist, perhaps, but never interpenetrate. Myth
preëmpts that set of concrete representations most suited to
the needs of the masses it seeks to influence. Ritual seizes
on some set of acts "pleasing to God." Diverse systems of
positive law draw out alternative paths for the good life,
and designate all others as sin. 'Why this way?' asks the
rational-mystic, "Why not a different representation, or the
truth itself?', 'Why not a foreign ritual or an imaginative innovation on the law?' Hayy rebels against the particularism
of mass religion: the reason in him, because it seeks the
universal; the mysticism, because it seeks the absolute. Agnosticism is a subjunctive mood; it prefaces all the "proposi-
tions" of traditional religion with 'What if . . .'. Rational-
mysticism is more generous; it prefers the concessive mood,
prefacing all of mass religion with 'Although . . .'.

Ibn Tufayl has no quarrel with Islam or any other religion
that bears the tradition of a divine revelation. All of them
are paths from different directions twisting up to the same
summit. All are veiled glimpses at the Truth. All are poetic
attempts to capture Divinity, catch a glimpse of God "as
through a glass darkly"; but the rational-mystic asks 'Why
see God through a glass darkly, when you can see Him *now*
face to face, if your mind has eyes to see? Why darken the
glass with positive dogma and positive law, a law that prevents searching and a dogma of representations purposely
placed by tradition between the mind and the truth? Clear
all this out of your mind and seek the Truth!'

But tradition is a cultural force more powerful in molding
minds, perhaps, than minds are to mold themselves. Is it
possible for man to void his mind of all the myths, conscious
and unconscious, which society has instilled in him since
birth? Should he even try? How can the mind possibly

transcend cultural categories of thought and value by which its own nature has been formed? How safe is man's soul outside society?

IV

Man and Society

If *Hayy Ibn Yaqzān* were no more than a mouthpiece for Ibn Tufayl's religious philosophy, or if his story were only a conveyance for the tenets of the author's educational philosophy, its interest would be at least historical, but at best academic. The book would detail the path only for those who already know the way; for those who do not, it would be of value only as a curiosity. Yet, from the way in which Ibn Tufayl makes Hayy's personal evolution recapitulate the intellectual development of the species and the step-wise growth of every individual, we suspect that Hayy himself is more a symbol than a didactic mouthpiece and begin to realize that one of the questions at the heart of Ibn Tufayl's concern when he wrote *Hayy Ibn Yaqzān* was 'what is essential in man?'

Now essence is a metaphysical notion. Having an essence is not like having a dog, or even like having a cold, for essence is not a thing or even something that happens to a thing. But we must not be misled by the fact that essence is not substantial into supposing that it is not objective. Everything that exists has an essence and has one by virtue of the fact that it exists. In fact everything that exists has the specific essence that it has by virtue of the fact that it is what it is. This is what we mean by saying essence is a metaphysical notion, for metaphysics is the study of being *qua* being. And one thing we do know about things purely in view of the fact that they exist is that if a thing (no matter what it is) did not have its own essence, it would not be itself. Thus to ask the essence of a thing is very similar to asking what the thing *really* is, or asking what set of characteristics allow us to identify it when they are present and make us very reluctant to call it by a certain name when they are absent. These characteristics we distinguish from those it may just *happen* to have without prejudice to its identity and those it does not have at all.

To ask 'What is essential in man?' or 'What is man essentially?', is thus to ask what man is *really*, what predicates are applied to him, not most often, but most truly, 'Are there any characteristics the lack of which would make us reluctant to call something a man? If so what are they?' This seems quite straightforward. If it is not the vocabulary of ordinary language, it is certainly the syntax of everyday thought. It is impossible to recognize anything without the mind going through a sparking, short-cut process that has a rough-and-ready resemblance to what medieval philosophers called distinguishing between essence and accident. Yet, for some reason, there has been an almost automatic tendency to translate 'Essence is a metaphysical notion' to 'Essence is a very difficult notion—and maybe even a little superstitious!' It is fashionable even among philosophers to claim not to understand what is meant by essence. Many purport to dispense with the notion altogether; others follow the fashion in their terminology, but reintroduce the notion, disguised as "necessary and sufficient criterion." Perhaps as a means of skirting the mental block to metaphysics, perhaps as an intellectual aid to grasping some genuine difficulty, philosophers have cloaked the concept of essence in figurative language. The word 'essence' itself has become a metaphor.

And around the concept conveyed by that word a number of other metaphors have sprouted up, rigidified and died, leaving behind dried stalks—points of mental association on which the fine abstract of essence can crystallize and so become visible to the human mind,

In reading *Hayy Ibn Yaqzān*, our concern is with a clump of five of these dead metaphors. One is that of the basic as opposed to the superstructure. The notion is that the real is what *lies at bottom*, no less real if distorted by the weight of the edifice that rises above it. For Descartes, the essence of knowledge, the most vital and important part, without which it would not be knowledge—and the part most worthy of philosophical investigation—was the foundation of assumptions that lay beneath the cathedral of medieval Christian knowledge. Marx too relied on the same metaphor: *real* historical causes are economic; culture and ideology are superstructure.

A second of these dead metaphors on which the essence-accident distinction has been crystallized is the imagery of natural versus artificial, a real distinction often figuratively applied, as if certain forms of human association, for example, were more organic, more plant-like as it were, while others are more like artifacts, "forged" or "molded"; and it seems somehow quite justifiable to illustrate the fact that the family is more essential to human association, more characteristic and less dispensable, than government by calling the family natural and the government artificial, although both are established by human beings to fill human needs.

Growing sophistication, however, happens upon the subtlety that artifice is just as natural, just as "plant-like" as anything else, and talk begins of cultural evolution. Furthermore it may begin to appear to the more pluralistically minded that the universe is not monocentric in every way: more than one "base" can be found. Ideology and attitude can be recognized for basic factors in history along with modes of production. Such developments call for a new metaphor to maintain a point of mental contact between the concept of essence and its image. This third metaphor lies in the distinction between element and complex: what is essential is what is simple, the elements out of which more complicated things are made. Thus the Marxian historian, facing pluralism, retrenches, saying that economic drives are the simplest if not the most basic or the most natural, and are, therefore, the essential drives in history. Ideology is merely the complex rationale of economy; the superstructure is *fashioned* of forces more elemental than the complex they make up; metaphorically there is still a build-up and fashioning of the elemental raw materials; so the metaphors of nature and foundation are restored.

A fourth metaphor is the primitive-civilized distinction. The use of 'primitive' to mean 'essential' may have arisen out of the metaphor of simplicity because of the popular notion that primitive life is somehow simpler than "civilized life." Be that as it may, we often discover ourselves saying or believing that real life is primitive, in some sense raw, while "sophisticated", urbane life may seem to some artificial, and thus unreal.

The fifth metaphor involves attributing to the essential a special locus, at the beginning for example, or the end of time. Thus theories begin "Originally . . ." or "Ultimately . . .". The thought here, closely related to the line of mental assumption in the case of the primitive, is that what comes first is more real and remains real, even if distorted by subsequent developments, or that what comes last comes at a moment of truth when trivial considerations are washed away.

Such metaphors as these five have more than a rhetorical and instructive function. They do help put across a point and promote learning by allowing reïfication, the mental equivalent to audio-visual aids. But in addition, perhaps because they serve at the pleasure of the imagination, these metaphors bring a good deal of color into the black and white world of abstraction. Even if they were not necessary or useful, they would probably remain as luxuries in conversation because they stand at the juncture between metaphysics and poetry. And yet, like many luxuries, these metaphors are dangerous.

There is a great danger in taking literally what was meant as a figure; and, although we confidently feel the danger is easily avoided, history has proved the opposite. It is one thing to associate metaphor and concept, another to identify them. What is the genetic fallacy if not such a confusion? Nietzsche seeks the essence of justice in primitive, Teutonic revenge. Freud seeks the essence of religion in primitive cults and finds the *real* psychic forces in infantile sexuality: the real is identified with what happened to come first. But the fallacy is double-edged. It is as wrong to presume that the logically prior must have come first in time as it is to infer from temporal to essential priority. The conceptual simplicity or presumptive essentiality of communism or social contract as the "natural basis" of human relations bestows no historical primacy on "primitive communism" or an actual compact in the first society. We demand external evidence. No matter how persuasive this interchange of metaphors may be—and it has seemed very persuasive—it confers no legitimacy on *a priori* history.

A double confusion of image with essence and essence with image seems possible in the case of all five metaphors parallel to the paradigmatic confusion of essence and origin, the genetic fallacy. If the danger is so great, and even those who consciously use this rhetoric are carried away by their own language, why do these metaphors continue in use? Their pedagogic helpfulness seems diminished when it is realized what confusion they can cause, and the dialectical advantage they afford may begin to seem an unfair advantage. Is not fallacy too great a price to pay for poetry? And yet it seems some benefit is to be had from these figures that outweighs the danger of confusion and requires philosophers to caution themselves against taking them literally but go on using them. One such benefit comes from the usefulness of figures like these in formulating a unique conceptual tool, the thought-experiment.

Essences cannot be distilled in any ordinary device, but the thought-experiment is one means of capturing them. In science, a thought-experiment postulates a hypothetical situation and then tries to "predict" the natural outcome. The same technique has been used for centuries by philosophers grasping for the intangible. If you want to reveal the essence of man, postulate a situation in which that essence is thought to be most able to develop purely, unimpeded by foreign influences. Make the environment natural, make it primitive and simple, fill it with all the concrete conditions we associate with essentiality. Then let the imagination go to work to discover what will follow, what seems most reasonable, what seems most likely. The poetry is no longer a collection of images but has become drama: symbolic figures have taken roles as active, even causal factors; and they can work out for themselves the dialectic of the action. The philosopher's hope is that if any intellectual process can capture any fraction of the essence of man, the resolution of this dialectic can.

Postulate the situation to which metaphor leads you and

watch what develops—it seems so easy, all the straightforward clarity of science. Isolate man in a primitive environment and discover his essence. The mind does all the work. But these metaphors mean many things; there is much room, since every thought experimenter establishes his own situative premiss, to slant the given toward a desired result. Besides, the premiss itself is inherently ambiguous, since "what follows" follows naturally, not by strict implication. No direct scientific "answer" can be given. Instead, as if in response to that same Rousseau who devoted himself to Emile, the state of nature, the social contract, and the noble savage, who pleaded that "a good solution" to the problem "What experiments would have to be made to discover the natural man?" would "not be unworthy of the Aristotles and Plinys of the present age"[99] and who argued for an intellectual "throwing aside" of "all those scientific books which teach us only to see men such as they have made themselves, and contemplating the first and most simple operations of the human soul . . .",[100] we find a whole literary genre in his age and in others, devoted to the discovery of man's essence by the use of thought-experiment, and displaying as much diversity as might be expected from any heterogeneous group of philosophers discussing such a question as 'What is man?'

It seems apparent that, no matter what else *Hayy Ibn Yaqzān* may be, it is a member of this genre of thought-experiments. It is an attempt to sketch the outlines of an answer to the question of man's essence. As gleaners and interpreters, we must not wear blinders: we cannot evaluate the validity or even assess the meaning of Ibn Tufayl's resolution of the human essence thought-experiment without juxtaposing that resolution with other answers that have grown out of other branchings of conceptual possibility, especially not after we have seen that from the same situative premiss radically different conclusions can be drawn.

Basic-ness is vital to the imagery of which the given in Ibn Tufayl's experiment is constituted. The foundation of Hayy's soul is his *fitra*, his congenital endowment of capacities. We have already seen[101] how Ibn Tufayl postulates this natural complement of excellences in Hayy. This is his

given. But we must not ignore just *how much* is given by
the conception of this endowment of capacities as a *basis*:
the experimental dialectic must then work itself out as the
successive realization of Hayy's potentials, the progress of
his soul *upward,* toward God. The Sūfī conception of degrees of beatitude, orders of divine intimacy, is adopted.
Each new spiritual experience "wafts" the soul a level higher.[102]   Each new septenary, like a Sūfī stage, is a plateau
from which old progress can be surveyed and a glimpse can
be had of what lies further up.   From Hayy's first spiritual
steps, scorning the carcass of his mother-doe as something
low and worthless compared to the soul that once lived in
it,[103] to his final beatific ecstasy, in which his mind arrives
at the highest sphere, looks down over the whole Universe
and reaches up toward union with God,[104] the progress of
his soul is upward along a path of which a simile is the
progress from rusted to clear mirror, from polished mirror
to burning glass, from burning glass to the sun,[105] but of
which the analogue is the hierarchy of the spheres themselves rising higher and higher towards God, who is exalted
above all material comparison.[106]   And thus, Ibn Tufayl is
able to draw out a doctrine of human perfectibility by expressing the given as foundation and allowing the metaphor
of construction to complete itself.

Nor is the model of rise and foundation from which to
rise confined to use on the cosmic scale; the microcosm of
Hayy's thought seems also to follow a path of upward progress from firmly set groundworks. Each new piece of knowledge arises in what went before and rests upon it; every
individual discovery is a step-by-step renewal of the same
upward building process.   Reason is Hayy's skill to climb
the ladder, careful exacting reason, which takes each premiss as a step to the next conclusion, which can chart the
courses of the stars as well as any astronomy book[107] and
prove the finitude of the heavens with professional preci-
sion: ". . . for if I just imagine to myself two lines, bounded
on one side, and stretching to infinity on the other . . ." and
thus to an elaborate *reductio ad absurdum.*[108]   Each step of
reason is a step upward, mounting from the basis of the

God-given nature and the conclusions gained by reason's own advances.

If Ibn Tufayl's situative premiss is replete with the imagery of basicness, has he not given himself too much? Is not the pattern of the dialectic that will unfold already implicit in the premiss itself? Does not talk about foundations already presume too much about the buildings they will support? If we fear that Ibn Tufayl's premiss has telegraphed his answer or begged his question, it may be comforting to know that another author, beginning from a premiss identically steeped in metaphorical "fundamentism" allowed himself to be carried to a violently different conclusion.

William Golding's *Lord of the Flies* implies much of the imagery of basicness; but what is basic, and therefore what is given, is far from a set of perfectible capacities. Is it any wonder that the basic residue of human essence distilled in Ibn Tufayl's thought-experiment is so different from that precipitated out in Golding's?

The Freudian conception of id and superego is adopted here, over-soul and cellar. We all know, says the Freudian, what man is at bottom. A hungry group of boys find a pig caught in the jungle creepers.[109] Jack's blade flashes over the struggling creature; and, while he hesitates, it escapes: "The pause was only long enough for them to understand what an enormity the downward stroke would be." That is the superego, the ages' built-up terror of "the unbearable blood"—but scratch the surface, as Ralph does: "'You should stick a pig,' said Ralph fiercely. 'They always talk about sticking a pig.'" Now it can be readily seen what lies beneath: "'I was going to, said Jack . . . I was choosing a place . . .' He snatched his knife out of the sheath and slammed it into a tree trunk. Next time there would be no mercy." For Golding, to give the basic is to give the bottom, to strip man down to the brute soul that lies beneath the civilized veneer: sluggishness, aggression, lust to kill: let these go into action and the drama of the thought-experiment will resolve itself into a dénouement quite different from that of *Hayy Ibn Yaqzān*.

What of Hayy's painstaking progress step-by-step out of

the low and toward the Most High? Golding writes ". . .
they ignored the miraculous throbbing stars," and in a single telling and credible sentence explodes the illusion of a
castaway child having the least concern for the precession
of the equinoxes or the finitude of the heavens and eliminates the possibility among his islanders of any spiritual or
emotional advance. How does Golding win his credibility?
Surely this is the realism of a shared assumption. We find
it easy to believe the island castaways ignored the stars for
the same reason we find it hard to believe Hayy studied
them: we rarely look on a passion for truth as a fundamental urge from deep underneath; we are more inclined
to accept lassitude as lying beneath the social accretions of
art and intellect. Likewise, shared experience of the blindness of competitive emulation and especially of children's
eagerness to find a scapegoat and a butt makes the boys'
cruelty to Piggy not merely a real-seeming portrayal but an
emotive lever supporting Golding's given: the basicness of
aggression. But if we share these assumptions and experiences with Golding, as Ibn Tufayl's immediate audience
shared others with him, we must not allow such prejudice
to obscure the fact that the persuasive metaphor of the fundamental can be slanted many ways, and note only in passing that 'realistic' need not mean 'cynical'—that perhaps a
brief can be made out for curiosity or a drive to truth as
basic, and that in view of the fact that man has progressed
at all it is not unreasonable to include an upward drive toward perfection among the foundations of man's soul.

No matter how remarkable a set of natural capacities may
be, they will be nothing according to the premisses of Ibn
Tufayl's philosophy without the activating causality of an
external efficient agent. This, in turn, must act through the
medium of matter. Here arises the role of nature in the
thought-experiment as Hayy's true foster-mother. A large
part of Ibn Tufayl's purpose in entertaining the notion that
Hayy was born by spontaneous generation was to allow us
to contemplate the earth itself as man's womb[110] providing
a milieu in keeping with the Aristotelian notion of excellence: excessive in no one direction but with elements and
qualities ideally blended so as to be perfectly fit for life:

as he puts it, the better the elements are blended, the more they neutralize one another's harsh effects and the better fitted they are to make up higher forms of life.

When Ibn Tufayl sets the stage with his portrayal of the ideal environment at the outset of his book, we should take it as a signal that just as a biologist breeding for a hearty species demands a rich medium of nutriments and mild toxins to select for resistance, so our physician, Ibn Tufayl, is ready to postulate whatever he needs to establish a fit environment for Hayy. A fit environment is a balanced one that will promote a balanced individual, for equilibrium is stability and an approach to self-sufficiency; what is balanced, Ibn Tufayl tells us, has no opposite to overturn it.[111] Thus we learn in the first words of the story that the climate is neither too hot nor too cold, but perfectly temperate, 'balanced'—ideal for the propagation and sustenance of higher life;[112] and this conception of nature as bounty and bounty as balance continues throughout the book. The island has rich pastures; Hayy's nurse-mother is a fat and ample doe, archetype of nature's bounty. She nourishes him on her good milk, looks after him, shades him and warms him; and her fostering is not limited to the physical, for she becomes the object of Hayy's trust, hope, affection, loyalty, and finally grief,[113] giving us some assurance that nature did not leave the emotional side of his endowment totally uncultivated.

The island is rich with fruit and has no predatory animals, but Ibn Tufayl readily recognizes the danger of giving Hayy everything, especially when the purpose is to develop his endowment into a self-reliant soul. Balance must be observed: there are fruits, but Hayy must find them; there are no beasts of prey, but there seem to be some animals willing to fight Hayy for his supper. Just as in Ibn Tufayl's physiology a need is thought to call for the organ whose end it is to fill the need,[114] so nature can, by creating a need, allow for the realization of man's capacities. Thus, gradually, she withdraws some of Hayy's benefits: the doe must weaken, to teach Hayy responsibility; finally, she must die, leaving him alone to face the world.

Nature, by not supplying Hayy with all he needs, draws

out his latent ingenuity.   He must make clothes for himself, unless he wants to be the only naked animal.[115]   If he
wants to protect his food he must learn to make weapons
and build a store-house and a door.[116]   This is the beginning
of artifice, which seems to be the metaphorical obverse of
the natural; yet artifice bears a strange relationship to nature when it means the apprenticed skill to make things,
rather than the talent of merely using the artifacts of others.
Making things yourself, taking them apart and putting them
together, seems a means of seeing down into their natures.
People who can make many different kinds of things see the
world less as a mystery or a trick, more as a natural place,
easy to get along in.   Thus Rousseau, whose father was a
watch-maker and whose Émile is to be educated from the
ground up, insists that his young scholar learn the fundamental crafts "the natural arts", by which one man, working alone can be self-sufficient.[117]   And apparently, the valu-
ation of ingenuity as a means of seeing into the nature of
things was not far from Ibn Tufayl's mind: he made nature
demand art of Hayy; and the culmination of Hayy's skills
in the material world was dissection,[118] the attempt to lay
bare, to discover the inner causes of things; it was from here
that Hayy was able to make his entry into the spiritual
world.

Thus Ibn Tufayl, in postulating a perfectly bountiful and
balanced natural environment for Hayy, means to provide a
milieu causally fit to promote the development of a human
essence that will be blessed by direct bounty, and grow
self-reliant and artful in its interplay with a more thoughtful, reserved bounty, an essence that will bear the mark of
excellence implied by balance.

Lord of the Flies, too, isolates the subject-group in a natural environment—but with what a difference!   The island
is plentiful in fruit, but the fruit causes diarrhea: "double
handfuls of ripe fruit", "an easy if unsatisfying meal";[119] the
alternative: pig-hunting and the birth of blood lust.   This is
a hard dilemma for nature to pose to children.   Here the
incessant jungle heat of the real tropics is not evaded by
subtle reasoning that proves the equator the world's most
temperate zone.   The heat is dwelt upon: "always, almost

visible, was the heat";[120] "A bath of heat"[121] is the first impact of the island on the boys. The heat is causal, as was the moderate climate for Hayy, it strips the boys down as a balanced nature built him up. Nature taught Hayy to make clothes, but the heat teaches the children to forget them;[122] it brings out their lassitude and strips away whatever skills they may have been taught, leaving only a few hands willing, and none able, to build shelters.[123] Sometimes the causality is reflected back from effect to cause and Golding invokes the pathetic fallacy: " 'We may stay here until we die.' With that word the heat seemed to increase till it became a threatening weight and the lagoon attacked them with a blinding effulgence."[124] As with Hayy, nature is the mirror as well as the matrix of the human qualities it projects. Always the heat is present as a constant symbol of a hostile nature that fosters no upward-striving, but strips away the outer coverings of the soul, exposing the ugly underside of man.

A bountiful nature provides Hayy with ingenuity that lets him see into things as he makes them, but nature in Golding's thought-experiment is destructive, and destruction has a way of making men see through things. Czeslaw Milosz, a Polish writer who lived through the Warsaw uprising, writes of man,[125] he "tends to regard the order he lives in as *natural.* The houses he passes on his way to work seem more like rocks rising out of the earth than like products of human hands."; but witnessing devastation ". . . he stops before a house split in half by a bomb, the privacy of people's homes—the family smells, the warmth of the beehive life, the furniture preserving the memory of loves and hatreds—cut open to public view. The house itself, no longer a rock, but a scaffolding of plaster, concrete and brick; and on the third floor, a solitary white bathtub . . ."

What difference is there between seeing *into* and seeing *through*? A tone, an attitude, an emotion: "His first stroll along a street littered with glass from bomb-shattered windows shakes his faith in the 'naturalness' of the world." Such destruction is what the children on the island must face. They have seen war; their plane has been destroyed;

all the artifacts and comforts of home life are gone and they are brought up to the face of brute nature. They debate frantically whether there is an unknown beast: There isn't, claims Piggy. Why not? " 'Cos things wouldn't make sense. Houses an' streets an'—TV—they wouldn't work." These are not Rousseau's children; they see *into* nothing; but having seen destruction, they see through everything: "But s'pose they don't make sense? Not here, on this island? . . ."[126] The world of artifact no longer seems to be nature, and the boys face alone the real nature which is cruel and will resonate with their own latent cruelty.

Once again, two premises identical in form have been loaded with a content calculated to yield radically different resolutions. Somehow, nature seems a more neutral force than either author will allow, but Golding is bent on his exposé, and Ibn Tufayl is anxious to postulate the optimum conditions for Hayy's development—the divergence can hardly be avoided.

How Ibn Tufayl implies the metaphor of elementality should already be fairly transparent. The soul manifests itself in a unified complex of simples, the hierarchically organized, progressively realized potentialities of the *fitra*. Hayy recognizes[127] in his soul a set of resemblances which brings him far beyond the Aristotelian scheme of animal, vegetable, and rational from which Ibn Tufayl allows his hero to depart.[128] In some ways he resembles animals; in some, heavenly bodies; in some, God himself.

At the service of each of these aspects of Hayy's soul are capacities for implementing its characteristic functions. These capacities are not concrete entities, but dispositions of the substantial soul. They stem from Ibn Tufayl's assumption of the distinctively Aristotelian line of argument[129] that the modality of possibility may be expressed in terms of the potentials of things. If a being is capable of something, that capability may be expressed in terms of its having a corresponding capacity.[130] Thus capacities are, in origin, the results of a perfectly allowable and purely syntactical shift to render the modality of possibility more vivid, a shift which Ibn Tufayl himself absorbs when he writes of the "power" of a thing to catch fire.[131] Likewise, as Hayy's physiology teaches him, each organ has its own "power" to effect its characteristic "action." The "action" is its function, its *ergon*, the actualization of its potentiality or capacity. What enables anything to realize its potential, to work as it should, is what Plato and Aristotle would both have called an *arete*, its good.

What is striking about the soul's capacities and excellences is that while they are not concrete, they are discrete; and perhaps the best evidence of their discreteness is that they must be given. Thus each new aspect of Hayy's *fitra* is introduced with the matter-of-fact tone of an accepted assumption. No more is said of his innate curiosity than that he "had a great desire" to study the anatomy of the animals[132] or that he wondered where the governing soul of his mother-doe had gone.[133] Of his natural imitation, little more is said than that he did in fact learn to imitate the animals[134] and came years later to imitate the heavenly bodies and God himself.[135] His moral sense, too, simply appears: "What a fine thing for that bird to bury the other's body—although it was wrong to kill it." And even his modesty[136] seems a bolt from the blue. Like the natural boldness[137] with which God formed Hayy's nature and which enables him to try to grasp fire the first time he sees it, all these virtues of Hayy's are placed in him by God; and this, as we have seen, is the significance to a rationalist radical monotheist of God's breathing life into man.

The fact that these excellences are part of the divine endowment enables Ibn Tufayl to take them as given in his thought-experiment; he need feel no compunctions about not reducing them to other terms. Each of these human faculties is atomic; each is a whole within itself. One may prepare the way for the next; all may be interrelated, and the more intellectual may enjoy precedence over the rest, but no detailed breakdown of each virtue's structure can be given, because all are irreducible: they are not "made of" anything. There is no brew of the elements, however well tempered, which is a recipe for the faculties of the soul, for these faculties themselves are elements.

Such thinking may seem antique to us, who devote so much energy to the enterprise of generating paradoxes by reducing thought to numbers, literature to syntax, philosophy to logic, human experience to color-blurs,—the soul to dispositions, and dispositions to behavior. But if truth rather than fashion is to be a criterion, a moment's thought about the radical denial of reductionism to be found in Ibn Tufayl's musty pages may serve as a breath of fresh air, demanding that we critically compare some of his unquestioned assumptions with our own. To do this honestly we must be prepared to discover that much of our effort and achievement—especially in the reductionist "findings" of social science—is far less substantial than it would like to appear. We certainly recognize that to reduce everything to everything is impossible. Perhaps we also see the danger, in reducing everything to one thing, of reducing all things to nothing. There is a way of "explaining" that explains too well and leaves nothing left in the pot of the peculiar flavor we were seeking to understand. If Gordon Allport can temper psychology's desire to reduce all motivation to a few simple drives by modestly asserting the functional autonomy of ideas—perhaps *some* things are done for their own sake; if G. E. Moore can probe repeatedly with his open-question method, seeking a "characteristically moral" flavor in purported reductions of 'good' to natural terms, asking, "But is it really good?", then certainly we should moderate our haste to "reduce man to terms", ask ourselves "Is this really man?", and be prepared to admit that more in the psyche is elemental than we may have thought.

Ibn Tufayl's attitude, stemming from his radical monotheism, is to treat all branches of the soul's action as activations of capacities granted by God, and therefore atomic to analysis, given in the situative premiss that makes the thought-experiment work. Golding too has a conception of elements in the soul: Freud is the source of Golding's elements; but, although both Freud's and Aristotle's conceptions of a hierarchical soul stem from the same Platonic source, the Freudian version is put to a vastly different use by Golding than is the Aristotelian by Ibn Tufayl. To follow down Golding's version of the soul's elements, we must examine the mimetic scheme adopted by him; for each of the lost children seems to stand for a single element of the psyche and the tiny society they form seems, like the Platonic state, to be the human soul, writ large.

Piggy is the superego, Freud's modified version of one facet of Platonic reason. He wants always to be sensible, to do the right thing; his first concern is for the censure of "My auntie—";[138] his constant thought is "What's grownups going to think?"[139] He watches in "disgust", the characteristic mood of the superego, as the boys run off, without thinking, to light a fire: " 'Like kids!' he said scornfully. 'Acting like a crowd of kids!' "[140]

Ralph is a Platonic guardian, the ego, proud, handsome, self-possessed, a bit vain: he "shut one eye and decided that the shadows of his body were really green."[141] When he throws a spear, it is for honor or "attention", not to kill.[142] His leadership is seemingly indisputable,[143] for he is the will, force, and ascetic drive, as his long speech[144] shows, behind Piggy's ideas.

Jack is the id, the fire of the Platonic passions, to which Freud adds an urge Plato did not know, the death wish, aggression and the lust to kill. He is "ugly without silliness",[145] the animal in man; he stalks his prey "his nose only a few inches from the humid earth. The tree trunks and the creepers that festooned them lost themselves in a green dusk thirty feet above him and all about was undergrowth. There was only the faintest indication of a trail here; a cracked twig and what might be the impression of one side of a hoof. He lowered his chin and stared at the traces as though he would force them to speak to him. Then doglike, uncomfortably on all fours he stole forward . . ."[146] "We want meat."[147] Jack speaks only demands. The black-cloaked choir he brings[148] are his minions, the forces of the id. The youngest children, the "littluns", are appetite. They eat fruit, bathe all day and play unhappily—'they don't know any better'; at night they know only fear.

Simon is the rudimentary spiritual, 'sublimation', as Freud would say. To him, the jungle flowers look like candles, "Candle buds" he calls them. " 'Green candles' said Jack contemptuously. 'We can't eat them. Come on.' "[149]

Simon's is the moral concern for the bullied Piggy: "We used his specs . . ."[150]   And it is he who seeks beauty and solitude in the heart of the jungle.[151]

Each element of the soul, for Golding, is a separate microcosm—and here the trouble begins.   For the working out of the island dialectic here is not Hayy's rising to perfection, directed by an internal drive, *conatus*, but a total breakdown that begins as a breakdown of communications. Each element of the soul has its special function, to be sure, but each is powerless to relate to the others: none of the boys can reach the others.   Ralph is so absorbed in blowing his conch that Piggy is unable to list the children's names.[152]   Jack's eagerness to start a fire drowns out Piggy's pathetic, weakling voice.[153]   Ralph's demands for common cleanliness and a spirit of work meet giggles, demurs from the littluns and angry shouts from the hunters,[154] for Ralph and Jack are "two continents of experience and feeling, unable to communicate."   And even the prophetic Simon, who has the courage to face the beast,[155] to see it covered with flies and learn that it is the Lord of the Flies, Beelzebub, "expanding like a balloon", expanding from an external threat to an inner depravity, meets the climactic frustration, is unable to explain, unable even to voice his discovery: " 'Maybe,' he said hesitantly, 'maybe there is a beast.' "   They laugh him down, "Simon became inarticulate to express mankind's essential illness."[156]   And even when his knowledge is complete and he sees the fouled lines of the dead parachutist that explain the phantom,[157] he cannot speak and will not be heard, but must be destroyed and destroyed by the hands of all.[158]   For the working out of the drama of the thought-experiment is, to Golding, the revelation of that same *essential* illness that Simon cannot relate.   The parts cannot connect—and worse they are at odds; but worst of all, their order, set from the time of Plato and confirmed by Ibn Tufayl, the higher ruling the lower as master rules servant,[159] has been subverted.   Plato's image[160] of man's neck as isthmus between the higher and the lower souls, the passions and man's reason, is not strong enough for Golding.   He pictures the isthmus as setting of a hopeless confrontation—an allegory on his favorite story, the Anglo-Saxon *Battle of Maldon*[161]—in which ego and superego, continents cut off by a narrow neck of land from stronger forces seeking to overwhelm them, reason with unreason, only to be shouted down. Piggy and Simon are destroyed and even Ralph must be hunted; the lower must rule, aggression must out because it is what lies at bottom. The children are not merely a society reaching anarchy but a man going mad: only madness is the natural condition! Here is the resolution of Golding's thought experiment: man is essentially evil.

To a medieval Arab, primitive means Bedouin. The desert life means to him courage, generosity, virility, simplicity of manners, the purest standard of language and the best poetry. Civilization, on the other hand, meant citification in medieval Arabic, as it did once in the West. Thus Ibn Khaldūn writes "Bedouins are closer to being good than sedentary people." And it is worthy of note how he defends this assertion. He has said in many places that settled and urban populations are weaker, more prone to luxury and less exempt from degeneracy. Here he explains: "The reason for it is that the soul in its first natural state of creation is ready to accept whatever good or evil may arrive and leave an imprint on it." He quotes a traditional saying of Muhammad: "Every infant is born in a natural state (*fitra*). It is his parents who make him a Jew or a Christian or a Magian",[162] and thus echoes the sentiment of his Maghribī predecessor, Ibn Tufayl, who as we have seen believed that crime and positive law, mass ritual and the need for ritual, and all the culturally specific traits of man, arise together under the social pressures of built-up centers of population. Thus Ibn Tufayl's thought-experiment endeavors to give man a fresh start, to choose ground far from the crowded tenements of the great cities—which have settled owners and restrictive traditions, and are not, like the desert, equally hostile or hospitable to all. The object of the exercise is to see whether a man by himself can build a better home, starting only with a firm, straightforward foundation, and the mind God gave him.

To us, it seems, if Golding is our spokesman, 'primitive' has come to mean 'savage'. And what of its correlative term, 'civilized'? Freud wrote

> . . . men are not gentle creatures who want to be loved, and who at the most can defend themselves if they are attacked; they are, on the contrary, creatures among whose instinctual endowments is to be reckoned a powerful share of aggressiveness. As a result their neighbor is for them not only a potential helper or sexual object, but also someone who tempts them to satisfy their aggressiveness on him, to exploit his capacity for work without compensation, to use him sexually without his consent, to seize his possessions, to humiliate him, to cause him pain, to torture and kill him. *Homo homini lupus.*[163]

We have seen how Golding accepts at face value this account of aggression as instinct. He follows Freud in suspecting that "instinctual passions are stronger than reasonable interests."[164] Freud argues that "Civilization has to use its utmost efforts in order to set limits to man's aggressive instincts and hold the manifestations of them in check. . ."[165] Words like these have profoundly changed the sense conveyed by 'civilized'—the word no longer means urban; and, for many of us, has long ceased to mean urbane. Where culture, knowledgeability, and human values were once implied by calling a man civilized, desperate pleas like Freud's, "The fateful question for the human species seems to me to be whether and to what extent their cultural development will succeed in mastering the disturbance of their communal life by the human instinct of aggression and self-destruction,"[166] have succeeded in putting civilization on the defensive, minimizing the positive achievements of the humanities and girding up the pragmatic arts as if to meet the exigencies of some battle. And yet this view of civilization as defender of man against himself is far more charitable to her, if less so to man himself, than that of Ibn Tufayl, which views civilization as obliged to bring cures to man's ills, since she herself is the cause.

Freud's theory of civilization, like his notion of personality, seems to be that adopted by Golding. Civilization re-presses the id; thus the thought-experiment: "Roger stooped, picked up a stone, aimed and threw it at Henry—threw to miss. The stone, that token of preposterous time, bounced five yards to Henry's right and fell in the water. Roger gathered a handful of stones and began to throw them. Yet there was a space round Henry, perhaps six yards in diameter, into which he dare not throw. Here invisible, yet strong, was the taboo of the old life. Round the squatting child was the protection of parents and school and policemen and the law. Roger's arm was conditioned by a civilization that knew nothing of him and was in ruins."[167] But when the boys paint their faces, when they become *savages*, then the repression is loosened; they lose their self-consciousness, perhaps their self-awareness; their natural hostility can be released.[168] By the end of the book Roger throws to hit and to kill. Apparently the veneer has been stripped away. Thus Golding does mirror Freud's social assumptions. And yet, in some ways, Golding's theory of civilization is less hopeful than Freud's; for Freud sees civilization as at least a defensive, stabilizing force, but Golding often vacillates to a more pessimistic image, in which he views civilization as merely a more articulated means for the expression of the same basic aggressions as isolated individuals express. Will not evil triumph in society as it does in man, society's micro-analogue? What other outcome could result in any society or institution each member of which was subverted from within by death-wish or aggression? The thought experiment seems almost to demonstrate just how aggression must rise to the surface even in the infant institutions of the island. Thus it is that Golding envisions civilization itself lying in ruins.

Hayy must recapitulate the progress of mankind for himself. All the truth established by human experience must once again be put to the Cartesian questioning of a genuine neophyte, because only thus can a truth be reached which is free of the particularisms of period and culture, and depends, not on tradition, but on the direct vision of reason and natural intuition. It is for this reason that Hayy is set alone in the place of Adam, in the garden of nature. Until

Absāl discovers him, Hayy might as well be the first man on earth. No social milieu deflects the progress of his soul toward the polarity of any over-stated half-truth; he is free. And, once again, we may see the symbolic significance of entertaining the hypothesis of Hayy's spontaneous generation: just as his environment puts no smoked glass before his eyes, no social filter against some colors of the sun, so too no heredity marks his birth. It must not be said that anything more or less is given to Hayy than the bounty a perfect-tempered nature and a gracious God would bestow. Hayy's symbolic place at the start of time gives special weight to his story: given life, and the seeds of his *fitra*, his soul can work out its own nature; but the development of that nature is the development of the human essence.

Golding's children stand at the end of time. Ralph's dim, quasi-messianic hopes of rescue by his father: "He's a commander in the Navy. When he gets leave he'll come and rescue us . . .,"[169] and his dimming recollection of the purpose of a signal-fire, seem meant by Golding as comments, in the tradition of Freud, on the origin in wish-fulfillment of a religious form opposed to Jack's savage cult, a religion that seems a vague form of hope, like the cargo cults of the South Seas; but of course it is too late. In spite of the dubious *deus ex machina* of a rescue in the book's last thousand words, we realize that the fatal stand-off[170] of Ralph and Piggy against the savages on the narrow neck of land is a Dunkirk or a Battle of Maldon,[171] end-game for a civilization already played out. Society has destroyed itself with bombs, and even the children recognize the symbolic resemblance to bombs of the boulders with which they come to murder Piggy.[172] The rest of the world has proved itself for what it is; when the children on the island are stripped down and assayed in the acid bath of nature—more a Hell than an Eden—the apocalyptic retrogression in which the end has become like the beginning, will have performed its last analysis. The children are the skimmings of the skimmings of man's essence, when their final nature is known.

The resolution of Ibn Tufayl's thought-experiment, which finds the soul of man to be essentially good and ultimately perfectible, if only society let him alone, implies a positive value in extrication of the individual from society; and indeed we have seen such a value to be equally implied by the Arab attribution of primacy to the self-reliance of the Bedouin way of life and by Ibn Tufayl's philosophy of religion that considers culturally oriented dogmas as squint-eyed views of the Truth. Like Absāl,[173] Ibn Tufayl's ideal man is anti-social. It is outside society, in solitude, that man will find his best opportunities of searching for the Truth. How can Ibn Tufayl share Golding's pessimism about society while rejecting Freud's pessimism about man? Paradoxically, Golding's "finding" that man is essentially evil and Ibn Tufayl's discovery that man is essentially good do not exclude each other. The two authors differ radically on the meaning of 'essential'; neither accepts the other's concept of 'real', for both are engaged in a moral polemic. Golding, like a Calvinist theologian, is castigating man for the Beelzebub that lies within him, original sin. For his hesitant readership, who may lack ears for preachments of fire and brimstone, Golding preaches in a different vein; his tone of absurdist pessimism only adds intensity to his rhetorical effect and impact to his appeal, for these moods echo their own quiet questioning thoughts. But the book is an appeal, and it works by the same old springs that make John Bunyan work: the more convinced man is of his inner depravity, the more convinced he is that "in reality," at bottom, he is evil, the more ready he is for salvation. On this, the only substantial modification demanded by Golding's pessimism is to make it read: "the less unready . . ." Behind the vehement assertion that 'Man is essentially evil' lies the same old unspoken warning: 'You'd better do something about yourself!'

To all this Ibn Tufayl speaks at cross purposes. He had no experiences that would contradict Freud's evidence of evil in man and in the world; but he too was involved in a moral polemic, the purpose of which was not to admonish sin but to awaken excellence. Islam has well established ways of dealing with sin; the needs of the run-of-the-mill worshipper, too, it can accommodate. But for the man of more than ordinary excellence, the supererogatory man, the *fādil*, a special path is needed, a path *upward* toward

greater perfection, a *higher degree of reality*. The beauty
Ibn Tufayl finds in Hayy, the grasping out for pure truth,
the natural goodness and the *irrelevance* of sin—which
makes it senseless to question the safety of his soul "outside
the civilized compound"—should show us in what sense
Hayy is man's essence. He is an ideal, a guide to the path
where the brave and hearty-minded can climb towards
truth and self-perfection. Why else is he given the bounty
of nature at its peak, incomparable talents, the intellectual
manliness that grows in solitude, a harmonious soul in the
perfect order of Platonic reconciliation with itself, and stat-
ure as a torch-bearer at the beginning of time? Surely not
to illuminate the ugly underside of man! Hayy's life is a
standard of the imagination toward which Ibn Tufayl points
as an ideal possibility.

An ideal possibility? Ideal perhaps, if man has a capacity in him for good—but is it really possible? We all know
that if a real infant is left alone and unsheltered, he will
grow up mentally and emotionally disturbed, if he grows
up at all. Common sense and human experience cannot
gainsay this prediction; and Golding himself, despite his
anxiety to show the innateness of evil in man, corroborates
it, by sketching the beginnings of autism in his "littluns".[174]
Ibn Tufayl is stopped at the postulation of the first item of
his premiss: there is no "basis," say the psychologists, out of
which any essence could arise. Man's *given* to begin with
is a *tabula rasa*, a blank slate. What he will be depends on
the circumstances of his life. The pessimism of Golding
and the optimism of Ibn Tufayl are both set aside. It is
as wrong to say man is essentially evil as it is to say he's
essentially good—man is essentially nothing.

This denial of a human essence may, at first blush, resemble Sartre's attack on essence. The radical difference
between the two becomes apparent when the determinism
of the tabula-rasa position is contrasted with the moral bootstrap individualism of Sartre: every man chooses himself,
makes himself what he will be, and, in so doing, chooses
for the world. To the tabula-rasa theorist, substantial souls
seem ghosts, phantasmata of old superstitions that still

haunt common thought. Man has no more existential basis than he has essential.

What then is left of man? Bundles of data? One trait, at least, remains: the blankness of the state itself! Adaptability, flexibility, a chameleon power of reflecting the surroundings, the protean, protozoan capacity to assimilate. And one trait more: man's social desire and social capacity to modify himself as well as his environment. Given flexibility and the communal power of control, nullity is left behind; there is a new basis from which to build; optimism again becomes the mood. Of that mood Robert Owen wrote the shibboleth:

> Any general character, from the best to the worst, from the most ignorant to the most enlightened, may be given to any community, even to the world at large, by the application of proper means; which means are to a great extent at the command and under the control of those who have influence in the affairs of men.[175]

This is the optimism of environmentalism, and out of such optimism arises a new thought-experiment, B. F. Skinner's *Walden Two.*

In trying to discover what man is, both Golding and Ibn Tufayl tried to discover what man can become, to what depths he can sink, to what heights he can rise. But if man is nothing in himself, nothing to begin with, society must create him. With the discarding of essence, Skinner's thought-experiment asks not what man is or might become, but what man can be *made.*

"We have no truck" says Frazier, Skinner's master experimenter, "with philosophies of innate goodness—or evil, either, for that matter. But we do have faith in our power to change human behavior. We can *make* men adequate for group living—to the satisfaction of everybody. That was our faith, but it's now a fact."[176] In Skinner's novel, unlike Golding's or Ibn Tufayl's, the structural framework of experiment rises to the surface and becomes explicit: the community is described as "an experiment in living",[177] and

Skinner leans heavily on the postulational character of his situative premiss. Castle, the "philosopher", asks for proof on a certain point; Frazier's response, "The proof of an accomplished fact? Don't be absurd! . . .", makes us almost forget that what we have here is no more than a *thought*-experiment. But 'experiment' itself has changed its meaning; to Skinner, it is no longer a means of distilling the elemental essence of man: no such essence exists, for the only constants of human nature are the malleability of man and the hammer-anvil force of society. Experiment is no longer the search for an answer; it is the answer. Experiment becomes a way of life, *experimentalism*, identified with "flexibility" itself![178]

Control is the new word, control of the forces of nature, from which nothing can be expected, control of man, from whose nature no more can be hoped than a due "response to conditioning." The engineer, then, takes the place of Ibn Tufayl's and of Golding's Nature as causal provider and symbolic representative of the milieu in which man is formed; which is to say that artifice becomes all, nature, nothing. Representative of the new attitude is Frazier's remark ". . . we can deal with the weather."[179] Neither beauty and generosity nor cruel pressures and mockeries are to be expected from nature; she is a "factor" to be controlled.

If engineering were confined to control of the environment *per se*, perhaps no further complaint could be added to the observation of latent alienation from nature, already laid at the Skinnerite's door, than that the demand for narrow specialization he rather arbitrarily associates with engineering[180] seems to discourage ingenuity and seeing-into-the-works-of-things, as Emile or Hayy does, and upgrades the tendency to view devices as "black-boxes", artifacts to be used blindly, instead of artifices to be devised and enjoyed. The trouble is that the crucial factor in the human environment is not the weather, but man himself; and, thus, the engineering would not fulfill its promise if it did not begin to tinker with man. Were Skinner's faith in engineering confined to the control of external nature, he would be no more than one of the many *laudatores* of technology. When he extends the method of engineering to man—as

Dewey, in *The Public and Its Problems*, extends it to the state—he takes on a tone of purpose which puts him in a more dangerous class.

Staggered schedules of eating, rising, and relaxation are "an amazing piece of cultural engineering . . .".[181] Architecture is used to establish moods,[182] and design is used to mold attitudes: using period and modern decors of diverse countries is intended, for example, to promote broad aesthetic tastes.[183] The tea service is designed to avoid the petty frustrations of formal tea,[184] and even the dishes are planned in glass to avoid having to turn them over and over in washing.[185] All things are calculated to avoid the slightest annoyance: the hostile nature of Golding and the tempered nature of Ibn Tufayl are both displaced by an artificial environment with thermostatic controls.

But the experiment goes further than to postulate a surrogate nature and to engineer the "bumps" out of life—the engineer dives down to the elemental level of the soul and makes man over again—man can be *made* anything. Imitation, which Ibn Tufayl gave as an element, becomes conformity in Skinner, identified with man's penchant for flexibility itself.[186] All the rest of man's capacities, for good or evil, society controls, since she created them. Burris, who is jestingly suspected for a Freudian,[187] is met at the elemental level with the assertion that hostility is not an inherent, atomic motivation of the psyche and confronted with "experimental" evidence that man can be free of aggression. Infants are raised at first with not the slightest annoyance, then with minor, but gradually increasing "traumatizations", physical and psychological.[188] Adults are taught by the "Walden Code" to use the fitting mixture of tact and tactlessness, decorum and informality which Skinner supposes will reduce tension to a minimum and blot out anger, jealousy, and boredom. The elements of man's soul are, so he thinks, compounded and re-compounded by society, and, thus, not really elements at all.

As for civilization, Skinner's position seems at first a peculiar cross between Ibn Tufayl and the Freudian. Rogers and Jamnic echo Freud's language, "we want to find out what's the matter with people, why they can't live together without fighting all the time. We want to find out what people really want, what they need in order to be happy, and how they can get it without stealing it from somebody else."[189]   But the matter-of-fact explanation Frazier eventually gives for the origin of crime and 'manifestations of aggression' is self-consciously non-Freudian: ". . . let's be realistic.   Each of us has interests which conflict with the interests of everybody else.   That's our original sin, and it can't be helped."[190]   Social conflict seems an odd origin for original sin, but postulating such an origin allows Skinner to make society the scapegoat for the hostilities Golding saw as inherent in man, as well as the Giver of the innate capacities for perfection Ibn Tufayl spoke for.   To society as well he attributes the constructive force Freud saw in eros and the inner weakness and blindness Ibn Tufayl feared in man, leaving the *tabula* itself in immaculate neutrality.   Postulating a social origin for crime, Skinner adopts all the more readily a Freudian concept of the task of civilization: "Society has made the criminal and must take care of him."[191]   He is thus able to accept the Freudian outline of social history as the history of protracted efforts to find means of repressing conflict and aggression:

> Each of us . . . is engaged in a pitched battle with the rest of mankind. . . . Each of us has interests which conflict with the interests of everybody else. . . . Now 'everybody else' we call 'society.'   It's a powerful opponent, and it always wins.   Oh, here and there an individual prevails for a while and gets what he wants.   Sometimes he storms the culture of a society and changes it slightly to his own advantage.   But society wins in the long run, for it has the advantage of numbers and of age.   Many prevail against one, and men against a baby.   Society attacks early, when the individual is helpless.   It enslaves him almost before he has tasted freedom.   The 'ologies' will tell you how it's done.   Theology calls it building a conscience or developing a spirit of selflessness.   Psychology calls it the growth of the super-ego.[192]

Yet Skinner, perhaps because he fears iatrogenic illnesses may result if he allows the poisoner to serve as physician, does not accept Freud's hope that civilized society can win its fight against aggression. Frazier says, "Considering how long society has been at it, you'd expect a better job."[193] Indeed, Frazier's talk about the enslavement of the individual and the taste of freedom is reminiscent of Ibn Tufayl's Arab scorn of *civil*-ization as the birthplace of weakness and decadence; as his rejection of society for creating problems it cannot solve resembles Ibn Tufayl's teaching that crime and law arise together in great cities, where mass mentality blinds everyone and man cannot get an unobstructed view of the truth. What then is Skinner's answer? Follow Hayy, as Absāl does, out of society? Free man at once from constraint and the need for constraint? On the contrary! If civilization means control of conflict, and civilization has not worked, what is needed is a larger dose of the same medicine, not the relaxation but the perfection of control,[194] in a totally engineered environment where engineered behavior governs artificial relationships, through the engineered specifications of artificial souls. "We see to it," says Frazier, "that they will do precisely the things which are best for themselves and the community."[195] The solution is not to extricate man from society, but to implode him into it, to build outside the failing walls of the old society, a new society where everything will be controlled, where every action will be "other-directed" and directed by other, an ultra-civilized, a trans-social, society.

There is no "basis"; nature is to be engineered; man's "elements" to be re-created; civilization must become a perfect control. How, then, does Skinner treat our fifth conceptual distillant of essence, time? Ibn Tufayl set his thought-experiment at the start of time, and Golding set his at the end, allowing for apocalyptic retrogression to the beginning. Skinner, for the sake of realism, set his novel in the present, at the end of the War.[196] But still, a latent use of temporal symbolism can be detected. Roberts, seeing that civilization's old methods have reached the end of their rope, wants to "start all over again the right way . . ."[197] "We look ahead, not backwards . ." says Frazier,[198] who archly calls Walden II "*il paradiso*".[199] Skinner's thought-experiment seems, like the workers' paradise, to mark the end of prehistory and the beginning of history; it is placed, like the first Garden, at the beginning and at the end of time.

Golding denied the conclusion of Ibn Tufayl's thought-experiment; Skinner denies the premiss. He postulates new conditions of his own, diametrically opposed to those arising out of the metaphors of primitive, basic, and the rest, and allows them to "produce" a new man, corresponding to his own concept of human perfection, a man of "invariable good humor",[200] for whom unhappiness, tension, fatigue, boredom, inhibitions, jealousy and "the destructive and wasteful emotions" are "almost unknown."[201]

How far Skinner has departed from any resemblance to existentialism should be apparent. It was the plea of Kantian ethics to treat men as subjects and ends in themselves, rather than means and objects, which prompted Sartre to denigrate the use of a concept of human essence and elevate that of existence. In response to the same primary moral claim, Camus, writing[202] against the background of resistance in Vichy France, went so far as to affirm "perhaps there is a human nature after all"; for the experience of rebellion had convinced him that man is not "infinitely malleable"; there are limits beyond which his moral endurance cannot stretch. Of this Skinner is blind.

For the mechanism by which Walden II works is the reduction of men to objects. Frazier speaks of children as "the Walden Two product"[203] and the reference is more than a joke: the people of Walden II are products, objects of "psychological management"[204] and artifacts of manufacture; the children behind the glass are not so much reared as cured, like plastic.[205] Yet both experience and morals tell us the way to raise children to emotional adulthood is to treat them as people not things—and can we not say *a fortiori!* for regulating the actions of adults?

A second flaw, as great as the object-ification of man is woven into the fabric of the society Skinner has designed; and in both cases, it seems, the attempt to undo the flaw would unravel the whole cloth. Frazier prides himself that Walden II can "train out destructive and wasteful emotions" when experiment has proved "they're no longer needed." Jealousy, for example: "a minor form of anger, I think we may call it. Naturally we avoid it. It has served its purpose in the evolution of man; we've no further use for it." Likewise, "sorrow and hate—and the high-voltage excitements of anger, fear, and rage—are out of proportion with the needs of modern life, and they're wasteful and dangerous."[206]

No one enjoys fear; no one likes to watch a jealous man —and yet we must ask ourselves what sort of man it would be who had no capacity for "high-voltage" passions. Is Frazier realistic to hope for a Golden Age of culture[207] in a society that molds men who cannot hate? Perhaps, if art means "hobbies, arts and crafts.", as Frazier seems to think,[208] then he is right to say: "Right conditions. All you need. . . . Give them a chance, that's all. Leisure. Opportunity. Appreciation."[209] But can this lukewarm life produce a Beethoven? Is Frazier honest to claim love is not on the exclusion list? Perhaps, if love and "Puppy love",[210] and "a sort of nesting instinct" are alike, as Frazier hints.[211] The men emerging from Frazier's mold are small, hollow men, incapable of passion. It was with a prophetic horror at what he saw around himself and what he saw to come that Nietzsche wrote:

> Behold! I shall show you the *Ultimate Man*. 'What is love? What is creation? What is longing? What is a star?' thus asks the Ultimate Man and blinks.
> The earth has become small, and upon it hops the Ultimate Man, who makes everything small. His race is as inexterminable as the flea; the Ultimate Man lives longest.
> 'We have discovered happiness,' say the Ultimate Men and blink.[212]

The strongest retort Skinner can find to the individualism behind Nietzsche and Kant's attacks is to call them antisocial: *Hayy Ibn Yaqzān* is an expression of a mood of "anti-social" thought that has bolstered rebellion and withdrawal for centuries. What contribution does Hayy make to society? What does he do for his fellow men besides bore them with his incomprehensible teachings? "It's a long, slow process—giving anyone a social conscience."[213]

Hayy has none. He feels for his fellow man, but cannot reach him. "We", says Frazier, "must always think of the whole group."[214] 'You,' he might continue, 'think only of yourself!' A harsh judgment, perhaps, but Ibn Tufayl might find it a step towards the truth to sigh, 'At last you are beginning to see the point: must we *always* think of the whole group?' Hayy is an epitome, an ideal, expressed as a possibility—the ideal of withdrawal.

And now the scientist in Skinner speaks: your "possibility" is not possible. 'The child, if it lived, would be a simpering, autistic schizoid with no sense of self, of the continuity of space, the flow of time, the uniformity of causality, or the rules of logic—and you expect it to do astronomy!' We are at the heart of the meaning of Ibn Tufayl's book: can we let ourselves forget the metaphorical structuring of the thought-experiment's premiss and Ibn Tufayl's explicit warning against taking his words literally, and superficially? Ibn Tufayl does not want us to expose our infants—he did not expose his own; he wants to show us what we can achieve if we extricate ourselves from society. The exposure is not a project of primitive science, but a symbol of the completeness of Hayy's independence. The point is not to live on an island—that too is imagery— the point is merely to achieve independence from social myth, civil coercion, and cultural blindness.

'Unless you are actually isolated, as your language led us to believe, how,' asks Skinner, 'can you possibly escape the influence of society? You cannot, by an act of will, evade the forces that created you and that mold your every action.' Again the scientist is speaking, this time the social scientist. 'Even if you ignore my model of a perfectly unified coherent field of social force and leave society as it is in struggling fragments, how can you "refuse" to be affected?' The only real question is whether the determinism be made systematic or remain "accidental."[215] The answer is in terms of freedom: freedom begins with plurality of choice. From Ibn Tufayl we learn that it does not end there. Ibn Tufayl is not ignorant of the forcefulness of social pressures—he saw how they distracted his predecessor,

Ibn Bājja—and it is precisely because of his awareness of their cogency that he urges withdrawal. 'But', demands Skinner, 'does withdrawal have a meaning?' Ibn Tufayl argues that it does: even given the "plural coercions", as Louis Hartz calls them, of an existing, non-monolithic society, there are other, unseen, un-given possibilities. If we have seen that to be a moral adult is to have attained a point of "take-off", after which no analysis of "input", no matter how complete the data, is a sure guide in predicting the outcome of human choice, then certainly we can learn here that to be imaginatively free is to achieve a certain power to choose what is not given but taken, what lies outside the hidebound volumes in which one culture lists what is past, not what is possible; to seek and find the truth and value that lie beyond the tables of the law and the scrolls of social ritual. It is this seeking and finding, of course, which Hayy is meant to symbolize.

Emancipation of the mind and spirit is all Ibn Tufayl asks: he sets it as an ideal that those whose minds are brave enough seek for themselves. But is even this possible? Even on a purely intellectual and spiritual plane, argues the social determinist, you cannot escape society. What could prove it better than Ibn Tufayl's own book? He sets out to disclose the truth not as revealed by any sect or tradition, but the truth that lies behind the veil of particularism; and he proceeds to give a partisan account of the doctrines advocated by an established intellectual circle, admitted to be an attempt at synthesis of the tradition of the Avicennan school of oriental philosophy with the Islam of Ghazālī, an effort openly showing the historical influences of the catholic Islamic tradition and revelation, not to mention of Plato, Aristotle, and the neo-Platonists. May I deflect the blow with a word? Ibn Tufayl did have a glimpse at the truth; there are things to be learned from his book— and our age, in particular, has a good deal to learn about rational-mysticism. But can this heal the bruise to his ideal? Why is no more than a glimpse promised us? Traditional religion has fragmentary glances, oriental philosophy was supposed to see beyond, to open a full-faced view

of the *truth*. Ibn Tufayl did not learn the number of the
spheres by rational speculation, or rational intuition, he
learned it in school.

And yet this says no more than that Ibn Tufayl is not
Hayy Ibn Yaqzān—not because he lacked a desert island or
a kindly doe, but because he himself had strength to attain
neither the fullness of emancipation nor the direct view of
the truth he praised in his hero. Let us be on our guard:
have we a right to be disappointed in *Hayy Ibn Yaqzān?*
Ibn Tufayl himself has warned us not to expect a direct
view of the truth;[216] this is something that requires a supreme effort,[217] and if we expect to learn all by reading
his little book, or any book, we deceive ourselves. Perhaps
Ibn Tufayl was more aware of his limitations than we might
have thought.

The limitations of Ibn Tufayl are the limitations of any
man. We are not perfect, we are not even remarkably self-
reliant. But the universality of such imperfections in beings that are admittedly finite does not constitute an argument against the desirability of an extra-cultural search for
truth or value. That one seeker of that ideal fails to realize
it indicates no more than his human-ness. The vital point
is that our very attempt to imagine what life and truth
would be like outside social walls is an implied argument
against the ineluctability of social forces. In this lies the
validity of Ibn Tufayl's thought-experiment: it proves that
we have a concept at least, of truth, value, and even beauty,
distinct from our concept of social myth, traditional revelation, positive law or fashion. No more than an examination
of what we mean by 'myth' and 'truth', 'beauty' and 'fashion' is needed to drive home the point. The thought-experiment proves not only that we already believe in trans-social
truths, and values; it also urges us to try to realize them
and hints how they can be discovered, for it lets us find
that we can conceive a human mind or a human will taking
paths that have not been followed before; and it reminds us
that, were such not the case, man would never have taken
his first step forward.

The Skinnerite's objections to Ibn Tufayl's efforts at ex-
tricating man from society arise in the tabula-rasa concep-

tion of humanity. If man is nothing, society must create him: *must*-ness in this judgment transfers an essence to man. Man is the social animal: if it is not social, then it is not man. Skinner's objections to the emancipation are partly bolstered by a natural reluctance to see an essential element abstracted away as contingent. And yet man is not an animal; and, if the thought-experiment can prove anything, it can prove that man is not *essentially* social.

The scientists of society have long stressed the importance of social forces in shaping man. Such diverse, but unmistakably human phenomena as humor, imagination, folk songs, epic poetry, and sound business decisions have been claimed, by one school or another, to originate with groups, rather than individuals. From the Ultramontane Bonald to the ultramodern élite of psycho-linguistics, claims are made for the crucial effect of language, an allegedly social product, on thought. It is remembered, one hopes, that this causality works both ways; but it takes the thought-experiment to remind us which of the two is essential: one can easily conceive, as Ibn Tufayl does, a man filled with thoughts, but never blessed by the "social gift" of language. It is thought that creates language; not language, thought. Likewise, one is logically and ontologically prior to many: no group has an idea or composes a refrain to the exclusion of its members. By the same token, it was man who created society, not society which created man.

Ibn Tufayl tells man to stand apart. No matter how intricate the relationship of accident and essence in man, we should preserve the capacity, which the thought-experiment proves we have, to tell them apart, to know where *I* ends and *other* begins, to learn what in me is most *me* and cultivate that. The thought-experiment points toward a truth to be learned and a beauty to be found, which society, by its lack of identity, can never capture.

Ibn Tufayl wants man to live the spiritual life of the natural first man. There is no ignorance here of the overarching forces that make such a life so difficult. The choice, of which Hayy is the pure and abstract ideal, is a moral imperative, not a pragmatic expediency. To believe in man's capacity to make such a choice may seem wishful thinking—

perhaps, but in view of the challenge implied, we might say will-ful thinking.

Both the Golding and the Skinner attack on Ibn Tufayl rely on claims of realism. Golding asks whether it is "realistic" to expect so much from man; his realism verges on cynicism, ignoring much that is good in man; and we must question whether Ibn Tufayl is not better aware of man's weakness than Golding is of his strength. Skinner uses 'realistic' in a different sense: he asks whether the withdrawal itself lies within the realm of possibility.

The thought-experiment is a means of establishing conceptual possibility; through it Ibn Tufayl constructs a maximally pure ideal of spiritual and intellectual self-reliance. To what extent is that ideal realizable? To answer such a question is to speak no longer of realism but of reality, and we must be clearly aware that the depth and complexity of real life admit the abstract ideal of a man who does nothing but "seek the truth" no more than they admit Golding's pure abstracts of aggression or Skinner's thin abstract of an artificial life. All ideals and abstracts, as such, are sections sliced from life; they *must* leave something out. But to be true to life is to allow the mind to re-synthesize the concepts it has divided, to flesh them out with substance, for life is big; stick figures can never picture it. One strange thing more is needed to cross the threshold of reality, *existence.* No thought-experiment can ever establish what exists and what does not. To find out what crosses the line between conceivable possibility and manifest actuality, a *real* experiment is needed and has always been needed. Only a real experiment can reveal to what extent Ibn Tufayl's ideal of withdrawal can be lived.

Henry David Thoreau, in the first *Walden*, leaves the record of the experiment he lived. "We chose our name," says Frazier, "in honor of Thoreau's experiment, which was in many ways like our own. It was an experiment in living, and it sprang from a similar doctrine of our relation to the state."[218] But if the two years Thoreau spent in the woods were an experiment, and if they involved withdrawal from the immediacy of external pressures, all resemblance to Skinner ends there.

Skinner removes his micro-society from the state, the better to achieve perfect control and unified direction, the implosion of each individual into a new society "for the good of the whole." Thoreau is an individualist, he withdrew one man from *society*, for his own good; he is an exemplar of the ideal of personal withdrawal.

A second great difference: the man Thoreau withdrew was himself; he was experimenting with his own soul, not talking about experimenting on others. He makes no one an object or a means: this is the heart of liberalism and at the heart of Thoreau's experiment.

But the most important difference is in what it was Thoreau discovered. Golding's children ignore the brilliant throbbing stars; the Ultimate Man cannot fathom a star— " 'what is love? . . . What is a star?' thus asks the Ultimate Man and blinks." But Thoreau, alone in the woods, can think:

> White pond and Walden are great crystals on the surface of the earth, Lakes of Light. If they were permanently congealed and small enough to be clutched, they would, perchance, be carried off by slaves, like precious stones, to adorn the heads of emperors; but being liquid, and ample, and secured to us and our successors forever, we disregard them, and run after the diamond of Kohinoor . . . They are too pure to have a market value; they contain no muck.[219]

What was it Thoreau found when he was alone? The beauty of nature? These are not ponds, but double-meaning symbols, these jewels in which there is no flaw, deep lakes whose bottoms have no mud: they stand for the pure and perfect knowledge of a truth beyond the pale:

> Let us settle ourselves and work and wedge our feet downward through the mud and slush of opinion, and prejudice, and tradition, and delusion, and appearance, that alluvion which covers the globe, through Paris and London, through New York and Boston and Concord, through Church and State, through poetry and philosophy and religion, 'till we come to a hard bottom and rocks in place which we call *reality*, and say This is, and no mistake.[220]

What is this Truth Thoreau discovers beneath the alluvia of tradition? His echo of the mystic Sanskrit phrase *'This is'* should leave us in no doubt: the soul is transcending itself, groping out towards "the Reality, the Truth, the necessarily existent." And, as if to prove the point, the jewel-lakes swing slowly round and take their places in the sky:

> In warm evenings I frequently sat in the boat playing the flute, and saw the perch, which I seemed to have charmed, hovering around me, and the moon travelling over the ribbed bottom, which was strewed with the wrecks of the forest . . . in dark nights, when your thoughts had wandered to vast cosmogonal themes in other spheres . . . It seemed as if I might next cast my line upward into the air, as well as downward into this element, which was scarcely more dense. Thus I caught two fishes as it were with one hook.[221]

Thoreau is reaching out of himself, towards beatitude. "Time," he wrote "is but the stream I go a-fishing in. I drink at it; but while I drink I see the sandy bottom and detect how shallow it is. Its thin current slides away, but eternity remains. I would drink deeper; fish in the sky, whose bottom is pebbly with stars. I cannot count one. I know not the first letter of the alphabet."[222]

Thoreau, like Hayy, has seen the stars as *jawāhir*, 'jewel-like substances,'[223] like him their essences have led him to the contemplation of a higher Truth, in which there is no flaw;[224] and like him, he finds that Truth in solitude. His inner sight can pierce the alluvia of tradition, for his soul can become like the pond "a perennial spring in the midst of pine and oak woods, without any visible inlet or outlet except by clouds and evaporation",[225] just as Hayy has pierced the veil of metaphor that hid the Truth with a soul like a fire or star that yearns upward.[226] What difference is there, then, which puts the flesh of substance on Thoreau's adventure?

First, Thoreau is an adult. No attempt is made to remove an unformed child from the womb of his family: the danger of destruction is too great; the harm from society too small to warrant such an attempt. When Thoreau went

to Walden, he was a man of established ideas. No one who
was not could have gone. Adulthood is a necessary of the
real experiment. Mowgli and Tarzan are children's stories
—the adult versions are in social-workers' files, labelled
'abandonment'. To face reality is to content ourselves with
the hope that the usual means of rearing children, or something just a little better, but within society, will suffice to
supply men capable of standing free of it.

Second, as has often been remarked, Thoreau's retreat
from society was by no means complete. The possibility of
complete social isolation has been established repeatedly by
monks and dervishes, but a life of utter solitude and silence,
as anyone knows who has lived it for even a few weeks,
takes on the unreal quality of an ordeal: Man's love of company is different from his need of food, but he loves it all
the same. Thoreau chose his place only a mile from the
town; and, in the days when 'society' still meant company,
and not coercive, molding force, he wrote "I think I love society as much as most . . . I had three chairs in my house;
one for solitude, two for friendship, three for society." "I
am no natural hermit," said he.[227] And yet, he did seclude
himself. His needs were no different from the needs we
find in ourselves, but he faced and overcame the need for
constant chaperones to his thoughts, and found another
value:

> I have never felt lonesome or in the least oppressed by a
> sense of solitude, but once, and that was a few weeks after
> I came to the woods, when, for an hour, I doubted if the
> near neighborhood of man was not essential to a serene and
> healthy life. To be alone was something unpleasant. But
> I was at the same time conscious of a slight insanity in my
> mood, and seemed to forsee my recovery. In the midst of
> a gentle rain, while these thoughts prevailed, I was sud-
> denly sensible of such sweet and beneficent society in Na-
> ture, in the very patterning of the drops, and in every sound
> and sight around my house, an infinite and unaccountable
> friendliness all at once like an atmosphere sustaining me,
> as made the fancied advantages of human neighborhood
> insignificant.[228]

A man needs friends, but he must also learn to discover the truth by himself, to find beauty alone, to live with himself. Unreal to be utterly alone, artificially 'sociable' to have not a moment to yourself; yet solitude and friendships are both necessary to the wholeness of a man; this is the kind of synthesis that makes ideals real.

Third, and most vitally, Thoreau's solitude in time itself is not complete. He is not alien to the culture he was born in—far from it!—or even to the distant cultures of other peoples. He would not have dreamed of going to the woods without his *"Bhagvat-Geeta"* his *Gulistan,* his *Harivansa,* his "mir Camar Uddin Mast", his Damodara, and Confucius[229]— not to mention his Testament, his Gospels, his Plato, and his *Iliad:* "A written word is the choicest of relics . . . Those who have not learned to read the ancient classics in the language in which they were written must have a very imperfect knowledge of the history of the human race . . ."[230] But food for thought is not the same as thought itself: there comes a time when the books must be closed and the mind must follow its own path; "build on piles of your own driving" says Thoreau,[231] "that way you rest on bed-rock." Cosmopolitan breadth of contact guarantees plurality of choice against cultural parochialism; but only the mind, which finds possibilities as yet unthought, can seek universality; only the soul, which finds its own beauty in solitude, can seek a truth which is absolute. Once again a synthesis is needed: there is a value in contact with other times and other minds—but there is a need, too, to "have a mind of your own", to come to an opinion—there is in Kohelet's words "a time to plant and a time to pluck."[232]

Would Ibn Tufayl reject these counsels of reality? To say so is to miss his point. Hayy is an ideal, a pure concept cut from the reality of a life which includes it but seems somehow to hold much more. Ibn Tufayl is not above realizing that other ideals exist. Absāl, before his mystic awakening, is the model of the scholarly, contemplative soul; Salāmān, the king of a rich and populous, settled land—Ibn Khaldūn would say a *civilized* island—symbolizes the ideal of involvement, devotion to public affairs and concern for public welfare. Hayy does not study; erudition is not what he is meant to represent. Nor does he serve the positive law; but in Ibn Tufayl himself we do find that synthesis of ideals that divides reality from fiction: he *was* a scholar of the ancient and medieval traditions, a physician and physiologist, a teacher and an active participant in national affairs as councilor to the Sultan of a powerful dynasty. And yet he knew that influence is not greatness and success is not fulfillment, that knowledge is not wisdom, and benevolence is not holiness. The Arab princes used to send their sons to the desert to learn generosity, the manly virtues, the purest language and the simplest life: there is something man can learn when he is alone. There is something blotted out in man when society devours his every waking moment: the apotheosis of society is the death of the transcendent soul. There are times when a man must draw back a bit and meditate—a moment of withdrawal to balance with the rest of life, a moment in which reason and the power of the soul can find a truth tradition can never impart. It was the ideal of that withdrawal embodied in the peaceful soul of Hayy Ibn Yaqzān which Ibn Tafayl singled out for praise.

Ibn Tufayl's
Hayy Ibn Yaqzān

HAYY IBN YAQZĀN a Philosophical Tale of IBN TUFAYL

In the name of God, the Merciful and Compassionate.   *3*
   God bless our master Muhammad,
  his house and companions and grant them peace.

Noble brother, my dear, kind friend, God grant you eternal life and everlasting happiness. You have asked me to unfold for you, as well as I am able, the secrets of the oriental philosophy[1]* mentioned by the prince of philosophers,   *4*
Avicenna.[2] Then you must know from the start that if you want the truth without flummery you must seek it and seek it diligently.[3]

Your request set off a stream of ideas in me—praise God—which lifted me to a state of sublimity I had never known before, a state so wonderful "the tongue cannot describe" or explain it, for it belongs to another order of being, a different world. But the joy, delight and bliss of this ecstasy[4] are such that no one who has reached it or even come near it can keep the secret or conceal the mystery.[5] The light-headedness, expansiveness,[6] and joy which seize him force him to blurt it out in some sweeping generality, for to capture it precisely is impossible. If he be the sort whose mind has not been sharpened by intellectual pursuits, he may speak unwisely.[7] Thus in this state one said "Praise be to me, great am I!"[8] Another said "I am the Truth";[9] another, "There is within this robe nothing but God!"[10] It was his own attainment of this ecstasy that Ghazālī[11] attempted to portray when he wrote:

* Notes to the Text begin on p. 167.

95

It *was*—what it was is harder to say.
Think the best, but don't make me describe it away.[12]

5   But his was a mind refined by learning and education.[13]

Look at the words Ibn Bājja appended to his discussion
of communion with the divine:[14] "Once these ideas are understood it will be clear that nothing learned in ordinary
studies can reach this level. For once this concept is
grasped the mind can see itself as cut off from all that went
before, with new convictions that cannot have arisen from
the world of matter, too splendid to have sprung from the
material since they are cleansed of all the compositeness
characteristic of the physical world. Surely it would be
more appropriate to call them divine ecstasies granted by
God to those He will."

The level to which Ibn Bājja refers is reached by use of
reason, and no doubt he reached it—but he did not surpass
it. The level of which I spoke at the outset is something
quite different,[15] although the two are alike in that nothing
revealed here contradicts what is revealed by reason.[16] The
6   difference is in an increase in what is seen and in the fact
that this is experienced through what I must, only figuratively, call a faculty:[17] For neither in popular language nor
in specialized terminology[18] can I find any expression for it.

This ecstasy, to the taste of which[19] I was brought by
your request, is one of a number of stages in the progress
of the devotee,[20] as reported by Avicenna: "Then, when
his training and willpower reach a certain point, glimmer-
ings of the light of Truth[21] will flicker before him, thrilling
him like lightning, flashing and going out. If he is diligent
in his ascetic practice, these spells grow more and more fre-
quent, until they come unasked, en-trancing him without
the use of exercises. No matter what he sees, he will turn
from it to the Sacred Presence, reminded of some aspect of
the Divine, and again he will be overwhelmed. Thus he
7   begins to see the Truth in everything.[22] Finally his efforts
bring him to a stage where his moment of recognition turns
to tranquil contemplation; his stolen glimpses, familiarity;
his spark, a limpid flame. He has gained an understanding[23] as unshakable as that of an old friendship."[24]

Avicenna goes on to describe the gradual progress[25] of the devotee, culminating as "his inmost being becomes a polished mirror facing toward the truth. Sublime delight pours over him and he rejoices in his soul at all the marks it bears of Truth.[26] At this level he sees both himself and the Truth. He still hesitates between them; but then, becoming oblivious to self, he is aware only of the Sacred Presence—or if he is at all aware of himself, it is only as one who gazes on the Truth. At this point communion is achieved."

Now these states, as Avicenna describes them, are reached not by theorizing, syllogistic deductions, postulating premisses and drawing inferences, but solely by intuition.[27] If you wish an analogy to make clear the difference between this sort of apprehension and all others, imagine a child, growing up in a certain city, born blind, but otherwise intelligent and well endowed,[28] with a sound memory and an apt mind. Through his remaining channels of perception he will get to know the people as well as all sorts of animals and objects, and the streets and alleys, houses and markets—eventually well enough to walk through the city without a guide, recognizing at once everyone he meets. But colors, and colors alone, he will know only by descriptive explanations and ostensive definitions.[29] Suppose after he had come this far, his eyesight were restored and he could see. He would walk all through the town finding nothing in contradiction to what he had believed, nor would anything look wrong to him. The colors he encountered would conform to the guidelines that had been sketched out for him. Still there would be two great changes, the second dependent on the first: first the daybreak on a new visual world, and second, his great joy.[30]

Those who merely think and have not reached the level of love[31] are like the blind. The colors, at that stage known only by accounts of their names, are those experiences which Ibn Bājja said are "too splendid to arise in the physical world", which "God grants to those of his worshippers whom He chooses." But to those who reach love, God grants what I purely metaphorically call another faculty. This corresponds to the restoration of sight. And some-

times, rarely, there comes a man whose eyes, as it were, are
always open, whose glance is always piercing, who does not
need to search.[32]

When I speak of the rationalists' method—God raise you
to the level of love!—I do not confine myself to their knowledge of the physical world, any more than I confine myself
to the metaphysical when I speak of intuition. The two
modes of apprehension are quite distinct and are not to be
confused, but what I mean by the rationalist's apprehension
includes his understanding of the metaphysical—for example, that of Ibn Bājja. It is a necessary condition of what
is reached by pure reason that it be true and valid. Thus
the difference between the rationalist and those who enjoy
intimacy is that while both are concerned with the self-same
things, the latter enjoy a clearer view and far greater delight.

10   Ibn Bājja censured them for the pursuit of this joy. He
claimed it was a product of their imagination and even
promised a clear and distinct description of just how ecstasy
ought to be enjoyed. Here is the answer he deserves: 'Do
not declare too sweet fruits you have not tasted, and do not
trample on the necks of the saintly.'[33] The man did not, in
fact, keep his promise or any such thing. What prevented
him, perhaps, was that, as he himself says, he was pressed
for time with the trouble of getting down to Oran. Or perhaps he felt that describing this state would force him to
say something derogatory to his own way of life or at odds
with his encouragement of amassing wealth and of the use
of various artful dodges to acquire it. But I digress.

It seems clear now that your request must fall within
either one or the other of these two objectives: You may be
asking what is actually seen by those who undergo the experience and reach intimacy. If so, this is something which
11   cannot be put into a book.[34] Whenever anyone tries to entrust it to words or to the written page its essence is distorted and it slips into that other, purely theoretical branch
of discourse. For, clothed in letters and sounds and brought
into the perceptible world, it cannot remain, in any way,
what it was. Accounts of it, thus, differ widely. Many
stray into error by trying to describe it, yet presume others

to have strayed who never left the path. All this is because it is something vast, infinite—encompassing, but unencompassed.[35]

But on the other hand you may desire a discursive, intellectualized introduction to this experience. And this— God honor you with His intimacy—is something that can be put into words and set down in books. But it is rarer than red sulfur,[36] especially in our part of the world.[37] For the experience is so arcane that only one lone individual and then another[38] can master the most trifling part of it. And even those who do win some bit of it, speak of it publicly only in riddles, because our true, orthodox and established faith guards against a hasty plunge into such things.

Do not suppose the philosophy which has reached us in the books of Aristotle and Fārābī or in Avicenna's *Healing*[39] will satisfy you if this is what you need, or that any Andalusian has written anything adequate on this subject. The reason is that before the spread of philosophy and formal logic to the West all native Andalusians of any ability devoted their lives to mathematics. They achieved a high level in that field but could do no more. The next generation surpassed them in that they knew a little logic. But study logic as they may, they could not find in it the way to fulfillment. It was one of them who wrote:

12

> How can it be that life's so small.
> Two sciences we have—that's all.
> One is truth beyond attaining;
> The other vain and not worth gaining.[40]

This generation was succeeded by a third, better thinkers and closer to the truth. Of these none had a sharper mind, a sounder method, or truer views than Ibn Bājja. But he was so preoccupied with material success that death carried him off before his intellectual storehouses could be cleared and all his hidden wisdom made known. Most of his extant books are unfinished and break off abruptly before the end like his *De Anima*, his *Discipline of the Solitary*, and his writings on logic and natural science. His only completed works, in fact, are outlines and hasty essays. He

13

himself admits this when he says that the argument for
the idea he was trying to convey in his *Essay on Communion with the Divine* was put into clear language only with
painful difficulty, that in places the organization is weak,
and that if he'd had more time, he'd have liked to have re-
written it.   This is as much as I can find out about the man,
since I never knew him personally.[41]

As for those of his contemporaries allegedly on a par with
him, I have seen none of their works.   Their successors,
however, our own contemporaries, are as yet at a develop-
mental stage, or else their development has halted prema-
turely—unless there are some of whom I don't yet have a
full report.[42]

Those of Fārābī's books that have reached us are for the
most part on logic, and those on philosophy are full of
doubts.[43]   In *The Ideal Religion* he affirms that the souls of
the wicked live on forever in infinite torments after death.
But in his *Civil Politics* he says plainly that they dissolve
into nothing and that only the perfected souls of the good
achieve immortality.   Finally in his commentary on Aristotle's *Ethics*, discussing human happiness, he says that it
exists only in this life, and on the heels of that has words to
the effect that all other claims are senseless ravings and old
wives' tales.[44]   This makes mankind at large despair of God's
mercy.   It puts the wicked on the same level with the good,
for it makes nothingness the ultimate destiny of us all.   This
is an unspeakable lapse, an unforgivable fall.   This on top
of his mis-belief, openly avowed, that prophecy belongs
properly to the imagination,[45] and his preference of philosophy to revelation—and many more failings which I pass
over.

As for the works of Aristotle, Avicenna undertook an exposition of their contents, in accordance with Aristotelian
thinking, and he followed Aristotle's philosophical approach
in his own *Healing*.   But at the start of the book he admits
that the truth for him is something quite different; this book
was written in the manner of the Peripatetics, but if you
want the truth without obfuscation you must study his writings on oriental philosophy.   If you take the trouble to
plough through the *Healing* and the Aristotelian corpus,

you will find that on most subjects they agree, although there are some things in the *Healing* that don't come down to us in Aristotle. But if you take everything in Aristotle and the literal reading of the *Healing* (without grasping its subtle, inner meaning) you will end up, as Avicenna warns, far from perfection.

Even Ghazālī's works, because he preached to the masses, bind in one place and loose in another. First he says a thing is rank faithlessness, then he says it's permissible.[46] One ground on which he charges the philosophers with unbelief in *The Incoherence of the Philosophers*[47] is their denial of the resurrection of the flesh and their assertion that only souls are meted out rewards and punishment. But at the beginning of *A Scale of Actions*[48] he definitely attributes this belief to the Sūfī masters, while in the *Rescue from Wrong and Discovery of Ecstasy*[49] he says that he accepts the Sūfī teaching although he came to it only after long searching.[50] Much of this sort of inconsistency will be found in his books by anyone who spends long studying them. He even offers some apology for this practice at the end of the *Scale of Actions*, in his tripartite division of ideas into those held in common with the masses, those exhorting all who seek the truth, and those a man keeps to himself and divulges only to people who share his beliefs.[51] Finally he writes "If my words have done no more than to shake you in the faith of your fathers, that would have been reason enough to write them. For he who does not doubt does not look; and he who does not look will not see, but must remain in blindness and confusion." He illustrates the point with this couplet:

> Forget all you've heard and clutch what you see—
> At sunrise what use is Saturn to thee?[52]

Such apothegms were characteristic of his teaching. Most of what he said was in the form of hints and intimations, of value to those who hear them only after they have found the truth by their own insight or to someone innately gifted and primed to understand. Such men need only the subtlest hints.[53]

17   In his *Gems of the Qur'ān* Ghazālī said that he had written certain esoteric books which contain the unvarnished truth. So far as I know no such book has reached Spain, although some claim that certain books we have received are in fact this hidden corpus. Nothing could be further from the truth. The books in question are *Modes of Awareness* and *The Smoothing, the Breath of Life, and Related Problems*. Granted that these books contain many hints, they still add little to what is disclosed in his better known works. His *Perfect Understanding of the Lovely Names of God*, in fact, has matter far more recondite than these, and Ghazālī himself tells us that this is not an esoteric book—which means that these which we have could not be among them.[54]

One of our contemporaries, basing himself on Ghazālī's statements at the end of *A Lamp for the Lights*, charges him with a crime monstrous enough to cast him into an inescapable pit. After discussing those "veiled by light,"

18   Ghazālī goes on to speak of those who achieve communion with the divine. He says they know this Being as characterized by an attribute which would tend to negate His utter unity. This critic wishes to impute that Ghazālī believed God, the First and the Truth—praised be He and far exalted above the aspersions of the wicked—has some plurality in His being.[55] I have no doubt that our teacher Ghazālī was among those who reached this sublime goal and enjoyed the ultimate bliss. Nonetheless, his esoteric books on mysticism have not reached us.

I myself would not have garnered what truth I have attained, the culmination of my intellectual efforts, without pursuing the arguments of Ghazālī and Avicenna, checking them one against the other, and comparing the result with the views that have sprung up in our era, so fervently admired by self-appointed philosophers, until finally I was able to see the truth for myself, first by thought and theory, and now in my first brief taste of the actual experience. I feel able now to set down a view to be preserved in my name; and because of our close friendship, I want you to be the first to whom I express myself.

Nonetheless, if I tell you of the highest levels I reached

without first going over the preliminary steps that lead there, it would do you no more good than blind faith[56]—as if you approved not because my arguments warrant acceptance, but because we are friends.   I expect better of you than that.   I won't be satisfied unless you go higher, for this much can't guarantee salvation, let alone conquering the highest peaks.   I want only to bring you along the paths in which I have preceded you and let you swim in the sea I have just crossed, so that it may bear you where it did me and you may undergo the same experience and see with the eyes of your soul all that I have seen.   Then you will not need to confine yourself within the limits of my knowledge.[57]

This will demand no small amount of time, free of all other concerns, for devotion to this endeavor.   But if you work hard, you'll be glad in the morning of the ground you gained at night.[58]   Your efforts will be blessed; you will please your Lord, and He will please you.[59]   I shall be at your side as long as you need me, to lead you where you wish to go by the shortest, safest, and most unobstructed route.

To give you a brief glimpse of the road that lies ahead,[60] let me tell you the story of Hayy Ibn Yaqzān, Absāl, and Salāmān, who were given their names by Avicenna himself. For the tale points a moral for all with heart to understand, "a reminder for anyone with a heart or ears to listen and to hear".[61]

* * *

Our forefathers, of blessed memory,[62] tell of a certain equatorial island, lying off the coast of India, where human beings come into being without father or mother.[63]   This is possible, they say, because, of all places on earth, that island has the most tempered climate.   And because a supernal light streams down on it, it is the most perfectly adapted to accept the human form.[64]   This runs counter to the views of most ordinary philosophers and even the greatest natural scientists.   They believe the most temperate region of the inhabited world to be the fourth zone,[65] and if

they say this because they reason that some inadequacy due
to the earth prevents settlement on the equatorial belt, then
there is some color of truth to their claim that the fourth is
the most moderate of the remaining regions. But if, as most
of them admit, they refer only to the intense heat of the
equator, the notion is an error the contrary of which is
easily proved.

For it is a demonstrated principle of physical science that
heat is generated only by motion, contact with hot bodies,
or radiation of light. The same sciences teach us that the
sun itself is not hot and is not to be characterized by any
such mixed qualities. Likewise they teach that it is the
highly reflective bodies, not the transparent ones, that take
up light best; next are opaque, non-reflecting bodies; but
transparent bodies with no trace of opacity do not take on
light at all. The foregoing point was proved by Avicenna,
using an argument which was his original work; his predecessors do not have it. If these premises are sound, they
imply that the sun does not warm earth the way bodies
22   warm each other, by conduction, because in itself the sun
is not hot. Nor is the earth warmed by motion since it is
stationary and in the same position at sunrise as at sunset,
although warming and cooling are apparent at these times.
Nor does the sun first warm the air and then the earth by
convection. How could it, since we find that when it's hot
the air close to the earth is much hotter than that higher
up? The only alternative is that the sun warms the earth
by radiation of light.

Heat invariably follows light. If focused in a burning-
mirror light will even set things on fire. It has been proved
with scientific certainty that the sun is spherical, as is
the earth, and that the sun is much bigger than the earth.
Thus somewhat more than half the earth's surface is perpetually lit by the sun, and of the sector of the earth il-
luminated at any given moment, the most brilliantly lit por-
23   tion is the center, since it is furthest from the darkness and
faces most directly into the sun. Toward the edges the il-
lumination is progressively less, shading into darkness at
the periphery. A place is at the center of the circle of light
only when those who live there can see the sun, at its ze-

nith, directly overhead. At this time the heat is as intense
as it will get. A place where the sun stays far from the
zenith will be very cold; places where it tends to linger at
the zenith will be very hot. But astronomy proves that in
equatorial regions the sun stands directly overhead only
twice a year, when it enters the Ram at the vernal equinox
and when it enters the Balances at the autumnal equinox.
The rest of the year it declines six months to the north and
six to the south. These regions, then, enjoy a uniform climate, neither excessively hot nor excessively cold. 24

I recognize that this statement demands a fuller explanation than I have provided,[66] but this would not further our
purpose. I bring it to your attention solely by way of cor-
roborating the alleged possibility of a man's being engen-
dered in this place without father or mother, since many
insist with assurance and conviction that Hayy Ibn Yaqzān
was one such person who came into being on that island by
spontaneous generation.

Others, however, deny it and relate a different version of
his origin, which I shall tell you. They say that opposite
this island there is a large island, rich and spacious, and inhabited by people over whom one, a proud and angry man,
was king. Now this king had a sister whom he forbade to
marry until he himself should find a fitting match.[67] But
she had a kinsman named Aware,[68] and he married her
secretly, but lawfully, according to their rite.[69] She soon
conceived and bore him a son, but fearing exposure of her
secret she took the infant after nursing him,[70] put him in a
tightly sealed ark; and, attended by a few trustworthy
friends and servants, brought him at nightfall down to the 25
sea, her heart aching with love and fear for her child. She
then wished the child farewell and cried "Almighty God,
you formed my baby 'when it was nothing, a thing without
a name.'[71] You fed him in the darkness of my womb and
saw that he was smooth and even[72] and perfectly formed.
In fear of that wicked tyrant I entrust[73] him to your care.
I beg you shed your bounty upon him. Be with him. Never
leave him, most merciful God!" She cast him into the sea.[74]

A powerful current caught the box and brought it that
very night to the coast of the other island of which I spoke.

At that very moment the tide reached a height to which it would not return for another year. It lodged the little ark in a pleasant thicket, thick with shady cover, floored by rich loam, sheltered from wind and rain and veiled from the sun, which "gently slanted off it when it rose and set."[75] The tide then began to ebb, leaving the ark high and dry.

26 Sand drifted up with gusts of the breeze, damming the watercourse into the thicket so the water could not reach it. The nails of the box had been loosened and the boards knocked akilter by the pounding of the surf against them in the thicket. When the baby had gotten very hungry, he began to cry and struggle. The sound of his voice reached a doe; and taking it for the call of her lost fawn,[76] she followed the sound until she came to the ark. She prodded with her hoof and the baby fought from inside until one of the top boards came loose. The doe felt sorry for the infant and nuzzled him tenderly. She gave him her udder and let him drink her own delicious milk. She became his constant nurse, caring for him, raising him and protecting him from harm.

This, according to those who deny spontaneous generation, is the story of his origin.[77] In a moment I shall tell you how he grew up and progressed from one phase to the next until he reached his remarkable goal. But first I should say that those who claim Hayy came into being spontane-

27 ously say that in a pocket of earth on that island, over the years, a mass of clay worked until hot and cold, damp and dry were blended in just the proper way, their strengths perfectly balanced. This fermented mass of clay was quite large, and parts of it were in better equilibrium than others, more suited than the rest for becoming human gametes. The midmost part was the best proportioned and bore the most perfect equivalence to the makeup of a man. The clay labored and churned, and in the viscous mass there formed what looked like bubbles in boiling water.

28 In the very middle formed a tiny bubble divided in half by a delicate membrane and filled by a fine gaseous body, optimally proportioned for what it was to be.[78] With it at that moment joined "the spirit which is God's,"[79] in a bond virtually indissoluble, not only in the purview of the senses,

but also in that of the mind. For it should be clear that this spirit emanates continuously from God—glory be to Him. It is analogous to the sunlight that constantly floods the earth. Some objects, like transparent air, are not lit by it at all. Others, opaque but not shiny, are lit partially, differing in color according to their different receptivities. Still others, polished bodies such as mirrors, take up light maximally; and if these mirrors have a certain concave form, fires start in them from the concentrated rays of light. The same holds for the spirit which flows eternally from God's word to all that is. Some beings, lacking any aptitude to receive it, show no trace of it. These, corresponding to the air of the analogy, are the lifeless, inanimate objects. Others, that is plant species, show its influence to varying degrees in proportion to their capacities; they are analogous to opaque objects. Still others show its impact greatly; these are animal species, and they correspond to the shiny objects of the analogy. The most reflective body, far outshining all others, is the one that mirrors in itself the image and pattern of the sun. In the same way with animals, the one that best takes on the spirit in himself and is formed and modelled in its pattern is man. There is reference to this in the words of the Prophet—God bless him and grant him peace—"God created Adam in His own image".[80]

If this image grows so strong in a man that its reality eclipses all other forms, the splendor of its light setting afire all it apprehends so that it alone remains, then it is like the mirror reflecting on itself, burning everything else. This happens only to prophets, the blessings of God upon them.[81] But all this will be made clear in due course. Let us return to the story they tell of his creation.

They say, "When this spirit was linked with that chamber all the powers of the latter submitted totally to it, bowing to its sway according to God's command.[82] Then opposite this chamber a second bubble formed, divided into three chambers, separated by thin membranes and joined by tiny ducts. This also was filled by gaseous material, like that which filled the first, only not as fine. In these three sacs, partitioned within one, lodged some of the powers that had subordinated themselves to the spirit, entrusted with its

preservation and care and with relaying to this first spirit,
linked with the first chamber, all their experiences, from the
subtlest to the most magnificent. Next to the first, opposite the second, a third bubble formed, filled with its own
gaseous matter, denser than either of the others, and with
its own set of subordinate faculties, devoted to the protection and sustenance of the spirit.[83]

31   "These chambers, first, second, and third, in the order I
have given, were the first to be created in that working mass
of clay. Although they all depend on each other, the dependence of the first on the other two is its need for service,
but their dependence on the first is the reliance of the led
on their leader or the controlled on what controls them.
Still the second and third in their own right are masters,
not servants, of all the organs formed after them; and the
second has a fuller share of rule than the third. The first
has the conical shape of a flame, since it is linked to the
spirit and burns with the spirit's heat. The dense matter
by which it was enclosed took on the same shape; it developed into solid flesh and was in turn covered by the
tough protective envelope of peritoneum. The whole organ
is what we call the heart.

32   "To survive the heart needed to be fed and maintained
to replenish the juices which constantly broke down in the
terrific heat. It needed also a sense of what was good and
bad for it so it would be drawn to the one and reject the
other. The first need was delegated to one organ with powers designed to serve that need, and its second to another.
Sensation was in charge of the brain and nutrition of the
liver. Each depends on the heart not only because its heat
keeps them alive, but also because their specialized powers
originate there. Meanwhile ducts and passages were woven
between them and the heart, some wider than others, depending on the need. These were the veins and arteries."
So, neglecting nothing, they go on to describe the whole
anatomy and all the organs, as physiologists describe the
formation of a foetus in the womb, up to the termination
of the development process when all the parts were fully
formed and the embryo was ready to be born.[84]
          In accounting for the success of this metamorphosis they

rely heavily on their mass of fermenting clay and on its suitability to be formed into all the protective membranes and the like which would be needed in the forming of a man.[85]

When the embryo was ready these coverings were sloughed off as if in labor; and the clay, which had already begun to dry, cracked open. His food supply thus vanishing, the newborn infant got hungrier and hungrier and began to cry, whereupon the doe with the lost fawn responded. From this point on both factions[86] give interchangeable versions of his upbringing.

They agree that the doe that cared for him was richly pastured, so she was fat and had plenty of milk, to give the baby the best possible nourishment. She stayed with him, leaving only when necessary to graze. The baby grew so fond of her he would cry if she were late, and then she would come rushing back. There were no beasts of prey on the island.

So the child grew, nourished by its mother-doe's milk, until he was two years old. By then he'd learned to walk; and, having his teeth, he took to following the doe on her foraging expeditions. She treated him gently and tenderly, taking him where fruit trees grew and feeding him the sweet, ripe fruits that fell from them. The hard-shelled ones she cracked between her teeth, or if he wanted to go back for a while to milk she let him.[87] She brought him to water when he was thirsty; and when the sun beat down she shaded him. When he was cold she warmed him, and at nightfall she would bring him back to the spot where she had found him, nestling him to herself among the feathers with which the little ark had been cushioned.

When they went out to forage and came back to rest they were accompanied by a troop of deer that went along to graze and stayed the night near where they slept. Thus the child lived among the deer, imitating their calls so well that eventually his voice and theirs could hardly be distinguished. In the same way he imitated all the bird calls and animal cries he heard with amazing accuracy,[88] but most often he would mimic the calls of the deer for alarm, courtship, summons or defense—for animals have different cries for these different contingencies.[89] The animals were used

to him and he was used to them, so they were not afraid of
each other.

Hayy discovered in himself an aversion toward some
things and an attraction to others even after the things
themselves were no longer objects of his immediate experience, for their images were fixed in his mind.[90] He observed the animals from this perspective and saw how they
were clothed in fur, hair or feathers, how swiftly they could
run, how fiercely they could fight, and what apt weapons
they had for defense against any attacker—horns, tusks,
hooves, spurs and claws. Then he looked back at himself
and realized how naked and defenseless he was. He was
a weak runner and not a good fighter. When the animals
grappled with him for a piece of fruit they usually wrested
it from him and got away with it. He could not defend
himself or even run away.

Hayy saw the fawns his age sprout horns from nowhere
and grow strong and swift. But in himself he could discover
no such change. He wondered about this but could not
fathom the cause. No maimed or deformed animal he could
find was at all like himself. All other animals, he observed,
had covered outlets for their bodily wastes—the solid by a
tail, the liquid by fur or the like. And the fact that the private parts of an animal were better concealed than his own
disturbed him greatly and made him very unhappy.[91]

When he was nearly seven[92] and had finally lost hope of
making up the deficiencies which so disturbed him he took
some broad leaves from a tree and put them on, front and
back. Then out of plaits of palms and grass he made something like a belt about his middle and fastened his leaves
to it. But he had hardly worn it at all when the leaves
withered and dried and, one by one, fell out.[93] So he had
constantly to get new ones and work them in with the old
in bundles. This might make it hold up a while longer, but
still it lasted only a very short time.

He got some good sticks from a tree, balanced the shafts
and sharpened the points. These he would brandish at the
animals that menaced him. He could now attack the weaker
ones and hold his own against the stronger. His self-
esteem rose a bit as he observed how superior his hands

were to those of an animal. They enabled him to cover his
nakedness and to make sticks for self-defense, so he no
longer needed natural weapons or the tail he had longed
for.

All the while, he was growing, and soon he was seven.
The chore of getting new leaves to cover himself was taking
too long, and he had an urge to get the tail of some dead
animal and fasten that on instead. But he had noticed that
the living wildlife shunned the bodies of the dead and fled
from them. So he could not go ahead with his plan, until
one day he came upon a dead eagle. Seeing that the animals had no aversion to it, he snatched the opportunity to
put his idea into effect. Boldly taking hold of the eagle,
Hayy cut off the wings and tail just as they were, all in one
piece. He stretched out the wings and smoothed down the
feathers, stripped off the remaining skin and split it in half,
tying it about his middle, hanging down, half in front and
half behind. The tail, he threw across his back; and he
fastened the wings to his arms. Thus he got a fine covering
that not only kept him warm but also so terrified the animals that not one of them would fight with him or get in
his way.[94] In fact, none would come near him except the
doe that had nursed and raised him.

She was inseparable from him and he from her. When
she grew old and weak he would lead her to rich pastures
and gather sweet fruits to feed her. Even so, weakness and
emaciation gradually tightened their hold, and finally death
overtook her. All her movements and bodily functions
came to a standstill. When the boy saw her in such a state,
he was beside himself with grief. His soul seemed to over-
flow with sorrow. He tried to call her with the call she
always answered, shouted as loud as he could, but saw not
the faintest flicker of life.[95] He peered into her eyes and
ears, but no damage was apparent. In the same way he
examined all her parts but could find nothing wrong with
any of them.[96] He hoped to discover the place where she
was hurt so he could take away the hurt and allow her to
recover—but he could not even make a start; he was powerless.

What made him think there was something he could

39

"take away" was his own past experience. He knew that
when he shut his eyes or covered them, he saw nothing until
the obstruction was removed; if he stopped his ears with
his fingers he could not hear until the obstacle was gone;
and if he held his nose he would smell nothing until the
passageway was clear again.

These observations led him to believe that not only his
senses, but every one of his other bodily functions was liable
to obstructions that might block its work. When the block
was removed it would return to its normal functioning.[97]
But when he had examined all her external organs and
found no visible wound or damage, considering meanwhile
that her inactivity was not confined to one part but spread
throughout the body, it dawned on him that the hurt must
be in some organ unseen within the body, without which
none of the external parts could function. When that organ
had been hurt, the harm was general. No part of the body
could carry on its work. Hayy hoped that if he could find
that organ and remove whatever had lodged in it, it would
revert to normal, its benefits would once more flow to the
rest of the body and all the bodily functions would resume.

40

He had observed in the past that the parts of animals'
dead bodies were solid, having no hollows except those of
the head, chest and abdomen. He felt certain that the vital
organ he was looking for must occupy one of these three
cavities, and it seemed to him most likely by far that it be
in the central of the three.[98] Surely it had to be centrally
located, since all the other organs were equally dependent
on it. Besides, in his own case, he could feel what must be
such an organ in his breast.[99] He could restrict the action
of his other organs—hands, feet, eyes, nose, and ears; he
could lose these parts and conceivably get along without
them. Conceivably he could get along without his head.[100]
But when he thought of whatever it was he could feel in his
breast he could not conceive of living for an instant without
it. For this reason, in fact, when fighting with animals, he
had always been especially careful to protect his breast from

41

their horns—because he could feel that there was something
there.

Certain that the organ where the hurt had settled must be in her breast, he decided to search for and examine it. Perhaps he would be able to get hold of the hurt and remove it. Still he was afraid this very operation might be worse than the original damage. His efforts might do more harm than good. He tried to think whether he had ever seen any animal recover from such a state; and, unable to do so, he lost hope of her getting better unless he did something. But there remained some hope of her recovery if he could find the critical organ and take away the hurt. So he decided to cut open her breast and find out what was inside.

He took chips of stone and dry splinters of wood, sharp as knives, and split her open between the ribs.[101] Cutting through the flesh, he reached the diaphragm. When he saw how tough it was he was certain that this covering must belong to some such organ as he was searching for. If he looked beneath he was sure to find it. Hayy tried to cut *42* through it, but this was difficult, since he had no tools but only stones and sticks.

He made fresh instruments and sharpened them. Then, cutting very carefully, he pierced the diaphragm and reached a lung. He supposed at first that this was what he was looking for and turned it round and round to see where it was impaired. What he found at first was only one lung, and when he saw that it was to one side (while the organ he was looking for, he was convinced, must be centered in the body's girth as well as in its length) he went on exploring the mid-chest cavity until he found the heart, wrapped in an extremely tough envelope and bound by the strongest ligaments, cushioned in the lung on the side where he had entered. He said to himself, "If this organ has the same structures on the other side as it does here, then it really is directly in the center and it must be the organ I'm looking for—especially since its position is so good, and it is so beautifully formed, so sturdy and compact, and better protected than any other organ I have seen."

He probed on the other side and there too found the dia- *43* phragm and the other lung, just as before. Now he was sure this was the central organ he wanted. He tried to split or cut its protective pericardial cover; and finally with a tremendous effort he was able to lay the heart bare.

On all sides it seemed firm and sound. He looked for any visible damage and found none. Squeezing it in his hand, he discovered it was hollow and thought, perhaps what I actually want is inside this organ and I have not yet reached it. He cut open the heart and inside found two chambers, a left and a right. The right ventricle was clogged with a thick clot of blood, but the left was empty and clear.

"What I'm looking for," he said to himself, "must live in one of these two chambers. In this one on the right I see nothing but clotted blood—which cannot have congealed until the whole body got the way it is—" for he had observed how blood thickens and clots when it flows out of the body, and this was simply ordinary blood, "I see that blood is found in all the organs, not confined to one as opposed to others. But what I've been looking for all along is something uniquely related to this special position and something I know I could not live without for the batting of an eye. Blood I have often lost in quantity fighting with the animals, but it never hurt me; I never lost any of my faculties. What I'm looking for is not in this chamber. But the left one has nothing in it; I can see that it is empty. I cannot believe it serves no purpose, since I have seen that every organ exists to carry out some specific function. How could this chamber, with its commanding position, have none? I can only believe that what I was searching for was here but left, leaving the chamber empty and the body without sensation or motion, completely unable to function."

Realizing that whatever had lived in that chamber had left while its house was intact, before it had been ruined, Hayy saw that it was hardly likely to return after all the cutting and destruction. The body now seemed something low and worthless compared to the being he was convinced had lived in it for a time and then departed.

Hayy turned the focus of his thoughts on that being.[102] What was it? What was its manner of existence? What had bound it to this body? Where had it gone, and how had it gotten out? What drove it away if it was forced to leave; or, if it left of its own free choice, what made it so loathe the body? His mind was filled with these questions. He soon dropped the body and thought no more of it, knowing that the mother who had nursed him and showed him so much kindness could only be that being which had departed. From that—and not from this lifeless body—all those actions had issued. The whole body was simply a tool of this being, like the stick with which he fought the animals.[103] His affection was transferred now from the body to the being that was its master and mover. All his love was directed toward that.

Meanwhile the body began to decay and give off dreadful odors, increasing his revulsion for it. He longed not to have to look at it. Not long afterwards he noticed two ravens fighting. They fought until one struck the other dead, whereupon it scratched a hole in the earth and buried the dead one. Hayy said to himself, "It surely was good of this bird to bury the other, although it was wrong to kill him. I ought to do the same for my mother."[104] So he dug a hole, threw in his mother's body, heaped earth upon it, and went back to thinking of what controls the body.

He had no idea what it was; but he observed that each individual deer had the same form and figure as his mother. In all probability each of them was moved and governed by something like what had once given motion and direction to his mother. He was friendly to the deer, treating them more kindly for their likeness to his mother.

He lived thus for a time, studying animals and plants and roaming along the island shore in search of some being like himself, since he saw that every animal and plant had many others like it. But he found none.[105] Seeing that the sea completely surrounded the island, Hayy believed that his island was the only land there was.[106]

A fire broke out one day by friction in a bed of reeds. When Hayy first saw it the sight terrified him. He had never seen anything like it.[107] For some time he stood staring at it, gradually moving nearer and nearer, awestruck by its piercing light and the way it attacked, overwhelmed, and turned to flame everything it touched. Carried away by his

amazement, and by the courage, not to say audacity, God
had compounded with his nature, Hayy reached out and
tried to grasp a piece of it. But when he touched it it burnt
his hand, and he could not hold on to it.   Then he got the
48   idea of taking a brand that was not wholly on fire.   He
picked it up by the end that wasn't burning, leaving the
fire at the other end.   This he could manage with ease, so
he took it home—for he had moved into a cave, which
seemed to him a fine place to live.

He kept the fire up with dry grass and a good supply of
firewood, tending it day and night because it seemed such a
wonderful thing. He liked it best at night when it took the
place of the sun, giving warmth and light.   It meant so
much to him he fell in love with it and was convinced that
of all the things he had, this was the best.   Seeing how it
always moved upwards, as though trying to rise, he supposed it must be one of those jewel-substances he saw shining in the sky.

Hayy tested the power of fire on everything by throwing
things in and watching how quickly or slowly it overwhelmed them, depending on the combustibility of the material.[108]   One thing he threw in, purely to experiment with
49   its propensity to burn, was a fish that had been cast up on
the beach by the sea. As it began to roast and the savory
odors spread, his appetite was aroused. He nibbled it and
liked it.   In this way he learned to eat meat and practiced
hunting and fishing until he became quite skilled in both.
He liked fire even more now that it brought him good
things to eat he had never had before.

His new infatuation with fire, based on its power and all
its beneficial effects, gave him the notion that what had
abandoned his doe-mother's heart was of the same or similar
substance. This supposition was reinforced by his observation that body heat in animals was constant as long as they
were alive, but that they grew cold after death. Besides he
felt quite a bit of heat in his own breast, just at the spot
where he had cut into the doe. It occurred to him that if
he took a live animal, cut open the heart and inspected the
same chamber he had found empty in the doe, he would
find the ventricle of a living animal still occupied by what-

ever had lived in it, and so determine whether it was of the same substance as fire, whether it had any heat or light or not.[109]   50

He got hold of a beast, tied it down and cut it open, as he had the doe, and reached the heart. This time he started on the left. Cutting into the heart, he saw the chamber, filled with a steamy gas, like white mist. He poked in his finger—it was so hot it nearly burnt him, and the animal died instantly. This satisfied him that the hot vapor was what imparted animation to the animal and that every animal has something corresponding: When this departs, the animal dies.

A desire was aroused in him to study all the other animal organs, their organization, placement, number, and interdependence, how the heat of that steam reaches them, giving life to them all, how it lasts as long as it does, where it comes from, and why its heat does not dissipate.

He followed this up by dissecting and vivisecting many animals, constantly learning and improving the quality of his mind until he had reached the level of the finest natural scientists.   51

By this time it was plain to him that each animal, although many in respect of its parts, its various senses and types of motion, was nonetheless one in terms of that spirit which stems from a single fixed place and diffuses from there to all the organs.[110] All parts of the body are simply its servants or agents. The spirit employed the body much as he himself employed the tools with which he fought, hunted, or dissected. His weapons could be classified as offensive and defensive. His hunting gear could be divided into those implements appropriate to land animals and those for fish. Similarly his dissecting tools could be classified as those suitable for cutting, breaking, or boring. The same body handled all these tools, using each appropriately for its own purpose.[111]

In the same way the one vital spirit uses the eye as a tool for seeing, the ear for hearing, the nose for smelling, the tongue for tasting, the skin and flesh for feeling, the limbs for moving, the liver for feeding and digestion. Every one of these organs is at the service of the spirit and would   52 be deprived of its functions were it not directed by this spirit through what we call the nerves: for when nerve pathways are cut or blocked, the functions lapse in the organ to which they lead.[112] These nerves do no more than transmit the animal spirit emanating from the brain, which in turn derives it from the heart. The brain has in it a great many spirits, since it is highly compartmentalized.[113] If for some reason any organ does not receive this spirit, like a useless, discarded tool, it can work no longer. And should the vital spirit leave the body altogether or in one way or another disintegrate or become extinct, the whole body is stilled and dies.[114]

This type of thinking had brought him to this point when he had completed three sets of seven, that is when he was twenty-one. By this time he had grown quite ingenious. He dressed in skins from his dissected animals. From these he also made shoes. He got thread from animal hair, hemp, and the pith of reeds and cattail stalks and other fibrous plants. The original idea of making thread came from his initial use of the tall grass. He made awls of tough thorns or splinters of reed sharpened on a stone. By watching swallows he got the idea of building himself a storehouse for surplus food, secured by a door of cane sticks tied together, against the intrusion of animals while he was away. He trained some birds of prey to help with his hunting and kept poultry from which he got eggs and chicken. He made some semblance of spearpoints from the horns of wild cows and mounted them on sturdy lengths of cane or beechwood shafts. After hardening in fire and sharpening with chips of rock, they were as good as real spears. He also made a shield out of several plies of hide. This was due to his realization that despite his lack of natural weapons, he could manufacture everything he wanted to make up the lack.[115]

Seeing that no animal would stand and fight with him, but all ran away and wore him out with running, he tried to think of some ingenious method of catching them, and came to the conclusion that the plan most likely to succeed was to gain the confidence of one of the swifter beasts and feed it well so as to be able to ride it in pursuit of other animals. There were wild horses on the island as well as

wild asses. Hayy found some that were suitable and trained
them as he had planned. Then out of thongs and rawhide
he contrived saddles and bridles. So, as he had hoped, he   55
was able to chase animals he had found difficult to catch.

He accomplished all these things during the time when
he was still engrossed with dissection and his one great passion was to understand the differentiation and the characteristic functions of all animal organs, that is within the
period I have sketched, ending with his twenty-first year.
At this point he took up another tack.

Hayy considered all objects in the world of generation
and decay—the various species of plants and animals, minerals, and every sort of rock and soil, water, water-vapor,
and ice, snow, sleet, smoke, flame and burning embers.
He saw that these had among them many different attributes with conflicting effects. They moved, some in the
same direction, some in opposite directions from each other.
Hayy saw that while physical things differed in some respects they were alike in others and after some study and   56
thought, he concluded that inasmuch as things differ they
are many, but inasmuch as they correspond they are one.[116]

At times he would concentrate on the peculiarities which
differentiate things from each other, and then things seemed
to be manifold and beyond number. Being seemed to pro-
liferate into an unmarshallable array. Even his own identity seemed complex and multiform, because he was view-
ing it in the perspective of the diversity of his organs and
the specialization of each by its own specific capacity to
perform its own specific task. Each organ, moreover, was
itself divisible into a great many parts. So he judged that
he himself was many and so was everything else.

But looking at it from the opposite point of view, he realized that, no matter how many parts he had, all were connected and contiguous. Thus they could be said to be one.
They differed only in having different functions, and this
was due solely to the disposition each received from the
animal spirit, to the discovery of which his earlier thoughts
had led him. This spirit itself was one, and it was this
which was his real self, all other organs serving as its tools.
He thus established for himself that he himself was one.

Shifting his attention to animal species in general, Hayy
found that each individual was one in this respect. He then
considered whole species at a time—deer, horses, asses, the
different species of birds. He observed the likeness among
individual members of each species in internal and external
organs, modes of perception, motion and appetite. What
differences he could find were negligible,[117] compared to
all the points of congruity. Hayy reasoned that the spirit
present throughout the species must be a single entity, un-
differentiated except through its division among numerous
hearts. If somehow what was divided among all those
hearts could be collected in one great vessel, then it would
be one thing, like one quantity of water or punch divided
into different bowls and then collected again.[118] Together
or separate, the identity is the same. Plurality is predicable of it only from a certain point of view. Hayy thus saw
whole species as one in this respect, likening the plurality
of individuals to the plurality of each individual's parts,
which are not really many.

Next Hayy mentally combined all animal species for consideration together. He saw that they were alike in having
sensation, nutrition, and voluntary motion in whichever direction they pleased. These activities, he had learned already, were characteristic of the animal spirit; whereas the
respects in which they differed, were not particularly essential to the animal spirit. These reflections made it apparent to him that the vital spirit in all animal genera is in
reality one being, despite the slight differences that differentiate one species from another. Just as water from a single
source may be divided into different bowls, and may be
cooler in some than in others, so the animal spirit is one;
its specific differentia are like the different temperatures of
the water, while the animal itself is like the water, which
remains one even though it happens to be divided. By
thinking in this way Hayy was able to see the whole animal
kingdom as one being.[119]

He turned his mind to the various plant species, observing
the likeness of all their members in leaf, branch, flower, and
fruit, and all the plant functions. By analogy with animals
he saw that, parallel to the animal spirit, plants too must

have a single substance in which all partake, and which makes them all one being. Likewise, considering the plant kingdom at large, he judged it must be one because of the universality of growth and nutrition. At this he joined plants and animals together in his mind, since they were alike in nutrition and growth, although the animals are higher than the plants in that they possess sense perception, locomotion, and sensation as well. Still plants seemed to have something roughly similar, as, for example, when flowers turn toward the sun, or roots towards food.[120] These considerations showed him that plants and animals are united by a single common entity, more perfectly represented in one and somehow impeded in the other. It was as if water were divided, part running freely and part frozen over. Thus he saw how animals and plants are one being.

Next he investigated bodies that do not sense or feed or grow such as stones, earth, water, air, and flame. He saw that these bodies are bounded in length, breadth, and depth, the sole differences among them being in terms of such contrarieties as that some were colored and others colorless; some hot, others cold. He perceived that warm bodies grow cold and cold ones hot; he watched water turn to steam, steam to water; burning things to embers, ashes, flame and smoke. When rising smoke was trapped in a hollow, it precipitated and in its place appeared bits of solid, rather like earth. This line of thinking, similar to the reasoning he had done on animals and plants, made evident to him that all physical things, despite the involvement of diversity in some respects, are one in reality.[121]

He then turned to that entity which in his belief united plants and animals. It had to be a body with length, breadth and depth and, like any ordinary body that does not feed or perceive, either hot or cold. The only differences between this archetypal living being and any inanimate objects, in fact, were the life functions it manifested through the use of "tools" in animals and plants. But perhaps these functions were not properly theirs, but came in from some other being. And if they came to other objects, perhaps these too would come to life! Hayy wondered what he himself might be, stripped of all the functions

60

61

which seemed at first glance to emanate from himself, and realized that he was no more than another body. These thoughts, then, brought him to the conclusion that all bodies —whether they are animate or inanimate—are one thing, although some exhibit certain special functions, which they implement by organs. But he did not know whether these activities were strictly speaking their own or had come from something else—for at this stage the only beings he knew were physical.[122]

In this way Hayy saw all being as one, although it had appeared at first glance boundless and without number. For some time he rested content at this stage.

But then he began to wonder about all these physical things, both living and non-living, which seemed sometimes to be one, sometimes to be infinite in number and diversity. He observed that all must either rise like smoke, flame, and air under water, or fall like water, particles of earth, and parts of plants and animals.[123] All such bodies must move in either one direction or the other and not come to rest unless stopped by something, as when a falling rock hits hard ground and cannot break through—for if it could, it would obviously have gone on falling: Thus you can feel it tugging downward against you if you try to lift it. In the same way Hayy found that smoke would not stop rising unless trapped; and even then it would curl around, left and right, and if there were an air passage, escape and continue rising, since air could not contain it. Hayy observed that if he filled a skin with air, tied it shut and pushed it under water it would try to wriggle free and rise until taken out and restored to air. Then it would stop wriggling upwards and lie quite still.

Hayy tried to find some body that neither rose nor fell or exerted no pull in either direction, but among the objects with which he was familiar he could find nothing of the kind.[124] He sought such an object purely in the hope of finding out what it was to be a body as such, free of all the qualities that give rise to plurality. After he had worn himself out looking, studying all the objects that bore the fewest predicates without finding one that could not be said to be either 'heavy' or 'light' as we express it, he began to investigate heaviness and lightness themselves. Did they belong to bodies *qua* body, or did both arise from something distinct from the physical?

It seemed plain to him that both must stem from some separate principle, for if they belonged to body in virtue of its being body, then every material object would have both.[125] In fact, however, we know that heavy objects have no buoyancy, and light ones no gravity; yet they remain bodies all the same. Thus over and above physicality each has its own differentiating factor. If not for this added factor, the two would be identical. Clearly the substantiality of objects both heavy and light was compounded of two factors, the physicality they have in common, and linked with it either gravity or buoyancy—that is what moves them either upwards or downwards and makes them different.

Regarding all bodies, living and non-living in the same light, Hayy saw that the being of each of them was made up in the same way of corporeality plus some factor or factors. Before him loomed the forms of physical things in all their diversity. This was his first glimpse of the spiritual world. For these forms cannot be apprehended by the senses, but only by reasoning.[126] And as he was awakening to these things, it dawned on him that the animal spirit, which lives in the heart and at which he had first probed with his dissections, must itself have a principle over and above its corporeality which would enable it to carry out all its wonderful tasks, as true subject of the various modes of sensing, apprehending and moving.[127] This is the form which differentiates it from all other bodies. Philosophers term it the animal soul.

The same holds for plants: whatever they have to fill the role of body-heat in animals would have its own special form, called by philosophers the vegetative soul. And even inanimate objects—that is all things in the world of generation and decay besides plants and animals—must have some special thing to make them behave in their own peculiar way, and give them their particular qualities to the senses and their ways of moving. This is the form, or as philosophers call it, the nature of the thing.

When Hayy understood, through this line of reasoning,

64

65

that the substance of the animal spirit, toward which all his love had been directed, was compounded out of the corporeal factor and another, non-physical factor, and that it had the former in common with every other body, while the latter, linked with it, belonged exclusively to this spirit, he felt contempt for physicality. He dropped the physical and his mind fastened on the other factor, which is called simply the soul.

66

He was now anxious to learn all he could about the soul. Turning his thought in this direction, he started off by going over in his mind all physical objects, considered not as bodies but as having forms from which emerge their distinguishing characteristics. Following this up in many specific cases, he was able to see how a great number of bodies participate in a certain form, from which emanates a given mode or given modes of behavior. Within this group a subclass, besides sharing the form of the rest, has an additional form from which further functions emerge. A still smaller class displays both of these plus a third form, generating still more special behavior.

67

For example, everything earthen, such as soil, rocks, minerals, plants, animals, and all other heavy objects, makes up a single totality which participates in a single form from which issues the tendency to fall when unimpeded or when lifted and let go. Plants and animals are a subclass of this group, but besides sharing this form with all the rest, they have an added form from which emanate the activities of nutrition and growth. Nutrition is an interchange by which the being nourished replaces matter that breaks down by ingesting material similar to itself and assimilating this to its own substance. Growth is movement in all three dimensions at once, according to a set proportion. These two functions are universal among plants and animals and must therefore issue from a form shared by both plants and animals. This form is what is called the vegetative soul. A still smaller subdivision, namely the animals, while sharing the first form with the whole group and the second with the subclass, surpasses both by the exclusive possession of a third form which gives rise to sensation and locomotion.

68

Further, Hayy knew that every animal species had its

own distinguishing characteristics. He now understood that this differentiating principle stemmed from the species' own distinctive form, superadded to the form it held in common with all other animals. Each plant species had something similar.

Plainly some of the objects of sense perception in the world of generation and decay were made up of many factors over and above physicality, while others had only a few. He recognized that it would be easier to grasp the simpler than the more complex, so he decided, to start with, to try to understand whatever had the fewest components to its make-up. Seeing that plants and animals must be composed of numerous factors because of the complexity of the tasks of life, he put off consideration of their forms for the present. By the same token he observed that some pieces of earth were simpler than others, so he directed his attention to the simplest of these he could obtain. Likewise he recognized that water must be very simple since so few activities issue from its form. The same was true of fire and air.

At first he had supposed not only that these four, fire, water, earth, and air, were interchangeable but also that all partook of one common entity, that is materiality, which was itself necessarily devoid of the factors which differentiate the four.[128] This must neither rise nor fall; it must be neither hot nor cold, moist nor dry. For all these predicates are inapplicable to body *qua* body, since none is applicable to all bodies. Therefore if an object could exist which had no form beyond physicality, not one of these predicates would be true of it, and no predicate at all could apply to it which did not apply to all physical things, regardless of their form.

He searched for some one characteristic common to all objects, animate and inanimate, but the only thing he could find in all physical objects was extension in three dimensions. This he recognized belonged to physical things purely by virtue of the fact that they were physical. But his senses did not so readily reveal any object with just this attribute of extension and no other.

He then examined this notion of extension, asking himself whether it was just this that belonged to material things or whether there was not perhaps, some further principle; and he realized that behind extension there must be another factor in which extension itself was grounded. For bare extension could no more subsist by itself than the extended object could exist without extension. Hayy tried out this idea on several form-bearing objects such as clay

71 for example. He found that if he molded clay into some shape, for example into a ball, it had length, width and depth in a certain ratio; if he then took this ball and worked it into a cube or egg shape, its length, width and depth took on different proportions. But it was still the same clay; and, no matter what the ratio, it could not be divested of length, breadth, and depth. The fact that one proportion could replace another made it apparent to him that the dimensions were a factor in their own right, distinct from the clay itself. But the fact that the clay was never totally devoid of dimensions made it plain to him that they were part of its being.

His experiment suggested to him that bodies, *qua* body, are really composed of two factors, one analogous to the clay of the example, the other to the length, width, and depth of the ball or block or other figure the clay might have. The truth was, he could not comprehend physical things at all unless he conceived of them as compounded of these two factors, neither of which can subsist without the

72 other.

The variable factor, which can present a succession of many different faces, that is extension, corresponds to the form of all other bodies. The other factor, which remains constant like the clay of the example,[129] corresponds to materiality in all other bodies. In philosophy the factor analogous to the clay is called *hyle*, or matter. It is entirely devoid of forms.

When his thinking had risen to this level and the sensory world had been left behind to some extent, just as he was mounting to a height from which he could gaze out toward the approaches of the world of mind, Hayy felt alien and alone. He longed for the familiar world of the senses, balked at the notion of unqualified body, a thing he could neither perceive nor possess, and fell back on the simplest objects he could see, the four he had already singled out.[130]

He examined water first and found that if left to itself, determined only by its own form, it was perceptibly cold and downward-seeking; but if warmed by fire or the heat of the sun, first its coldness would pass, leaving only its proclivity to fall; then, if it were heated strongly, this too would vanish, and it would seek to rise, leaving it without either of the characteristics which had sprung from its form. Yet all he knew of that form was that these functions issued from it. When they were gone the rule of that form must have ended. The form of water must have left this body, since it now exhibited behavior characteristic of some other form. A new form not previously present must have come into being here, giving rise to behavior unlike that it had shown under its original form.

Now Hayy knew by necessity that all that comes into being must have a cause. From this consideration he gained a vague and general notion of the cause of this form. One by one he went over the forms he had known before and saw that all of them had come to be and all must have a cause. He then considered that in which the forms inhere and found it to be no more than a body's propensity for such and such an action to arise from it. Water, for example, has a propensity to rise when strongly heated. This propensity is due to the form, for there is nothing there but body and certain perceptible things—qualities and ways of moving, for example—which come into being, and the cause who creates them. Thus the proneness of a body to certain kinds of motion as opposed to others must be due to its disposition or form.[131]

Hayy realized that the same would be true of all forms. Clearly the acts emerging from forms did not really arise in them, but all the actions attributed to them were brought about through them by another Being. This idea to which he had now awakened is the meaning of the Prophet's words: "I am the ears He hears by and the sight He sees by."[132] As it is written in the unshakable Revelation "It was not you but God who killed them; and when you shot, it was not you who shot, but God."[133]

Possessing now a broad if indistinct notion of this great Subject, Hayy found in himself a burning desire to know Him more fully. But, having as yet not left the sensory world, he tried first to find this Cause among the objects of his senses. Besides, he did not yet know whether He was one or many. Accordingly he scrutinized all the physical things he knew and to which his thinking had always been confined.

All of them, he perceived, develop and decay. Those which are not destroyed completely are destroyed at least in part. Water and earth, for example, are at least in part destroyed by fire. Air too, he saw, can be destroyed by a severe chill and turn to snow or water. None of the physical things around him was exempt from change, thus none could exist without there being a cause of all this change.[134] Seeing that this was the case Hayy left behind all these things and turned his mind to the heavenly bodies. He reached this level at twenty-eight, having completed four seven-year phases in his development.

He knew that the heavens and all the stars in the skies were bodies because without exception they were extended in three dimensions, and whatever is always extended in three dimensions is a body, therefore they were all bodies.[135] He wondered whether they extended infinitely in all directions or were finite, bounded at some point beyond which no extension was possible. The problem perplexed him more than a little, but ultimately his inborn talent and brilliance led him to realize that an infinite body is a pseudo-entity which can neither be nor be conceived. This conclusion was bolstered in his mind by a number of arguments that he reached quite independently in the course of his reflections.

"This heavenly body," he said to himself, "is bounded on the near side, without doubt, since I can see it with my own eyes. Only the far side admits of doubt. Nonetheless I know it is impossible for it to extend forever. For if I imagine two lines beginning on this finite side, passing up through the body to infinity, as far as the body itself supposedly extends, and imagine a large segment cut from the finite end of one and the two placed side by side with the

75

76

cut end of one opposite the uncut end of the other, and my mind travels along the two lines toward the so called infinite end, then I must discover either that the pair of lines really do extend to infinity, the one no shorter than the other, in which case the cut line equals the intact one, which is absurd—or else that the one does not run the full length of the other, but stops short of the full course, in which case it is finite. But if the finite segment that was subtracted is restored, the whole is finite. Now it is neither shorter nor longer than the uncut line. They must be equal then. But one is finite, so the other must be finite as well— and so must the body in which these lines were assumed to be drawn. Such lines can be assumed in any physical thing. Thus to postulate an infinitely extended physical body is fallacious and absurd."

77

Once the exceptional mind which had made him aware of such a remarkable argument[136] had demonstrated to him the finitude of the heavens, Hayy wished to know what shape they had and how they were divided by their limiting surfaces.[137] To start with he watched the sun, moon and other stars, observing how all rose in the east and set in the west. Those which passed directly overhead inscribed a great arc; those inclining north or south from his zenith inscribed a smaller arc. The further they lay from the zenith and the closer to the poles, the smaller the arc they described, the smallest orbits in which stars moved being those of Ursa Minor and Canopus, two little circles about the North and South Poles respectively.

78

Since Hayy's home, as I mentioned at the outset, was on the equator, the orbital planes of all the stars were perpendicular to his horizon and their orbits equally large at a given deflection north and south. What is more, both polar axes were visible to him. He observed that when a star with a large orbit and one with a small one rose together, they also set together; and seeing this repeated constantly with all stars, he realized that the firmament must be spherical. The conviction was strengthened by his seeing the sun, moon and stars return to the east after disappearing in the west, and by the fact that their apparent sizes at rising, peak, and setting were constant. For if their motion fol-

79

lowed any path other than along a sphere, they would have
to be closer to view at some times than at others, and if so
their magnitudes or apparent sizes would vary. They would
seem bigger when closer than when farther off. But since
there was no such variation to be seen, he was certain that
their motion was in a spherical course.

He continued to study the motion of the moon, observing
that this was from west to east, and he even observed the
retrograde motion of the planets.[138]   Thus he eventually
learned a great deal of astronomy. He now knew that the
80 courses of the stars could be set only in a number of spheres,
all enclosed in one great sphere above them all, which
moves the whole from east to west in a day and a night.
But to explain each step in his progress in astronomy would
be a protracted task. And this, after all, is treated at length
in books. For our purpose no more is needed than what I
have already set down.

Having reached this point, Hayy understood that the
heavens and all that is in them are, as it were, one organism
whose parts are joined organically together. All the bodies
he had known before such as earth, water, air, plants and
animals were enclosed within this being and never left it.
The whole was like an animal.[139]   The light-giving stars
were its senses. The spheres, articulated one to the next,
were its limbs. And the world of generation and decay
within was like the juices and wastes in the beast's belly,
where smaller animals often breed, as in the macrocosm.

81   Seeing the whole universe as in reality one great being,
and uniting all its many parts in his mind by the same sort
of reasoning which had led him to see the oneness of all
bodies in the world of generation and decay, Hayy wondered whether all this had come to be from nothing, or in
no respect emerged from nothingness but always existed.
On this question he had many misgivings. Neither position
seemed to prevail.[140]   For whenever he assumed the eternity
of the universe, numerous difficulties arose due to the fact
that any actual infinity could be shown to be impossible by
the same sort of reasoning which had shown him the impossibility of an infinite physical body. Besides he knew
that the world could not exist without temporal events, thus

it could not precede them.   But what cannot precede temporal events must itself come to be in time.[141]

When, on the other hand, he assumed that the universe arose in time, other objections assailed him.   Thus he realized that the notion of the universe coming to be from nothing could be made sense of only in terms of a time before there was a universe—but time itself is an inseparable part of the universe.   Therefore it is inconceivable that the origin of the universe came before the origin of time.[142]

"Furthermore," he said to himself, "if the universe came to be in time, there must have been some cause to bring it into being.[143]   Why did this Cause bring about a world now rather than before?   Had some outside force disturbed Him? Nothing existed but He.   Had some change, then, occurred within Him?   But what brought about *that* change?"[144]

For some years Hayy pondered over this problem, but the arguments always seemed to cancel each other.   Neither position could outweigh the other.   Baffled and exhausted by this dilemma, he began to wonder what each of the beliefs entailed.   Perhaps the implications were the same![145] For he saw that if he assumed that the universe had come to be in time, *ex nihilo*, then the necessary consequence would be that it could not have come into existence by itself, but must have had a Maker to give it being.   This Maker could not be perceptible to the senses; for if it could be apprehended by sense perception, then it would be a material body, and thus part of the world, itself in time and in need of a cause.   If this second cause were physical, it would need a third; the third, a fourth, and so *ad infinitum* —which is absurd.

Thus the world must have a non-corporeal Cause.   Since He is not a physical being there is no way of perceiving Him through the senses, as the five senses can grasp only physical objects and their attributes.   But if He cannot be perceived, He cannot be imagined either, since imagining is no more than the mind's projection of images belonging to sense objects no longer present.[146]   Furthermore, if He is not a material body, then it is impossible to apply to him any of the predicates of physical things.   Chief of these is extension in length, width, and depth.   He transcends these

82

83

and all the physical characteristics that follow from them. Finally as Maker of the universe He must know it and have sway over it: "Can it be that the Creator does not know? He is Kindly and Aware."[147]

Alternatively, Hayy saw that if he assumed the eternity of the world, that is that it had always been as it is now[148] and not emerged from non-being, this would imply that its

84   motion too was eternal and had never begun, never started up from rest. Now every motion requires a mover.[149] This mover can be *either* a force distributed through some body —self-moving or externally moved—or a force which is not distributable or diffusible in physical bodies. But the type of force which is diffused and distributed through material things is divided when they divide and augmented proportionately as they increase. Weight, for example, in a stone is what causes its downward motion. If the stone is split in half, so is its weight; and if another is added, equal to the first, the weight increases by an equal amount. If it were possible to keep adding stones forever, then the weight would mount to infinity; but if the stones reached a certain number and stopped, then the weight would reach a corresponding point and stop. Yet it has already been proved that every material body must be finite. So every force in a material body must be finite. Should we discover a force engaged in an infinite task, that force cannot belong to a physical thing. But we have found the motion of the heav-

85   ens to be ceaseless and eternal, for *ex hypothesi* it has gone on forever and had no beginning. *Ergo* the force that moves them must be neither in their own physical structure nor in any external physical being. It can only belong to some Being independent of all material things and indescribable by any predicate applicable to them.

When first reflecting on the world of generation and decay, Hayy had become aware that the substantiality of any material thing rests in its form, that is its propensity for certain types of motion. Its being, on the material side, is defective at best, and in itself scarcely conceivable. If so, the being of the whole universe is ultimately no more than its capacity to be moved by this great Mover, who is free

of matter and all its attributes and transcends all that sense
can perceive or imagination approach. If He brings about
the sidereal motions, each in its kind and all without discontinuity, never halting, never tiring, then He must know
them all and hold absolute power over them.

So this train of thought brought him exactly where the
other had. He was no longer troubled by the dilemmas of
creation versus eternity, for either way the existence of a
non-corporeal Author of the universe remained unscathed, a
Being neither in contact with matter nor cut off from it,
neither within nor outside it—for all these terms, 'contact'
and 'discontinuity', 'inside' and 'outside' are merely predicates of the very physical things which He transcends.[150]

Since matter in every body demands a form, as it exists
through its form and can have no reality apart from it, and
since forms can be brought into being only by this Creator,
all being, Hayy saw, is plainly dependent on Him for existence itself. Nothing can subsist except through Him.
Thus He is the Cause of all things, and all are His effects,
whether they came to be out of nothing or had no beginning in time and were in no way successors to non-being.
In either case they are His effects, dependent on Him for
their existence, since He is their Cause and Maker. If He
did not endure, they would not endure. If He did not exist,
they would not exist. If He were not eternal, they could
not have been eternal.[151]

But He, in Himself, has no need of them and is utterly
independent of them. How could this not be so, when it
has been proved that His force and power are infinite, while
all physical things and everything connected with them or
in the least related to them are truncated and finite? The
whole Universe, then, and all that is in it—heaven and earth
and all that lies above, beneath and between—is His work
and creation, ontologically, if not temporally, posterior to
Him.

Suppose you held something in your hand while moving
your arm. The object you held would undoubtedly move
with your hand, subsequently not in time, but in fact—for
in time the two motions are simultaneous.[152] It is in this

way, out of time, that the universe is caused and created
by its Maker "Whose command, when He desires a thing
is simply to tell it 'Be!' and it is."[153]

The moment Hayy realized that all that exists is His work,
he saw things in a new and different light. It was as an
expression of its Maker's power that he saw each thing now,
marvelling at His wonderful craftsmanship, the elegance of
His plan and ingenuity of His work.[154] In the least of things
—not to speak of the greatest—Hayy found marks of wisdom
and divine creativity that exhausted his powers of admira-
tion and confirmed his belief that all this could issue only
from a Cause of consummate perfection—beyond perfection! "Not an atom's weight escapes Him in heaven or on
earth."[155]

Hayy considered how the Creator had given each sort of
animal its makeup and showed how these were to be used
—for if He did not teach animals to use their parts for their
intended purposes, they would do the animals no more good
than if they did not have them.[156] From this Hayy learned
that He is most good and merciful. From then on, whenever he saw a being that was good, or beautiful, or strong,
or perfect in any way, he would recognize, on considering,
that this must be its Maker's work and stem from His overflowing abundance and liberality.[157] Thus he knew that
what He Himself possesses must be greater and more perfect, fuller, better, and more lasting out of all proportion,
than what He gives. And so, continuing the sequence of
perfections, Hayy saw that all belong to Him, proceed from
Him, and are more truly predicated of Him than of any
other being.

He surveyed the privations and saw that He is clear of
them and transcends them all. How could He not transcend
privation when the very concept means no more than absolute or relative non-being—and how could non-being be associated or confused with Him Who is pure being, Whose
essence is necessary existence, Who gives being to all that
is? There is no existence but Him. He is being, perfection,
and wholeness. He is goodness, beauty, power, and knowledge. He is He. "All things perish except His face."[158]

By the end of his fifth seven-year span, his awareness had

brought him to this point. He was thirty-five. By now thought of this Subject was so deeply rooted[159] in his heart that he could think of nothing else. He was distracted from his prior investigation of created being. For now his eye fell on nothing without immediately detecting in it signs of His workmanship—then instantly his thoughts would shift from craft to Craftsman, deepening his love of Him, totally detaching his heart from the sensory world, and binding it to the world of mind.

Having gained an awareness of this eternally existing Being, Whose existence is uncaused, but Who is the cause of all existence, Hayy wished to know how this knowledge had come to him. By what power had he apprehended such a being? He counted off his senses—hearing, sight, smell, taste, and touch. None of these could grasp anything but the physical or the attributes subsisting in it. Hearing catches only sounds which are generated by the vibrating waves of air when bodies strike together.[160] Sight knows only colors; smell, odors; taste, flavors; touch, textures—hard or soft, rough or smooth. Imagination too can apprehend only things with length, breadth, and depth. All these are qualities predicable only of physical things. Only these can be objects of the senses because the senses themselves are powers diffused in material things, and thus divisible with their substrates. The senses, for this reason, can apprehend only divisible objects, that is physical things. For these faculties are spread thoughout a divisible thing and their object must be capable of a corresponding division. Thus any faculty in a physical body can apprehend only physical bodies and their attributes.[161]

But it was already quite clear to Hayy that this necessarily existent Being transcends physical attributes in every respect. The only way to apprehend Him, then, must be by some non-physical means, something which is neither a bodily faculty nor in any way bound up with body—neither inside nor outside, neither in contact with it nor disjoined from it. Hayy had also realized that what had brought him his awareness of this Being would be his true self, and now that his understanding of Him was better, he recognized that this self too, by which he had come to know Him, was non-corporeal and not qualifiable by any physical predicate. The whole outward self, the objective, corporeal being he could perceive, was not his true self; his true identity was that by which he had apprehended the Necessarily Existent.

Knowing now that this embodiment, apprehended by the senses and enveloped in the skin was not himself, he thoroughly despised his body and set eagerly to thinking of that higher self by which he had reached an awareness of the sublime Being, Whose existence is necessary.[162]

Was it possible that this other, nobler being, which was himself, could perish—or was it everlasting? Disintegration and decay are, he knew, predicates of physical things indicating simply that they have taken off one form and put on another, as when water turns to air, or air to water, or when plants become soil or ashes, or soil becomes a plant. This is the meaning of breakdown. But the destruction of a non-physical being which does not depend for its existence on any body, and which completely transcends the physical, is utterly inconceivable.

Satisfied that his true self could not perish, he desired to know what its fate would be once it had freed itself of the body and left it behind. Clearly this being would not abandon the body until no further use could be derived from it as a tool.[163]

Hayy surveyed all his powers of perception and saw that each works actually at one time, potentially at another.[164] The eye, for example, when closed or averted from its object still sees potentially. The meaning of 'seeing potentially' is that while it is not seeing now, it will in the future. When open and turned toward its object, it actually sees. 'Seeing actually' means seeing now.[165] The same holds for all these faculties, they all work either actually or potentially.

Any faculty of apprehension which at no time actually perceives but remains "forever potential", never desiring to grasp its appropriate object because that object has never been encountered by it, is like a man born blind. If such a faculty actually does perceive for a time and then relapses into potentiality, but even in the potential state still yearns for actual perception, since it has known its proper object and grown fond of it, then it is like a sighted man gone blind who still longs for what he used to see. The more beautiful, whole, or good the objects he once knew, the greater his longing for them and grief at their loss. For this reason the sorrow of a man who has lost his sight is greater than that of one who has lost his sense of smell, for the objects of sight are higher and better than those of smell.

If there is a Being Whose perfection is infinite, Whose splendor and goodness know no bounds, Who is beyond perfection, goodness, and beauty, a Being such that no perfection, no goodness, no beauty, no splendor does not flow from Him, then to lose hold of such a Being, and having known Him to be unable to find Him must mean infinite torture as long as He is not found. Likewise to preserve constant awareness of Him is to know joy without lapse, unending bliss, infinite rapture and delight.

Hayy had already realized that while He transcends all privations, every attribute of perfection can be applied to the Necessarily Existent. He also knew that what in him had allowed him to apprehend this Being was unlike bodies and would not decay as they did. From this he saw that, leaving the body at death, anyone with an identity like his own, capable of awareness such as he possessed, must undergo one of these three fates: If, while in command of the body, he has not known the Necessarily Existent, never confronted Him or heard of Him, then on leaving the body he will neither long for this Being nor mourn His loss. His bodily powers will go to ruin with the body, and thus make no more demands or miss the objects of their cravings now that they are gone. This is the fate of all dumb animals— even those of human form. If, while in charge of the body, he has encountered this Being and learned of His goodness but turned away to follow his own passions, until death overtook him in the midst of such a life, depriving him of the experience he has learned to long for, he will endure prolonged agony and infinite pain, either escaping the torture at last, after an immense struggle, to witness once again what he yearned for, or remaining forever in torment, depending on which direction he tended toward in his bodily life. If he knows the Necessarily Existent before departing

95

96

the body, and turns to Him with his whole being, fastens
his thoughts on His goodness, beauty, and majesty, never
turning away until death overtakes him, turned toward Him
in the midst of actual experience, then on leaving the body,
he will live on in infinite joy, bliss, and delight, happiness
unbroken because his experience of the Necessarily Existent
will be unbroken and no longer marred by the demands of
the bodily powers for sensory things—which alongside this
ecstasy are encumbrances, irritants and evils.

97   Seeing that self-realization and happiness meant constant
actual experience of the Necessarily Existent, turning away
not for an instant so that when death came it would find
him rapt in ecstasy and the continuity of his delight would
remain unbroken by pain, Hayy considered how he might
maintain continuous, actual awareness without distraction.
He would concentrate on that Being[166] for a time, but as
soon as he did some sensory thing would present itself to
view, some animal cry would split his ears, some image
would dart across his mind, he would feel a pain some-
where, or get hungry or thirsty or hot or cold,[167] or have to
get up to relieve himself. His thoughts would be disrupted,
and he would lose what he had begun to reach. It was impossible for him to recapture the experience without tremendous effort; and he feared death might surprise him in
 a moment of distraction, leaving him to sink into the everlasting misery and torment of deprivation.[168] The malady
was grave, and he did not know the cure.

98   Hayy went back over all the animal species, checking all
their doings and strivings to see whether he might not find
one that was aware of this Being and made Him its goal, to
learn from it how to save himself. But all animals, he saw,
struggled day and night simply getting enough to eat, satisfying their appetites for food, water, mates, shade, and
shelter, until their span of time was up and they died.[169]
Not one could be seen to diverge from the pattern or ever
strive toward anything else. Apparently, then, none of them
was aware of this Being, desired Him, or had any notion of
Him. All of them would turn to nothing, or next to nothing.

Having judged this to be true of animals, Hayy recognized that it would be all the more so with plants, which

have only a fraction of the avenues of perception open to animals. If animals whose apprehension is the better and more complete, are incapable of reaching this level of consciousness, then beings whose perception is stunted are all the further removed from such an attainment. After all, the whole of plant functioning goes no further than nutrition and reproduction.

He looked to the stars and spheres then, seeing how all circled in an ordered array of rhythmic motion. They were diaphanous and luminous, far above all change and decay, and he made a strong surmise that they too had identities apart from their bodies, identities which knew this necessarily existent being and were neither physical nor imprints on anything physical. How could they not have such identities, free of all that is bodily, when, with all his weakness, his desperate dependence on sensory things, and despite the fact that he lived among decaying bodies, even he had such a self? His inadequacy did not prevent his true being from standing independent of all physical things and incorruptible. Clearly the heavenly bodies must be all the more so. Thus Hayy knew that they would know the Necessarily Existent and that their awareness of Him would be continuously actual since they are not subject to such hindrances as the sensory distractions that interrupted his own contemplation.[170]

He asked himself then why he of all living beings should be singled out to possess an identity that made him very like the stars. He had seen how the elements changed into one another. Nothing on the face of the earth kept the same form. All was in a constant alternation of build-up and breakdown. Most bodies were mixtures, compounded of conflicting things, and so all the more prone to degeneration. No physical thing was pure, although those which came closest to untainted purity, such as gold and sapphire,[171] lasted longest. The heavenly bodies *were* pure and uncompounded, and for this reason not subject to a succession of forms, and virtually beyond destruction.

Hayy had learned, moreover, that of bodies in the world of generation and decay some, namely the four elements, were made up of just one form besides physicality, while others, such as plants and animals, comprised more than one additional form. Those with the fewest forms to compose their reality showed the least activity and were at the furthest remove from life. If form were absent complete-

101 ly, life was totally impossible; the result was something very like non-being.[172] Beings composed of a greater number of forms showed more activity and a closer approach to life. When form became inseparable from matter, then life was present at its strongest, stablest, and most unmistakable.

What has no form at all is *hyle*, matter. It is not in the least alive, but next to non-existent. Composed with just one form are the four elements, occupying the lowest ontic rungs in the world of generation and decay. From these are compounded things with more than one form. The elements have a very weak claim on life, not only because each has only one mode of motion, but also because each has an opposite working directly against it, tending to cancel its effects and eradicate its form. For this reason its existence is unstable and its "life" tenuous. The purchase of plants on life is stronger, however; and animals are plainly more

102 alive than they. The reason is that in ordinary compounds the nature of one element predominates. Its strength in the composite overwhelms the other elements and destroys their capacities to function. Such a compound passes under the sway of the prevailing element and thus becomes unsuited for life to any but a trivial degree—just as that element alone makes a negligible bid for life.

In those compounds, however, which are not dominated by the nature of one element, where the elements are mutually tempered and counterbalanced (and for this reason one element does not wipe out the effective force of its opposite to any greater degree than its own power of action is checked by the other), each element's potential will do its work on the other to just the right extent, allowing the activity of one to show up no plainer than that of any other. No one element will take over the whole, so the whole will bear little resemblance to any of them. Its form, then, will have virtually no direct opposite—thus it will be ideally suited for life.

103 The stronger and stabler the equilibrium, the harder it

is to find any opposite to work against it and the fuller its share in life. Since the vital spirit situated in the heart is securely balanced in such an equilibrium, being finer than earth or water, but denser than fire or air, it is a middle so to speak, and no one element is in direct conflict with it. This fits it well for life.

The implication Hayy drew from this was that the vital spirit with the stablest equilibrium would be fit for the highest form of life to be found in the world of generation and decay. The form of such a spirit could virtually be said to have no opposite. In this it would resemble the heavenly bodies, the forms of which have none at all. The spirit of such an animal, being truly at a mean among the elements, would have absolutely no tendency up or down. In fact, *104* if it could be set in space, between the center and the outermost limit of fire, without being destroyed, it would stabilize there, neither rising nor falling. If it moved in place, it would orbit like the stars, and if it moved in position it would spin on its axis. Its shape could only be spherical. Thus it would bear a strong resemblance to the heavenly bodies.[173]

Hayy had considered all phases of animal life and found none that gave him reason to suspect it was aware of the Necessarily Existent. But his own consciousness informed him that it was aware of Him. He was sure, for this reason, that he himself was the ideally balanced animal, kindred spirit of the celestial bodies. Apparently, he was a species set apart from all other animal species, created for a different end than all the rest, dedicated to a great task which no animal could undertake.

Sufficient to establish his superiority was the fact that *105* even his lower, bodily half bore the closest resemblance to those heavenly starsubstances that lived beyond the world of generation and decay, far beyond all change and want.[174] As for his nobler part, it was by this that he knew the Necessarily Existent Being. This conscious part was something sovereign, divine, unchanging and untouched by decay, indescribable in physical terms, invisible to both sense and imagination, unknowable through any instrument but itself, yet self-discovered, at once the knower, the known and

knowing, the subject and object of consciousness, and consciousness itself.[175] There is no distinction among the three,
for distinction and disjunction apply to bodies. But here
there is no body and physical predicates and relations do
not apply.[176]

Seeing that what made him different from all other animals made him like the heavenly bodies, Hayy judged that
this implied an obligation on his part to take them as his
pattern, imitate their action and do all he could to be like
them.

By the same token, Hayy saw that his nobler part, by
which he knew the Necessarily Existent, bore some resemblance to Him as well. For like Him it transcended the
physical. Thus another obligation was to endeavor, in
whatever way possible, to attain His attributes, to imitate
His ways, and remold his character to His, diligently exe-
cute His will, surrender all to Him, accept in his heart His
every judgement outwardly and inwardly. Even when He
caused harm or pain to his body, even if He destroyed it
completely, he must rejoice in His rule.[177]

He recognized, however, that he was like the lesser animals in his lower half, the body, for it belonged to the world
of generation and decay. It was dull and dark and demanded sensory things of him—food, drink, intercourse.[178]
Still he knew that this body had not been created for him
idly. It had not been linked with him for nothing.[179] He
must care for and preserve it, even though in so doing he
would do no more than any animal.

His duties, then, seemed to fall under three heads, those
in which he would resemble an inarticulate animal, those
in which he would resemble a celestial body, and those in
which he would resemble the Necessarily Existent Being.
He had to act like an animal to the extent that he had a dull,
sublunary body with differentiated parts and conflicting
powers and drives. He had an obligation to imitate the
stars in virtue of the vital spirit in his heart, which was command point for the rest of the body and all its powers. It
was his obligation to become like the Necessarily Existent
because he was (and to the extent that he was) himself,[180]
that is to the extent of his identity with that self which

brought him his awareness of the Necessarily Existent Being.

Hayy had learned that his ultimate happiness and triumph over misery would be won only if he could make his awareness of the Necessarily Existent so continuous that nothing could distract him from it for an instant. He had wondered how this might be achieved and now came to the conclusion that the means would be to practice these three forms of mimesis.

The first would by no means give him this ecstasy. On the contrary, it would hinder the experience and distract him from it, since it meant handling sensory things, and all sense objects are veils blocking out such experience. This type of imitating was needed only to preserve the vital spirit, by which he might accomplish the second sort of assimilation, that by which he would become like the heavenly bodies. Thus the first type was a necessity despite its inherent drawbacks. His second type of imitation, however, did bring a large measure of continuity to his contemplation. Still the experience was not altogether untainted, for at this level of experience, one remains self-conscious and self-regarding, as will be made clear shortly.

The third sort of imitation is attainment of the pure beatific experience, submersion, concentration on Him alone Whose existence is necessary. In this experience the self vanishes; it is extinguished, obliterated—and so are all other subjectivities. All that remains is the One, True identity, the Necessarily Existent—glory, exaltation, and honor to Him.[181]

Hayy knew that his supreme goal was this third form of mimesis; but this would not be his without a long stint of training and self-discipline through the second, and this itself would not hold up for long if he neglected the first. He knew also that serving his first likeness, although necessary and *per accidens* helpful, would hamper his true self. So he made himself a rule to impose on himself no more of this first form of imitation than was necessary to keep the vital spirit on the brink of survival. Necessity called for two things to preserve this spirit: one to sustain it from within and replace what broke down, that is food; and the

109

other to protect if from without and keep off various sorts of harm such as heat and cold, rain, too much sun, and harmful animals.

If he heedlessly allowed himself these necessities when and where he found them, he might well go too far and take more than he needed. Without his realizing it, his efforts might work against him. The prudent thing, Hayy saw, would be to set himself a limit he would not overstep. There would be certain fixed quantities he would not surpass. He must make rules about what to eat, how much, and how often.

He first considered what to eat. There seemed to be three sorts of food: plants that had not yet reached peak maturity, that is various edible green vegetables; fruits of plants that had completed their life cycles and were ready to produce a new generation, comprising fresh and dried fruit; and animals, terrestrial and marine.

All these he was certain were the work of that Necessarily Existent Being, whom he must endeavor to be like, as he now saw clearly, if he were to attain happiness. Feeding on them would unavoidably cut them off from their own fulfillment and prevent them all from achieving their intended purpose. This would mean opposition to the work of the Creator and defeat the whole aim of drawing near Him and becoming like Him.

The answer, apparently, was, if possible, to give up eating completely. Unfortunately he could not do so because not eating tended to make his own body waste away, which was even more glaring a contradiction to the work of his Creator, since he was superior to those other beings whose destruction meant his survival. So Hayy chose the lesser of evils. He was forced to condone in himself the slighter form of opposition to His work.

He decided that if some varieties of food were unavailable, he would take whatever came most readily to hand in a quantity he would set. But if all were available, then he would have to decide carefully what to eat so as to bring about the least opposition to the work of the Creator. Thus he could eat such things as the meat of fully ripened fruits, with seeds ready to reproduce, provided he was certain not to eat or harm the seeds or throw them in places unfit for vegetation—among rocks or in salt flats or the like. If it was hard to find fruit with nourishing meat, such as apples, plums, and pears, then he would have to eat either fruits in which only the seed had food-value, such as nuts and chestnuts, or else green vegetables—on condition that he pick only the most abundant and prolific and be sure not to uproot them or destroy the seeds. If none of these were available, then he must eat meat or eggs, again being careful to take only from the most abundant and not root out a whole species. So much for his notion of what he should eat.[182]

As for the amount, he felt it should be enough to stave off hunger, but no more. For the time to be allowed between meals, he considered he should eat what he needed *113* and then look for no more until he began to feel too weak to carry out some of the tasks imposed on him by his second mode of imitation, which will be spoken of in a moment.

In terms of protection, the requirements for keeping alive the vital spirit were easily taken care of. He wore skins and had a house to guard against any incursion of the environment. This was enough for him.[183] He did not consider it worth his while to spend a great deal of time on it. He did keep the dietary rules he'd made for himself, which I have described.

Having secured the needs of his body, inside and out, Hayy took up his second duty, to become like the celestial bodies, to do as they did, and model himself on their attributes. Their properties, in his judgement, fell into three classes: First, their attributes in relation to the world of generation and decay below, giving warmth essentially, and *per accidens* cooling, radiation of light, thickening and thinning and all the other things they do to prepare the world *114* for the outpouring of spirit-forms upon it from the Necessarily Existent Creator.[184] Second, the properties they had in and of themselves, transparency, luminescence, purity from all taint, and transcendence of all tarnish, their circular motion, whether on their own axis or around some other center. Third, their attributes in relation to the Necessarily Existent, their continuous, undistracted awareness of Him,

their longing for Him,[185] their total submission to His rule
and devoted execution of His will, moving only at His pleasure and always in the clasp of His hand.[186]

Hayy exerted every effort to be like them in these three
ways. For the first, he imitated their action by never allowing himself to see any plant or animal hurt, sick, encum-
bered, or in need without helping it if he could. If he noticed a plant cut off from the sun, he would, if possible,
remove what was screening it. If he saw one plant tangled
in another that might harm it, he would separate the two
so carefully that not even the weed was damaged. If he
saw a plant dying for lack of water, he would water it as
often as he could. When he saw an animal attacked by a
predator,[187] caught in a tangle, or stuck by a thorn, or with
anything harmful in its eye or ear, or under pressure of hunger or thirst, Hayy did all he could to alleviate the situation
and gave it food and water. Chancing to see an animal or
plant's water-supply cut off by a fallen rock or a fragment
swept away from the overhanging riverbank, he would always clear away the obstacle. He kept up his practice at
this particular variety of imitation until he reached peak
proficiency.[188]

To be like the heavenly bodies in the second respect,
Hayy made sure always to be clean, washing frequently
with water, getting all the dirt and grime off his body,
cleaning his teeth, nails, and every nook and cranny of his
body—even scenting it as best as he could with plant frag-
rances and various pleasant smelling oils. He took great
care to see that his clothes were always clean and fragrant,
and soon he did begin to sparkle with vitality, cleanliness,
and beauty.[189]

In addition, Hayy prescribed himself circular motion of
various kinds. Sometimes he would circle the island, skirting along the beach and roving in the inlets. Sometimes he
would march around his house or certain large rocks a set
number of times, either walking or at a trot.[190] Or at times
he would spin around in circles until he got dizzy.[191]

His method of becoming like the heavenly bodies in the
third respect was to fix his mind on the Necessarily Existent
Being, cut away the bonds of all objects of the senses—shut

his eyes, stop his ears, use all the force at his command to restrain the play of imagination[192]—and try with all his might to think only of Him, without idolatrously mixing any other thought with the thought of Him.[193] Often he would aid himself by spinning around faster and faster.

If he spun fast enough, all sensory things would vanish; imagination itself, and every other faculty dependent on bodily organs would fade, and the action of his true self, which transcended the body, would grow more powerful. In this way sometimes his mind would be cleansed, and through it he would see the Necessarily Existent—until the bodily powers rushed back, disrupting his ecstasy, and reducing him once more to the lowest of the low.[194] Then he would start over again.

When he became so weak that he could no longer work toward his goal, he would take a little nourishment, always following his rules, and return to his three ways of imitating the celestial bodies. Tirelessly he battled against the drives of his body—and they fought back. But when for a moment he had the upper hand and rid his mind of tarnish, he would see with a flash what it was like to reach this third type of likeness to the stars.[195]

He then began to explore in the endeavor to achieve the third type of imitation. He considered the attributes of the Necessarily Existent. Already at the purely intellectual stage, before taking up active practice,[196] Hayy had learned that these attributes are of one of two kinds: either positive, like knowledge, power, and wisdom, or negative, like transcendence of the physical and all that even remotely pertains to it. This transcendence implies that the list of positive attributes can include no attribute proper to physical things—as is plurality. Thus His positive attributes do not render His identity plural, but all must reduce to one principle, which is His real self.[197]

Hayy then took up the task of becoming like Him in both these ways. For the positive attributes, knowing they all reduced to His identity (since plurality, belonging to physical things, was totally out of place here) and thus realizing that His self-awareness was not distinct from Himself, but His identity was Self-consciousness and His Self-knowledge

was Himself, Hayy understood that if he himself could learn
to know Him, then his knowledge of Him too would not be
distinct from His essence, but would be identical with
Him.[198]   Thus Hayy learned that to become like Him in His
positive attributes is simply to know Him, without sacrile-
giously associating anything physical with Him.   This he set
out to do.

The negative qualities all reduced to transcendence of
physicality.   So Hayy set about eliminating the physical in
himself.   The exercises by which he approached some likeness to the heavenly bodies had already brought him quite
a way in this direction.   Still, many vestiges remained:
For example, his circular motion, since 'motion' was a predicate appropriate only to physical objects.[199]   His compas-
sion and solicitude for animals and plants and his eagerness
to remove anything that hampered them were themselves
characteristic of the physical, since he would not have seen
the objects of his concern in the first place without using a
corporeal faculty; and to help them too required use of his
bodily powers.

So Hayy undertook to expel all this from himself, for none
of these things was conducive to the ecstasy he now sought.
He would stay in his cave,[200] sitting on the stone floor, head
bent, eyes shut, oblivious to all objects of the senses and
urges of the body, his thoughts and all his devotion focused
on the Being Whose Existence is Necessity, alone and without rival.   When any alien thought sprang to his imagination, Hayy would resist it with all his might and drive it out
of his mind.

He disciplined himself and practiced endurance until
sometimes days could pass without his moving or eating.
And sometimes, in the midst of his struggles, all thoughts
and memories would vanish—except self-consciousness.
Even when immersed in the beatific experience of the
Necessarily Existent Truth, his own subjecthood would not
disappear.   This tormented Hayy, for he knew it was a blot
on the purity of the experience, division of his attention as
if with some other God.   Hayy made a concerted effort to
purge his awareness-of-the-Truth, die to himself.   At last

it came. From memory and mind all disappeared, "heaven and earth and all that is between them,"[201] all forms of the spirit and powers of the body, even the disembodied powers that know the Truly Existent. And with the rest vanished the identity that was himself. Everything melted away, dissolved, "scattered into fine dust."[202] All that remained was the One, the True Being, Whose existence is eternal, Who uttered words identical with himself: "Whose is the Kingdom on this day? God's alone, One and Triumphant!"[203]

Hayy understood His words and "heard" the summons they made. Not knowing how to speak did not prevent him from understanding.[204] Drowned in ecstasy, he witnessed "what no eye has seen or ear heard, nor has it entered into the heart of man to conceive."[205]

Now do not set your heart on a description of what has never been represented in a human heart. For many things that are articulate in the heart cannot be described. How then can I formularize something that cannot possibly be projected in the heart, belonging to a different world, a different order of being?

Nor by 'heart' do I mean only the physical heart or the spirit it encloses. I mean also the form of that spirit which spreads its powers throughout the human body. All three of these might be termed 'heart', but there is no way of articulating this experience in any of them, and only what is articulate can be expressed. The ambition to put this into words is reaching for the impossible—like wanting to taste colors, expecting black as such to taste either sweet or sour.[206]

Still I shall not leave you without some hint as to the wonders Hayy saw from this height, not by pounding on the gates of truth, but by coining symbols,[207] for there is no way of finding out what truly occurs at this plateau of experience besides reaching it. So listen now with the ears of your heart and look sharp with the eyes of your mind, for what I shall try to convey to you. Perhaps in what I say you will find guideposts to set you on the main road. My only condition is that you now demand of me no further

explanation of this experience than I set down in these pages.
For it is dangerous to make pronouncements on the ineffable, and the margins in which I work are narrow.

To continue, Hayy had "died" to himself, and to every
other self. He had witnessed his vision and seen nothing
in all existence but the everliving ONE. Recovered now
from his seemingly intoxicated ecstasy, he saw other things
once more, and the notion came into his head that his identity was none other than that of the Truth. His true self
was the Truth. What he had once supposed to be himself,
as distinct from the Truth, was really nothing in itself, but
was in reality in no way discrete from the Truth.[208] When
sunlight falls on opaque bodies and becomes visible, it may
bear some relation to the object it lights up, but it is never
really anything other than sunlight. When the body is
gone, so is its light, but the sun's light remains the same,
not increased by the object's absence or diminished by its
presence. If an object comes along capable of taking on
this type of light, then it receives it; if no such object is
present there is no reflecting and no occasion for it.

Hayy was confirmed in the notion by his awareness that
the Truth, glorified and exalted be He, was not in any sense
plural and that His Self-knowledge was Himself. It seemed
to him to follow that whoever gains consciousness of His
essence wins that essence itself. Hayy had attained His
identity. This identity could be reached only by Himself;
indeed this very Self-awareness was His identity. If so,
then Hayy must be identical with Him, and so must every
disembodied being that knows Him. These he had once
seen as many; but now, in the light of this presumption,
they seemed to merge into one entity.

This specious thinking might well have taken root in his
soul, had not God in His mercy caught hold of him and
guided him back to the truth.[209] He then realized that he
would never have fallen prey to such a delusion unless some
shadows of the physical or taint of sensory things still lurked
within him. For 'many', 'few', and 'one'; 'singularity' and
'plurality'; 'union' and 'discreteness', are all predicates applicable only to physical things.[210] But those non-material
beings who know the Truth, glorified and exalted be He,

precisely because they are free of matter, need not be said to be either one or many. The reason is that there is multiplicity only when there is otherness and unity only where there is contact. Both of these make sense only for things that are compounded—and confounded—in matter.

Expression on this subject, however, is extremely difficult. If you speak of the non-material beings in the plural, as I have, it suggests that they are many. But they are entirely free of plurality. If, on the other hand, you use the singular, it suggests absolute unity, which is equally impossible for them. 125

What is this? It seems to be a bat that interrupts me, its eyes blinded by the sun,[211] baffled in the meshes of its own mad confusion, crying "This time your hair-splitting has gone too far. You have shed what the intelligent know by instinct and abandoned the rule of reason. It is an axiom of reason that a thing must be either one or many!"

Now if he could just calm himself and curb the rashness of his tongue—if he could only suspect himself and consider the vile, sensory world in which he lives, consider it as Hayy Ibn Yaqzān did, when from one point of view it seemed plural beyond number or term; and from another, a monolith. Hayy could not decide one way or the other, but remained oscillating between the two descriptions. 126 Such a quandary over the sense world, the birthplace and proper home of whatever legitimate understanding is conveyed by 'singular' and 'plural', 'discrete' and 'continuous', 'separate' and 'conjoined', 'identical' and 'other', 'same' and 'different'. What then was Hayy to think of the divine world, where 'whole' and 'part' are inapplicable, a world indescribable without misrepresentation, which no one can know or fully understand without actually reaching it and seeing for himself.

He says I have "left what every sound mind is born with and abandoned the rule of reason."[212] I shall grant him that. I have left him and his reason and his "sound minds." What he means by reason—he and his ilk—is no more than the power to articulate, to abstract a general concept from a number of sensory particulars, and his "men of sound reason" are simply those whose minds work the same way. But

the kind of understanding I am speaking of transcends all this.[213] The man who knows only sense particulars and universals drawn from them had better stop up his ears and
127   go back to his friends, who "know only the surface of this life and are heedless of the next."[214]

Still, if in your case a hint and a glimpse will be enough to give you some idea of the divine world, and if you can avoid construing my words in their ordinary senses,[215] then I can tell you a bit more of what Hayy Ibn Yaqzān saw in his ecstasy. Passing through a deep trance to the complete death-of-self and real contact with the divine,[216] he saw a being corresponding to the highest sphere, beyond which there is no body, a subject free of matter, and neither identical with the Truth and the One nor with the sphere itself, nor distinct from either[217]—as the form of the sun appearing in a polished mirror is neither sun nor mirror, and yet distinct from neither. The splendor, perfection, and beauty he saw in the essence of that sphere were too magnificent to be described and too delicate to be clothed in written or spoken words. But he saw it to be at the pinnacle of joy,
128   delight, and rapture, in blissful vision of the being of the Truth, glorious be His Majesty.[218]

Just below this, at the sphere of the fixed stars, Hayy saw another non-material being. This again was neither identical with the Truth and the One, nor with the highest sphere, nor even with itself, yet distinct from none of these. It was like the form of the sun appearing in one mirror, reflected from a second which faced the sun. Here too were glory, beauty, and joy as in the highest. Lying just below he saw the identity of the sphere of Saturn, again divorced from matter and neither the same as nor different from the beings he had seen—as it were, the reflection of the reflection of the reflection of the sun; and here too he saw splendor and rapture as before.
129   Thus for each sphere he witnessed a transcendent immaterial subject, neither identical with nor distinct from those above, like the form of the sun reflected from mirror to mirror with the descending order of spheres.[219] In each one Hayy sensed goodness, beauty, joy, and bliss that "no eye has seen, or ear heard, nor has it entered the heart of man to

conceive," until finally he reached the world of generation and decay, the bowels of the sphere of the moon.[220]

Here too was an essence free of matter, not one with those he had seen—but none other. Only this being had seventy thousand faces. In every face were seventy thousand mouths; in every mouth, seventy thousand tongues, with which it ceaselessly praised, glorified, and sanctified[221] the being of the One who is the Truth.

In this being, which he took to be many although it is not, Hayy saw joy and perfection as before. It was as though the form of the sun were shining in rippling water *130* from the last mirror in the sequence, reflected down the series from the first, which faced directly into the sun. Suddenly he caught sight of himself as an uncmbodicd subject. If it were permissible to single out individuals from the identity of the seventy thousand faces, I would say that he was one of them.[222] Were it not that his being was created originally, I would say that they were he. And had this self of his not been individuated by a body on its creation I would have said that it had not come to be.[223]

From this height he saw other selves like his own, that had belonged to bodies which had come to be and perished, or to bodies with which they still coëxisted. There were so many (if one may speak of them as many) that they reached infinity. Or, if one may call them one, then all were one. In himself and in the other beings of his rank, Hayy saw goodness, beauty, joy without end, the like of which eyes cannot see, ears hear, or human hearts conceive, ineffable, known only by the aware, who arrive.[224] *131*

He saw also many disembodied identities, more like tarnished mirrors, covered with rust, their faces averted and their backs to the brilliant mirrors in which shone the image of the sun. They were ugly, defective, and deformed beyond his imagining. In unending throes of torture and ineradicable agony, imprisoned in a pavilion of torment, scorched by the flaming partition,[225] they were tossed about like chaff by pitchforks, now frantically scattered, now huddled together in fear.

Besides these tortured beings he saw others which had

once been tightly knit and shone brightly, but had now
dimmed and grown loose and ravelled. Hayy scrutinized
these, studied them well. He saw a terrible sight, a great
confrontation, scattering creatures and a grave sentence, the
fashioning of man and the raising up of creation, the outflow of the breath of life.[226] Little by little he pulled himself together. His senses came back. He regained consciousness from what seemed to have been a faint and lost
his foothold on that plane of experience. As the world of
the senses loomed back into view, the divine world vanished, for the two cannot be joined in one state of being—
like two wives: if you make one happy, you make the other
miserable.[227]

You may object, "Your treatment of his experience shows
that if these non-material identities belong to eternal, indestructible bodies like the spheres, they too will endure
forever. But what if they belong to bodies subject to decay, such as that of the rational animal? Then they too
ought to perish. By your own analogy of the reflecting
mirrors, the image has permanence only so long as there is
a mirror. If the mirror is ruined, then the image is obliterated."

I can only reply, it certainly did not take you long to forget our bargain and break my conditions! Did I not just
tell you how narrow my scope for expression is here and
warn you that my words would make a false impression in
any case. Your misapprehension is due solely to your confusing my symbol with what it represents. You expect a
one-for-one correspondence. Such literalism is not tolerable
with ordinary figures of speech, and it is all the less tolerable in this special context. The sun, its light, its form and
image, the mirrors and the forms reflected in them are all
inseparable from physical bodies, unable to subsist without
them, thus dependent on them for existence itself, and of
course destroyed when they are destroyed.

But these divine, sovereign spirits all utterly transcend
the physical and everything dependent on it. There is no
tie of any kind between the two. To these beings, whether
bodies endure or perish, whether they exist or not, is all the
same. Their sole bond is to the One, the Truth, the Neces-

sarily Existent, Who is the first of them, their origin and cause, the ground of their existence, Who gives them being, allows them to endure and even to be eternal. They have no need of bodies. On the contrary, all bodies depend on them. If they could conceivably go out of existence, then all material objects would go with them, for all physical things originate from them. In the same way, assuming the Truth Himself were to become non-existent—sanctified be He and exalted above all such thoughts!—then not one of these essences would exist, no physical things, no sense world, nothing! For all things are bound one to the next.[228]

Yet even though the sense world mimics the divine like a shadow, and the divine world is self-sufficient and totally independent, still it is impossible to postulate complete non-existence for the sensory world, for the very reason that it does reflect the world of the divine. The destruction of the world, then, can mean only that it is transformed, not that it goes out of existence altogether. The Holy Book speaks clearly to this effect in describing how the mountains will be set in motion and become like tufts of wool, and men like moths, the sun and moon cast down, the seas split open and spilled out, on the Day when the earth turns to what is no longer earth, and the heavens to what is no longer heaven.[229]   *134*

These hints and no more I am able to relate concerning what Hayy Ibn Yaqzān witnessed at this lofty plane. Do not ask me to add anything more in words. That would be next to impossible. But I will tell you the rest of the story. Returned to the world of the senses from his wandering, Hayy grew weary of the cares of this world and longed still more for that other life. He tried to return as before, and found he could reach this higher level more easily and remain longer. He returned to the sense world and set out   *135* again, finding he could reach this station still more easily and stay still longer. Again and again he returned to that sublime state, more and more easily, more and more sustainedly, until he reached the point that he could attain it whenever he wished and remain as long as he liked.

He would stay riveted to his station, turning away only to attend the needs of his body, which had by now so wasted away that a more meagre figure could scarcely be found.[230]   All the while, Hayy longed that God—glory to Him—would ease him altogether of his body,[231] which constantly called him away from his post, and let him enjoy bliss untrammelled and undisrupted, free of the painful need of leaving his vantage point to tend to the body.   In this fashion Hayy lived until he had passed his seventh septenary and reached the age of fifty.   It was then he chanced to make the acquaintance of Absāl.   God willing, I shall tell you the tale of their friendship.

136   Near the island where, according to one of the two conflicting accounts of his origin, Hayy was born, there was, so they say, a second island, in which had settled the followers of a certain true religion, based on the teachings of a certain ancient prophet—God's blessing on all such prophets. Now the practice in this religion was to represent all reality in symbols, providing concrete images of things and impressing their outlines on the people's souls, just as orators do when addressing a multitude.   The sect spread widely throughout the island, ultimately growing so powerful and prominent that the king himself converted to it and made the people embrace it as well.[232]

There had grown up on this island two fine young men of ability and high principle, one named Absāl and the other Salāmān.[233]   Both had taken instruction in this religion and accepted it enthusiastically.   Both held themselves dutybound to abide by all its laws and precepts for living.[234] They practiced their religion together; and together, from time to time, they would study some of that religion's traditional expressions describing God—exalted be He—the angels He sends, and the character of resurrection, reward and punishment.   Absāl, for his part, was the more deeply concerned with getting down to the heart of things, the more eager to discover spiritual values, and the more ready to attempt a more or less allegorical interpretation.   Salāmān, on the other hand, was more anxious to preserve the literal and less prone to seek subtle intensions.   On the whole he avoided giving too free rein to his thoughts.[235]   Still each of them executed the express commands of the text fastidiously, kept watch over his soul, and fought his passions.[236]

In the Law[237] were certain statements proposing a life of

solitude and isolation and suggesting that by these means salvation and spiritual triumph could be won. Other statements, however, favored life in a community and involvement in society. Absāl devoted himself to the quest for solitude, preferring the words of the Law in its favor because he was naturally a thoughtful man, fond of contemplation and of probing for the deeper meanings of things; and he did find the most propitious time for seeking what he hoped for to be when he was alone.[238] But Salāmān preferred being among people and gave greater weight to the sayings of the Law in favor of society, since he was by nature chary of too much independent thinking or doing. In staying with the group he saw some means of fending off demonic promptings,[239] dispelling distracting thoughts, and in general guarding against the goadings of the devil. Their differences on this point became the cause of their parting.   *138*

For Absāl had heard of the island where it is said Hayy came to be. He knew how temperate, fruitful and hospitable it was and how easy it would be, for anyone who so desired, to live there in solitude. So he decided to go there and remain in isolation for the rest of his life. He took what money he had,[240] and with some hired a boat to take him to the island. The rest he divided among the poor; and, saying goodbye to his friend, he set sail. The sailors brought him to the island, set him down on the beach and left. Absāl remained there on the island, worshipping, magnifying, and sanctifying God—glory to Him—contemplating His most beautiful names and sublime attributes.[241]

His reveries were undisrupted; his thoughts, unsullied. When he needed food, he would take some of the island fruits or game, just enough to hold his appetite in check. He lived in this way for some time in most perfect happiness and intimacy with his Lord. Each day he could see for himself God's splendid gifts and acts of grace—the ease with which He allowed him to find not just his food but all his wants, confirming his trust and putting a sparkle in his eye.[242]

All this while Hayy Ibn Yaqzān was deeply immersed in his supernal ecstasies, emerging from his cave no more than once a week for whatever food came to hand. For this rea-   *139*

son, Absāl did not come across him at first, but surveyed the
whole island without seeing a soul or even a footprint—
which made him all the happier, since his intention had
been to be alone. But once, when Hayy had come out to
look for food, Absāl happened to be nearby and they saw
each other. Absāl had no doubt that this was another anchorite who had come to the island, as he had, in search of
solitude. He was anxious not to disturb the other by intro-
ducing himself, for fear of disrupting his frame of mind and
preventing his attaining the goal he would be hoping to
reach.

140   Hayy, for his part, had not the least idea what Absāl was,
since he had the form of no animal he had ever laid eyes
on. Besides, he was wearing a long, black cloak of wool and
goat hair, which Hayy took to be his natural coat.[243] Hayy
simply stood gazing at him in amazement; but Absāl, still
hoping not to distract him, took to his heels and ran. Always naturally eager to find out about things, Hayy set out
after him. But, seeing Absāl run still faster, he fell back and
dropped out of sight, letting Absāl suppose he had lost the
trail and gone elsewhere. Absāl then took up his devotions
and was soon completely absorbed in invocations, recitations, weeping, and lamentations. Little by little Hayy
crept up without Absāl's noticing, until he was in earshot of
his praises and recitations and could make out how he was
humbling himself and weeping. The voice he heard was
pleasant and the sounds somehow clearly patterned, quite
unlike the call of any animal he had ever heard before. On
closer inspection of the other's features and the lines of his
body, Hayy recognized the form as his own and realized
141   that the long coat was not a natural skin, but simply a garment intended for use like his own.

Seeing how abject Absāl made himself, Hayy had no doubt
that he was one of those beings who know the Truth.[244] He
felt drawn to him, and wanted to know what was wrong,
what was it that made him cry. He approached closer and
closer, but Absāl caught sight of him and fled. Hayy ran
after him, and with the power and vigor God had given
him, not just mentally, but physically as well, he caught up

with him and seized him in a grip from which he could not escape.

When he got a good look at his captor, clothed in hides still bristling with fur, his hair so overgrown that it hung down over a good part of his body, when he saw how fast he could run and how fiercely he could grapple, Absāl was terrified and began to beg for mercy. Hayy could not understand a word he said. But he could make out the signs of fright and did his best to put the other at ease with a variety of animal cries he knew. Hayy also patted his head, rubbed his sides, and spoke soothingly to him, trying to show how delighted he was with him. Eventually Absāl's trepidation died down and he realized that Hayy did not mean him any harm.

Years before, in his passion for the study of the more   *142* sophisticated level of interpretation, Absāl had studied and gained fluency in many languages,[245] so he tried to speak to Hayy, asking him about himself in every language he knew. But Absāl was completely unable to make himself understood. Hayy was astounded by this performance, but had no idea what it might mean—unless it was a sign of friendliness and high spirits. Neither of them knew what to make of the other.

Absāl had a little food left over from the provisions he had brought from the civilized island. He offered it to Hayy, but Hayy did not know what it was. He had never seen anything like it. Absāl ate a bit and made signs to Hayy that he should eat some too. But Hayy was thinking of his dietary rules. Not knowing what the proffered food might be or what it was made from, he had no idea whether he was allowed to eat it or not, so he would not take any. Absāl, however, kept trying to interest him in it, in an effort to win him over. And Hayy, liking him and afraid to hurt his feelings by persistently refusing, took the food and ate some. The moment he tasted how good it was, Hayy knew he had   *143* done wrong to violate his pledged dietary restrictions. He regretted what he had done and wanted to get away from Absāl and devote himself to his true purpose, a return to sublimity.[246]

But this time ecstasy would not come so readily. It seemed best to remain in the sense-world with Absāl until he had found out so much about him that he no longer felt any interest in him. Then he would be able to go back to his station without further distraction.[247] So he sought out Absāl's company. When Absāl, for his part, saw that Hayy did not know how to talk, the fears he had felt of harm to his faith were eased, and he became eager to teach him to speak, hoping to impart knowledge and religion to him, and by so doing earn God's favor and a greater reward.[248]

So Absāl began teaching him to talk, at first by pointing at some basic objects and pronouncing their names over and over, making him pronounce them too and pronounce them while pointing, until he had taught him nouns. Then he progressed with him, little by little and step by step, until in no time Hayy could speak.

144 Absāl then plied him with questions about himself and how he had come to the island. Hayy informed him that he had no idea of his origins. He knew of no father or any mother besides the doe that had raised him. He told all about his life and the growth of his awareness, culminating in contact with the divine. Hearing Hayy's description of the beings which are divorced from the sense-world and conscious of the Truth—glory be to Him—his description of the Truth Himself, by all His lovely attributes,[249] and his description, as best he could, of the joys of those who reach Him and the agonies of those veiled from Him, Absāl had no doubt that all the traditions of his religion about God, His angels, bibles and prophets, Judgement Day, Heaven and Hell were symbolic representations of these things that Hayy Ibn Yaqzān had seen for himself. The eyes of his heart were unclosed.[250] His mind caught fire.[251] Reason and tradition were at one within him. All the paths of exegesis lay open before him. All his old religious puzzlings were solved; all the obscurities, clear. Now he had "a heart to understand."[252]

145 Absāl looked on Hayy Ibn Yaqzān with newfound reverence. Here, surely, was a man of God, one of those who "know neither fear nor sorrow."[253] He wanted to serve as his disciple, follow his example and accept his direction in

those things which in Absāl's own view corresponded to the religious practices he had learned in his society.[254]

Hayy then asked him about himself and his life; and Absāl, accordingly, set out to tell him about his island and the people who lived there. He described how they had lived before the advent of their present religion and how they acted now.[255] He related all the religious traditions describing the divine world, Heaven and Hell, rebirth and resurrection, the gathering and reckoning, the scales of justice and the strait way.[256] Hayy understood all this and found none of it in contradiction with what he had seen for himself from his supernal vantage point. He recognized that whoever had offered this description had given a faithful picture and spoken truly. This man must have been a "messenger sent by his Lord." Hayy believed in this messenger and the truth of what he said. He bore witness to his mission as apostle of God.[257]

What obligations and acts of worship had he prescribed, Hayy asked.[258] Absāl described prayer, poor tax, fasting, and pilgrimage, and other such outward practices.[259] Hayy accepted these and undertook to observe them. He held himself responsible to practice these things in obedience to the command of one whose truthfulness he could not doubt.

Still there were two things that surprised him and the wisdom of which he could not see. First, why did this prophet rely for the most part on symbols to portray the divine world, allowing mankind to fall into the grave error of conceiving the Truth corporeally and ascribing to Him things which He transcends and is totally free of (and similarly with reward and punishment) instead of simply revealing the truth? Second, why did he confine himself to these particular rituals and duties and allow the amassing of wealth and overindulgence in eating, leaving men idle to busy themselves with inane pastimes and neglect the Truth.[260] Hayy's own idea was that no one should eat the least bit more than would keep him on the brink of survival. Property meant nothing to him, and when he saw all the provisions of the Law to do with money, such as the regulations regarding the collection and distribution of welfare or those regulating sales and interest,[261] with all their statu-

146

147

tory and discretionary penalties, he was dumbfounded. All this seemed superfluous. If people understood things as they really are, Hayy said, they would forget these inanities and seek the Truth. They would not need all these laws. No one would have any property of his own to be demanded as charity or for which human beings might struggle and risk amputation. What made him think so was his naive belief that all men had outstanding character, brilliant minds and resolute spirits. He had no idea how stupid, inadequate, thoughtless, and weak willed they are, "like sheep gone astray, only worse."[262]

148 Hayy deeply pitied mankind and hoped that it might be through him that they would be saved. He was eager to go to these men to reveal and explain the Truth. He spoke about it with his friend Absāl, asking if he knew any way of reaching them. Absāl warned him how defective they are in character and how heedless of God's Word, but this was not easy for Hayy to understand. His heart was set on what he hoped to accomplish. Absāl himself had hopes that through Hayy God might give guidance to a body of aspiring acquaintances of his, who were somewhat closer to salvation than the rest.[263] He agreed to help with the idea.

The two men decided to stay by the shore day and night, in hopes that God might give them some ready means of crossing over. And so they stayed, humbly praying God to fortify them with sound judgment. By God's command it 149 happened that a ship lost its course and was driven by the winds and the beating of the waves to their shore. When it came close to land the men on board saw two men on the beach, so they rode in closer and Absāl hailed them and asked if they would take them along. The men answered yes and brought them on board. No sooner had they done so than God sent a favorable wind that brought the ship with all possible speed to the island where the two had hoped to go. They debarked and went up to the city. Absāl's friends gathered, and he told them all about Hayy Ibn Yaqzān. They all marvelled at the story. They crowded around him, making much of him, and in fact deeply in awe of him. Absāl informed Hayy that of all men this group approached nearest to intelligence and understanding. If

Hayy were unable to teach them, it would be all the more impossible for him to teach the masses. The ruler of the   *150* island and its most eminent man at this time was Salāmān, Absāl's friend who believed in living within society and held it unlawful to withdraw.

Hayy Ibn Yaqzān began to teach this group and explain some of his profound wisdom to them. But the moment he rose the slightest bit above the literal or began to portray things against which they were prejudiced, they recoiled in horror from his ideas and closed their minds. Out of courtesy to the stranger and in deference to their friend Absāl, they made a show of being pleased with Hayy, but in their hearts they resented him. Hayy found them delightful and continued his exposition of the truth, exoteric and esoteric, night and day. But the more he taught, the more repugnance they felt, despite the fact that these were men who loved the good and sincerely yearned for the Truth. Their inborn infirmity simply would not allow them to seek Him as Hayy did, to grasp the true essence of His being and see Him in His own terms. They wanted to know Him in some   *151* human way. In the end Hayy despaired of helping them and gave up his hopes that they would accept his teaching. Then, class by class, he studied mankind. He saw "every faction delighted with its own."[264] They had made their passions their god,[265] and desire the object of their worship. They destroyed each other to collect the trash of this world, "distracted by greed 'til they went down to their graves."[266] Preaching is no help, fine words have no effect on them. Arguing only makes them more pig-headed. Wisdom, they have no means of reaching; they were allotted no share of it.[267] They are engulfed in ignorance. Their hearts are corroded by their possessions.[268] God has sealed their hearts and shrouded their eyes and ears. Theirs will be an awesome punishment.[269]

When he saw that the torture pavilion already encircled them and the shadows of the veil already enshrouded them,[270] when he saw that all but a very few of them adhered to their religion only for the sake of this world[271] and   *152* "flung away works, no matter how light and easy, sold them for a bad price",[272] distracted from the thought of God by business, heedless of the Day when hearts and eyes will be turned inwards,[273] Hayy saw clearly and definitely that to appeal to them publicly and openly was impossible. Any attempt to impose a higher task on them was bound to fail. The sole benefit most people could derive from religion was for this world, in that it helped them lead decent lives without others encroaching on what belonged to them. Hayy now knew that only a very few win the true happiness of the man who "desires the world to come, strives for it and is faithful."[274] But "for the insolent who prefer this life—Hell will be their refuge!"[275]

What weariness is heavier, what misery more overburdening than recounting all you do from the time you get up to the time you go to bed without finding a single action that did not amount to seeking one of these vile, sensory aims:

153   money making, pleasure seeking, satisfying some lust, venting rage, saving face, performing religious rites for the sake of honor, or just to save your neck![276] All these are only "cloud upon cloud over a deep sea."[277] "Not one among you will not descend there—this from your Lord, decreed and sealed."[278]

Hayy now understood the human condition. He saw that most men are no better than unreasoning animals, and realized that all wisdom and guidance, all that could possibly help them was contained already in the words of the prophets and the religious traditions. None of this could be different. There was nothing to be added.[279] There is a man for every task[280] and everyone belongs to the life for which he was created. "This was God's way with those who came before, and never will you find a change in the ways of God."[281]

So Hayy went to Salāmān and his friends and apologized, dissociating himself from what he had said.[282] He told them that he had seen the light and realized that they were right. He urged them to hold fast to their observance of all the statutes regulating outward behavior and not delve into things that did not concern them, submissively to accept all

154   the most problematical elements of the tradition[283] and shun originality and innovation,[284] follow in the footsteps of their

righteous forbears and leave behind everything modern. He cautioned them most emphatically not to neglect religion or pursue the world as the vast majority of people do.

Hayy Ibn Yaqzān and his friend Absāl now knew that even this aspiring group fell short and could be saved only in their own way. If ever they were to venture beyond their present level to the vantage point of insight, what they had would be shattered,[285] and even so they would be unable to reach the level of the blessed. They would waver and slip and their end would be all the worse. But if they went along as they were until overtaken by death, they would win salvation and come to sit on the right. *But* "those who run in the forefront, those who run in the forefront, *they* will be brought near."[286]

So, saying goodbye to them, the two left their company and discreetly sought passage back to their own island.[287] Soon God—exalted be He—gave them an easy crossing. Hayy searched for his ecstasy as he had before, until once again it came. Absāl imitated him until he approached the same heights, or nearly so. Thus they served God on the island until man's certain fate overtook them.

And this—may God give you spirit to strengthen you—is the story of Hayy Ibn Yaqzān, Absāl and Salāmān. It takes up a line of discourse not found in books or heard in the usual sort of speeches. It belongs to a hidden branch of study received only by those who are aware of God and unknown to those who know Him not. In treating of this openly I have broken the precedent of our righteous ancestors, who were sparing to the point of tightfistedness in speaking of it. What made it easy for me to strip off the veil of secrecy and divulge this mystery was the great number of corrupt ideas that have sprouted up and are being openly spread by the self-styled philosophers of today, so widely that they have covered the land and caused universal damage. Fearing that the weak-minded, who throw over the authority of prophets to ape the ways of fools, might mistake these notions for the esoteric doctrines which must be kept secret from those unfit to know them, and thus be all the more enticed to embrace them, I decided to afford them a fleeting glimpse of the mystery of mysteries to draw them to true understanding and turn them away from this other, false way.[288]

Nonetheless I have not left the secrets set down in these few pages entirely without a veil—a sheer one, easily pierced by those fit to do so, but capable of growing so thick to those unworthy of passing beyond that they will never breach it.

Of my brothers who read these words[289] I ask indulgence for my loose exposition and lack of rigor in demonstration. My only excuse is that I had risen to pinnacles higher than the eye can see, and I wanted to try, at least, to approach them in words so as to excite desire and inspire a passion to start out along this road.

Of God I ask forgiveness, and pray Him to purify our knowledge of Him, for He is bountiful and it is He Who bestows all blessings. Farewell my brother, whom it was my duty to help. The blessings and the mercy of God upon you!

Notes to the Text

(Numbers in italics refer to pages of Gauthier's edition of the Arabic text of *Hayy Ibn Yaqzān* and correspond to the numbers shown marginally in the present translation.)

1. Just what is meant by 'oriental philosophy' has been a minor *cause célèbre* among the students of that philosophy. See Nallino "Filosofia orientale ed illuminative" *Rivista degli Studi Orientali* X pp. 433 ff. Henri Corbin in *Avicenna and the Visionary Recital,* New York and London, 1960, and S. H. Nasr in *Three Muslim Sages,* Cambridge, Massachusetts, 1964, make a strong case for fluidity in the shift from 'orient' in Avicenna to 'illuminative' in Suhrawardī, but they cannot surmount the fact of a shift. Initially and primarily Avicenna and with him Ibn Tufayl give the word a literal geographical sense. Ibn Tufayl's expressions of a sense of isolation from the eastern centers of learning, and his contrasting of oriental with Peripatetic philosophy are sufficient evidence of this. Léon Gauthier, then, would seem to be mistaken in choosing the reading 'illuminative'—see his French translation of *Hayy Ibn Yaqzān*, Beirut, 1936, p. 1 note 3 and *Ibn Thofail sa vie, ses œuvres*, Paris, 1909, p. 59 note 1. He does, however call attention to a passage in *The Incoherence of the Incoherence* where Ibn Rushd seems to confirm the drift of the internal evidence. In the context of a discussion of the difficulties in Avicenna's contingency argument for the existence of God, Ibn Rushd writes: "In our own time I have seen many followers of Ibn Sīnā who interpret him in this way on account of this difficulty. They say . . . that this is the meaning he gave to 'oriental philosophy.' He called it oriental, they argue, only because it was the view of people in the east. . ." *Tahāfut at-Tahāfut* X ed. Bouyges p. 421, ed. S. Dunya pp. 639-40, tr. S. van den Bergh p. 254 and van den Bergh's notes *ad loc.*

Ibn Tufayl's consistent reliance on the light imagery of neo-Platonism and his repeated warnings that his words are not to be taken literally show that the term is not without overtones in the direction Gauthier senses. But one crucial premiss of illumi-

167

nism, the divinity of the soul of the aware, is vehemently denied by Ibn Tufayl and the imagery of light associated with *this* is explicitly rejected by him, see pp. *122-124*.

What we have here seems less a play on words than a particularly playful word. The cause of the difficulty is the natural expectation or hope that what comes from the east will be something more than another day. The goods of the orient will be something finer and better than our domestic product. The hope of "western man" is that the east will somehow provide a sort of intellectual sunrise that will clear the mind and vitalize the drowsy academic air that seems to shroud the powers of our thought. This hope was not born with Ibn Tufayl's Sūfī and Platonic antecedents and did not die with the Enlightenment in the West. The unfulfilled promise represented by such a hope is by no means the special province of the orientalist; for like any other "exile" he will find that his remote east will supply him with no more truth than he brings to it. The real orient is within. But to the extent of Ibn Tufayl's success, that province belongs to Hayy Ibn Yaqzān.

2. Avicenna, in Arabic, Abū 'Alī Ibn Sīnā (980-1037), the great Persian physician and philosopher, was born near Bukhara, where he was educated. He boasted that he mastered medicine in two years and that by age 18 he knew all the philosophy he ever learned. At 17 Avicenna successfully treated an ailment of the Prince of Bukhara and was admitted to the royal library. He became a councilor of state in Hamadan and Isfahan and was a member of the court at Rayy. Over 250 works of Avicenna are extant. Most are in Arabic, but some were composed in the author's native Persian. They include the great *Canon* on Medicine, one of the world's longest lived medical textbooks, a number of scientific and religious studies and poems, including a mnemonic poem on medicine, and the philosophical works: the *Shifā'* or "Healing" and its summary, the *Najāt* or "Salvation," systematic expositions of Aristotelian thought in the Islamic context. His works on "Oriental Philosophy," attempting a departure from the strictures of philosophy as practiced among the Greeks, include the allegories, *Hayy Ibn Yaqzān, The Bird*, and *Salāmān and Absāl*, tr. with commentary and other texts by Henri Corbin in *Avicenna and the Visionary Recital*, New York and London, 1960, also an "Essay on Love," *Ishārāt wa tanbīhāt* ("Hints and Pointers"), and the *Logic of the Orientals*, as well as a little known MS entitled "Oriental Philosophy."

Avicenna's thought is portrayed in cameo by S. H. Nasr in *Three*

Muslim Sages Cambridge, Massachusetts, 1964, pp. 20-51, and Introduction to *Islamic Cosmological Doctrines* pp. 177-274. Book-length studies include S. M. Afnan's *Avicenna, His Life and Works* and the millenary symposium edited by G. M. Wickens. For full bibliographical references, see G. C. Anawati, *Essai de bibliographie avicennienne*, Cairo, 1950.

3. Enlightenment will not come easily and it is surely not a prize to be passively awaited. It is one possible outcome of a long and difficult struggle involving tremendous moral and intellectual efforts. Cf. Ghazālī *Al-Munqidh min ad-Dalāl* tr. Wm. Montgomery Watt in *The Faith and Practice of Al-Ghazali* London, 1963, p. 54; cf. Plato Letter VII 340BC and *Republic* VI 490AB. See also Maimonides *Guide to the Perplexed* I 34.

4. Artfully Ibn Tufayl introduces the theme with which the piece will climax, *hāl*, ecstasy, a word which meant no more than 'mood' or 'state of mind' before it was remolded in the crucible of Sūfī practice. Under Sūfī influence the word becomes a "hint," through its very banality indicating the ineffability of an experience the term does not even attempt to characterize.

5. A mystery in pagan antiquity was a ritualized, sacramentalized drama in which the initiate played the symbolic role of what he was to become—a god, a god reborn, a sinless soul, or simply a man. Cf. A. D. Nock *Conversion*, Oxford, 1933 and A. J. Festugiere *Personal Religion among the Greeks*, Los Angeles, 1960. With the renaissance of personal religion and the rise of spirituality in the Hellenistic era, mystery was reappropriated by the individual. It became possible for the aspirant to hold his rites in some private society or at home (see *Conversion* p. 116), and ultimately in the temple of his own heart: See E. R. Dodds *Pagan and Christian in an Age of Anxiety*, Cambridge, 1965, pp. 79-101. To Hebraic and Islamic religion, the internalization meant less an appropriation of rites of initiation and purification than the attachment of an "inner," spiritual meaning to the external acts commanded by the Deity. Thus the secrecy which had been essential to the emotional impact of the pagan mysteries was reinterpreted as the intimacy of the soul in dialogue with itself: The Hebrew *seter* and the Arabic *sirr* no longer denote secrecy, but the inmost core of being. The new stress on the heart as seat of spirituality, common to Bahya Ibn Paqūda and Ghazālī, provides poetic language in which the demand for an inner dimension to the oldest mysteries can be voiced.

6. Elation, or "expansion" of the spirit, and "construction," its depressive correlative, are among features of the mystic experi-

ence noted not only by its practitioners, but also by its natural historians, and more recently, in attempts at a "supernatural history" of the phenomenon. R. C. Zaehner in *Mysticism Sacred and Profane*, Oxford, 1957, pp. 84-95 alludes to William James' treatment of the depressive phase, translates Qushayrī's treatment of the dialectic between expansiveness and oppression of spirit (transliterating the Arabic on p. 237) and warns of the danger of being trapped, oscillating between the two in what he calls "nature mysticism"—a simulation of the experience of the true mystic, which lacks only God to make it real.

7.   Intoxicated by the mystic experience, the uninitiated may utter paradoxical, heterodox, or even blasphemous words, for a man may become the subject of such experience even though he has not the intellectual capacity adequately to interpret it.   For such a man expression becomes a danger.   The attempt to express the ineffable invariably leads to error, see Ghazālī *Munqidh*, tr. Watt, p. 61; cf. Hujwīrī: "Expression of the meaning of reality is futile.   If a meaning exists it is not lost by expression, and if it is non-existent it is not created by expression.   Expression only produces an unreal notion and leads the student mortally astray by causing him to imagine that the expression is the real meaning."   *Kashf al-Mahjūb*, tr. R. A. Nicholson, London, 1967 (first edition, 1911), p. 153.   Despite his acceptance of the Sūfī belief that no human language is adequate to the full expression of the truth, Ibn Tufayl maintains the rationalist's faith that men of adequate understanding and superior intellect will be able to provide hints that will direct the understanding to the experience.   Transmissibility thus remains possible, even if only on a reduced scale; for, as Hujwīrī himself admits, "the fault lies soley in the expression, not in the idea it attempts to convey." *op. cit.* p. 152.

8.   This ecstatic cry is attributed to Abū Yazīd Bistāmī (d. ca. 875), one of the most famous Muslim mystics.   His awareness was characterized by the mystic's combined sense of nullity before his Judge and Creator and identity with the Fountain of all being.   Thus while he wrote nothing, many of the some 500 sayings ascribed to him are *"shatahāt"*—mixtures of piety and blasphemy such as the one quoted by Ibn Tufayl.   "I am the throne and the footstool," "I saw the *Ka'ba* walking around me," were among his boasts, and he claimed to have risen, like Muhammad, to the celestial world.   As a rationalist, Ibn Tufayl is anxious to defend his philosophico-religious enterprise from the dangerous

toying with pantheism and nihilism that such men's thoughts represented to him; cf. pp. *123* ff., *155-156*.

9. Hallāj, called the martyr, was crucified in 922 for his alleged identification of himself with the Godhead. See Louis Massignon *La passion d'al-Hallaj, martyr mystique de l'Islam* Paris, 1922, passim esp. p. 62. Massignon questions the validity of the charge against Hallāj, and Ibn Tufayl would seem to agree that Hallāj was not guilty of the precise crime charged to him. His fault was an intellectual one: he did not adequately interpret and thus could not accurately express the content of the experience he underwent. He was neither a clear pantheist or incarnationist, nor a clear blasphemer, but a man confused in mind and language. The source of his confusion is apparent: He interpreted his feelings of at-oneness as evidence of actual identity with God. Ibn Tufayl hopes to see his reader clear of this confusion see pp. *122* ff.

10. These words have been attributed to Abū Saʿīd Ibn Abī l-Khayr, as well as to Hallāj. See Massignon *La Passion d'al-Hallaj* pp. 399, 451. The former (967-1049) was a Khorasanian Sūfī, whose memory is almost totally obscured by the gilt of pious legends with which it has been encrusted. See R. A. Nicholson *Studies in Islamic Mysticism* I, London, 1967 (first edition 1921) for a full treatment of his life and thought.

11. Abū Hāmid Ghazālī (1058-1111) is traditionally regarded as having pumped new life into Islam at the start of its sixth century. His numerous works on theology, philosophy, and Muslim jurisprudence include the forty books of the *Ihyā' ʿUlūm ad Dīn* ("Revival of Religious Studies"), in which a comprehensive effort is made to refound Islamic faith, practice, and spirituality; and the *Tahāfut al-Falāsifah* ("Incoherence of the Philosophers"), a systematic refutation of some 20 major points of Islamized neo-Platonic philosophy. Commonly called "The Destruction of the Philosophers," this latter work utilizes the non-Aristotelian traditions of philosophy and original techniques of argumentation to rise to a high pitch of coherence and philosophical effectiveness. Ghazālī's talents included a keen perception of what might be acceptable to Islam from such initially alien and potentially dangerous traditions as mysticism and philosophy. He was thus capable of extracting from both these traditions a core that might be assimilated to the new orthodoxy which he helped found, while at the same time ruthlessly excising the remnant extremes. Despite the fact that the thoughts favored by Ghazālī were to

rigidify into an orthodoxy, and despite his opposition to some of the central doctrines of the mainstream of Islamized Greek philosophy, it remains possible to say that far from writing the death warrant of philosophy in Islam, Ghazālī, by questioning the dogmas of philosophy and opening the door to further fusion, gave Islamic philosophy a new breath of life. If so, it is in this aspect of Ghazālī's achievement, the hope he gave to independence of mind, not only by what he practiced, but also by what he preached, that Ibn Tufayl is his true heir.

12. Ibn Mu'tazz, quoted by Ghazālī in his autobiography, *Al-Munqidh min ad-Dalāl*, tr. Wm. Montgomery Watt in *The Faith and Practice of Al-Ghazālī*, p. 61.

13. Ghazālī was the recipient of the best education to be had in his day and country. Born at Tūs in Persia, his years covering roughly the same span as those of Anselm of Canterbury, he received the traditional Muslim training, including, of course, memorization of the *Qur'ān* and numerous other books. He studied in his teens with one Ahmad b. Muhammad ar-Radakānī and at Jurjān with masters of whom little is known. In his mature years, Ghazālī was to turn on the Isma'īlīs, but from his book against them, the *Fadā'ih al-Bātiniyya*, it appears that it was from them he had his first exposure to philosophical interchange. He returned to Tūs for three more years of study and went on to Nīshāpūr to study under Juwaynī, the foremost theologian of the day, whose position Ghazālī's works reveal him to have transcended. He studied also with the Sūfī Faramdī, who died in 1084 and remained under Juwaynī until the latter's death in 1085, when he began life as a follower of the great prime minister Nizām al-Mulk. He mastered philosophy, he says, in less than two years, while lecturing to 300 students at the Nizāmiyya College in Baghdad, for it was his nature always to want to understand things, never to be satisfied with blind faith: See *Munqidh*, tr. Watt, pp. 29-30, 21. For the works of Ghazālī, see Maurice Bouyges *Essai de Chronologie des Œuvres de Al-Ghazali*, ed. Michel Allard, Beirut, 1959.

14. Known to the schoolmen as Avempace, Ibn Bājja (d. 1138) authored a book on human contact with the Active Intelligence: *Risālah fi Ittisāl al-'Aql bi-l-Insān*. Islamic thinkers of conservative persuasion attempted to avoid the theological difficulties inherent in the mystic notion of union with God by relying instead on the notion of *ittisāl*, contact or communion with the divine. The contact is with the Godhead, neither identical with nor yet distinct from the lowest of the disembodied celestial

minds. Thus even when the identity of the beholder is "lost" in the divine, he does not become one with God. See pp. *129, 155-156*.

15. Ibn Bājja's talk of 'concepts' and 'understanding' and his suggestion that merely comprehending an idea will be sufficient to allow ecstasy lead Ibn Tufayl to suspect that his predecessor was attempting to assimilate the true mystic experience to some purely intellectual process of apprehension; cf. p. *10*. Fārābī had identified the source of prophetic and mystical enlightenment as intellectual contact with the Active Intellect through which understanding becomes immediate and the deductive process becomes unnecessary. To Ibn Sīnā this had seemed inadequate, and he superadded to Fārābī's scheme of the perfection of man's mind a higher level, the "Sacred Intellect" by which prophets might attain transcendence of their human limitations. To Ibn Tufayl, as to Ghazālī, recognition of the wider extension and deeper certainty derived from the immediate awareness characteristic of the mystic state demanded that this source of knowledge not be classed with the ordinary modes of thought. But for both men the experience did remain a mode of thought, a noetic state. Neither was content to retreat to the irrationalism of untempered mysticism.

16. Both reason and ecstasy are spoken of here as revelation. Reason is not "disproved" by revelation as it might seem to have been for Ghazālī: see *Munqidh* tr. Watt, pp. 24-25. Ecstasy cannot contradict reason: if it does, the subject's intellectual abilities are at fault, not the logic of the object of his experience. The theme will be a major one: Reason must not abdicate, but transcend itself; cf. pp. *124-126*. For a brief history of the relations between the divine and intellectual sources of knowledge in Islam see A. J. Arberry, *Revelation and Reason in Islam*, the Forwood Lectures of 1956, London, 1957 (in Books in Print).

17. Summing up the Sūfī position, Hujwīrī writes "God causes man to know Him through Himself without his knowledge being dependent on any faculty, a knowledge in which the existence of man is purely metaphorical. Thus to the aware, egoism is rank faithlessness." *Kashf al-Mahjūb*, tr. after Nicholson p. 271. Ibn Tufayl's stand is not as strong: Still to see the self and the world is not faithlessness but merely inadequacy, for to see God alone is the task of the supererogatory man. Nor will human existence be dismissed as a metaphor. But the immediate awareness of God must come immediately from God. It cannot inhere in a faculty or power. The "power" by which God is known must be

such only metaphorically. The reality is the immediate contact of the self with the divine.

18. Ibn Tufayl has in mind not so much the argot of professional philosophy as the highly developed technical terminology of the Sūfīs. That the experience of which he speaks and its mode of apprehension should elude both ordinary language and specialized usage is taken by Ibn Tufayl not as evidence of inadequacy in language, still less as symptomatic of some logical difficulty in the notions he hopes to deal with, but rather as a sign of a category difference; the experience he speaks of belongs to another world, another order of being, and the predicates in use in our ordinary world, the world of sense and imagination, simply do not apply.

19. The "metaphorical faculty" is now given its (metaphorical) name, *dhawq*, the taste, *i.e.* intuition, of God. "The distinctive thing in mysticism," writes Ghazālī, "cannot be grasped by study, but only by immediate experience *(dhawq)*." *Munqidh*, tr. Watt, pp. 54-55; cf. pp. 62-64. Technically, *dhawq* is the first stage of enlightenment beyond the ordinary; cf. Jurjānī *Kitāb at-Taʿarīfāt* ed. Fluegel, Leipzig, 1845, p. 112; and Qushayrī *Risālah*, Cairo, 1346 A.H., p. 39.

20. That is the aspirant to Sūfī awareness; cf. p. *148*.

21. The Active Intellect in neo-Platonic thinking was the condition of understanding, much as light is the condition of sight. God, the ultimate source of light, *will* be understood: that is He will be seen, not easily as some Sūfīs had supposed, but with difficulty, breaking through doubt and obscurity, in Ibn Sīnā's apt imagery, as the sun breaks through a clouded and stormy sky.

22. As Ghazālī explains in *Ihyā' 'Ulūm ad-Dīn* XXXV, the monotheism of the mystic is monism. He sees nothing in all being but God, the object of his love, whom he calls the Truth. The self becomes a barrier between the mystic and his God and the task of the Sūfī is to strip away this last veil and lose himself in God. The emotional "overwhelming" which the mystic undergoes is symptomatic of the initiation of the process in which the self is lost. The process would seem to be totally destructive. But for Ibn Tufayl, as for Ghazālī, the mind provides safeguards against total self-annihilation: loss of self is not loss of consciousness, but rather the highest form of consciousness. Thus the self remains: beyond the dying unto self is found the death of death, which to Ghazālī, as to most Muslim mystics, is the birth of life eternal. cf. p. *117, 119-120*.

23. Like most languages, Arabic reserves a special term for

the knowledge by which we know friends, which renders naturally the equivalent of *gnosis*: the term, *ma'rifa*, awareness, recognition, suggests a degree of intimate immediacy that renders this one form of knowledge at least proof against the ploys of skepticism. See Ghazālī *Munqidh* passim; also Farid Jabre *La notion de la ma'rifa chez Ghazali* Beirut, 1958, and *La notion de Certitude selon Ghazali*, Paris, 1958.

Gnosticism and agnosticism seem to live in a sort of symbiosis, each supplying the deficiencies of the other: Gnosticism respects and uses the "negative theology" of the agnostic, providing in return an answer to the demands of skepticism. The union breaks down when the credentials of gnostic certainty or the significance of content-less gnostic theology are held to critical scrutiny. What remains when the alliance is broken is the notion of a relationship with God that goes deeper than mere knowledge, a relationship more akin to friendship, or as Spinoza calls it, the intellectual love of God.

24. The passage quoted will be found in M. A. F. Mehren *Traités Mystiques d'Ibn Sina*, Leiden, 1889-1899, fasc. 4, ii, pp. 15 ff., corresponding to pp. 13 ff. of Mehren's French translation. (*Ishārāt wa-t-Tanbīhāt Livre des Directives et Remarques* tr. Goichon, p. 493.) The contrast of the flicker of enlightenment with the steady glow of understanding is developed in Matthew Arnold's poem "Despondency"—but the theme has now changed. Calm enjoyment of the truth is no longer readily won. Ibn Tufayl quotes at length from Avicenna in hopes of showing the congruity of the philosopher's views on the mystic experience with those of Ghazālī.

25. The mystic envisages his progress as the gradual ascent of a mountain by a road (cf. p. *20*), each stage of which has its own character, its own ways, and its own truths, as the ultimate and absolute truth is approached. Among the stages mentioned by Ibn Tufayl are the following: blind faith in authority pp. *19, 154*; doubt p. *72*; the joy of discovery p. *8*; elation p. *4*; the first "taste" of ecstasy p. *6*; ecstasy p. *116*; the "igniting of the mind" p. *144*; transcendence of self p. *5*; "contact" or communion with the divine p. *5, 127*; active involvement p. *118*; "entrenchment" pp. *7, 90*; concentration p. *116*; *imitatio Dei* pp. *34, 106* ff., *117* ff.; absorption p. *6*; death to self p. *109*; life eternal p. *4*.

26. To the rationalist, the argument for God's existence based on immediate experience is never fully satisfying; for there always remains, before any conclusion can be safely reached, the task of interpreting experience. Thus Avicenna assimilates the

argument from awareness of God to a form of design argument:
man's awareness of his Maker is not direct proof of God's existence, but evidence the Creator's design, a benchmark that is explicit where other signs of craftsmanship are present but not
articulate.

27.   No formal deduction or mechanical "truth test" can reveal the truth as discovered in the immediate experience of awakening to God.   The demand is not for a rejection of reason, but
for an expansion by reason of man's categories of thought, lest
there turn out to be "more things in heaven and earth"—and in
human experience, Ghazālī would add—than are dreamed of in
our philosophies.

28.   Man in the natural state is capable of finding God.   Inability to do so is a defect like inability to run or fight (cf. pp.
140-141) or like blindness.   The blind man of Ibn Tufayl's example is "strong" in all but the one faculty that he lacks.   Hayy
Ibn Yaqzān, on the other hand, is powerful in all his faculties:
his endowment is full.   Above all he has a thirst for the truth
which will not be satisfied until the last "veil" is stripped away;
cf. Ghazālī *Al-Munqidh min ad-Dalāl* tr. Watt p. 21.

29.   Just as ostensive definitions convey some notion of reality
but can never convey its full meaning, since they fail to confront
—let alone formulate—the nature of the reality they are intended
to define, so second-hand knowledge of religious truths will be of
value only to those who already have their own knowledge of
its object.   To others it will serve only as pointers do for the
blind, keeping them on the right path, but by no means giving
them the missing power of seeing and enjoying the road in which
they walk.

30.   Ibn Tufayl's audience is not totally unaware of the content of religious experience, but their understanding of the mystic state is like the blind man's knowledge of colors.   The analogy
is borrowed from Ghazālī's autobiography *Al-Munqidh min ad-
Dalāl*, "Deliverance from Error" ed. Farid Jabre, Beirut, 1959,
p. 42, Jabre's French tr. p. 104, tr. Wm. Montgomery Watt in
The Faith and Practice of al-Ghazali, p. 64.   Ghazālī applies the
analogy to prophecy, but its reapplication to the "private revelation" of the mystic is fully in keeping with the spirit of Ghazālī's
philosophy and that of his antecedents; cf. p. 62.   See also F.
Shehadi, *Ghazali's Unique Unknowable God* p. 16 and John
Wisdom "The Logic of God" in *Paradox and Discovery* Oxford,
1965, p. 15, and in *The Existence of God* ed. J. Hick, London,
1964, p. 291, originally broadcast for BBC, 1950.   The joy of the

man whose sight is restored is due not only to the fact of his awakening to a new world but also to his newfound ability to enjoy and appreciate that world, to live more fully in a world that is itself more real than the shadow world in which he has lived.

31. As Gustave von Grunebaum points out, "The concept of the 'friend of God' is an heirloom of the Hellenistic world." He compares Epictetus *Dissertations* IV iii 9 and Augustine *Confessions* VIII 6 with *Qur'ān* X 63. In popular thought, as von Grunebaum shows, intimacy with God was identified as a source of charisma (*karāmāt*). Ibn Abī'l-Khayr as well as Bistāmī are said to have denigrated such feats as walking on water or flying through air as easily accomplished by birds or insects. As for instant translocation to far off places, the devil himself has mastered that trick. "The true friend of God goes among people, eats and sleeps with them, buys and sells in the market, marries, and lives on good terms with his fellow men, and never forgets God for a single moment." See *Medieval Islam*, Chicago, 1961 (first edition, 1946), pp. 139, 352 quoting R. A. Nicholson *Studies in Islamic Mysticism* 1967 (first edition 1921), p. 67. Ibn Tufayl's position would seem to be midway between the two extremes mentioned by the Sūfī tradition: He is, of course, not overly impressed with the popular conception of the miracle; his "saint" is a natural man, but he does live alone, not in society: His intimacy with God depends on solitude. Yet, setting ideal types aside, Ibn Tufayl would not seem to deny the Sūfī notion that solitude can be achieved while living among men; cf. also pp. 137, 145, 154.

32. The archetype of the innately gifted, "self-taught" man is, of course, Hayy Ibn Yaqzān, Life Awareson. What he is taught is the nature of the Universe, the truth about being, about himself and above all about God. In this he has no need of help. Indeed help would be a hindrance, for no human conception can adequately convey the fulness of the truth as revealed to the man whose teacher is God. Men are born in a state of nature; and if they are well formed, as is Hayy, their natural endowment or *fitra* will bring them to the highest level of understanding a human being can attain. Traditional representations would only cloud the keenness of their perceptions. See Ghazālī's discussion of the *hadīth* "Everyone is born in a state of nature. His parents make him a Jew, Christian, or Magian" *Al-Munqidh min ad-Dalāl*, tr. Watt in *The Faith and Practice of Al-Ghazali*, p. 21; cf. Wang's remark in the article on "Fraud" in

Voltaire's *Philosophical Dictionary*, tr. Peter Gay, New York, 1962, p. 280. (First French articles begun 1752.)

33. The rationalist (justly) fears that the elation of "contact" may lead to loss of control by reason. The thrill of communion, the irrational joy at loss of self may become destructive forces; the means by which "contact" is sought may become ends in themselves. Against all these dangers Ibn Tufayl has only the self-authenticating experience itself to offer. Only those who have actually known this experience, he argues in true mystic-empiricist style, can judge its validity or its source. Ibn Bājja's criticism is discussed by Miguel Asin Palacios in "El Filosofo zaragozano Avempace" *Revista de Aragon*, 1901, p. 245.

34. "There is no writing of mine about these matters, nor will there ever be one. For this knowledge is not something that can be put into words like other sciences; but after long-continued intercourse between teacher and pupil, in joint pursuit of the subject, suddenly, like light flashing forth when a fire is kindled, it is born in the soul and nourishes itself." Plato Letter VII 341C, *et seq.* to 344. The ineffability of the truth as seen by the enlightened is not only a constant theme of Ibn Tufayl's, but also a main problem he confronts in the writing of *Hayy Ibn Yaqzān*.

35. For Ghazālī, God's unity was a sea of infinite extent, see *Ihyā' 'Ulūm ad-Dīn* XXXV, Introduction.

36. That is, idiomatically speaking, rare as hens' teeth. Red sulfur is identified with the philosopher's stone, by which the alchemist was enabled to perform his transformations. Cf. Ibn Hazm *Los caracteres y la conducta*, ed. M. Asin Palacios, Madrid, 1916, p. 99 note 1, and Ghazālī *Ayyuha 'l-Walad* ed. Purgstall p. 21. For the Stoic tradition that the wise man is as rare as the Phoenix see Seneca Letter 42.1. It was Socrates who remarked that the philosopher (combining as he does so many virtues) is a rare plant indeed: *Republic* VI 491.

37. Andalusia, in the time of Ibn Tufayl, comprised Muslim Spain, that is about half the Iberian penninsula, which was united with Northwest Africa, and governed from the Almohad capital of Marrakesh. The dynasty, under Abū Ya'qub Yūsuf (r. 1163-1184) was at the apogee of its power.

38. Islamic (notably Shi'ite) tradition assigns the task of leading each generation to a succession of charismatic figures of greater or lesser historicity. Prophets, Shi'ite Imāms, saints, and semi-legendary eschatological figures make up the successions by

which the dialectic of history is marked or controlled. See for example Ibn 'Arabī's *Fusūs al-hikam* ("Bezels of Wisdom") discussed by S. H. Nasr in *Three Muslim Sages*, Cambridge, Massachusetts, 1964, pp. 98 ff. The notion of a succession of religious teachers forming a dialectic of revelation is applied by Eusebius to prophets of the Jews *Praeparatio Evangelica* I. Ibn Tufayl interprets the traditional view of a succession of (soteriologically) necessary figures as applying to the wise, providing an interesting parallel to the remark of Socrates: "many, as they say in the mysteries, are the thyrsus-bearers, but few are the mystics, —meaning, as I interpret the words, the true philosophers." *Phaedo* 69. Ibn Tufayl's specific interpretation of the idea of succession is modeled on the practice of the Sūfīs.

39. The philosophy mentioned here by Ibn Tufayl is *falsafa*, i.e. philosophy on the Greek model, as opposed to the oriental philosophy (*hikma*) mentioned in the opening sentence. Avicenna's *Shifā'*, the "Book of Healing," that is, a therapeutic approach to philosophy, deals systematically with logic, physics, and metaphysics. The book, which formed a main basis for Ghazālī's understanding of Islamized Aristotelian philosophy (as outlined in the *Maqāsid al-Falāsifa* or "Aims of the Philosophers" and dealt with in the *Tahāfut al-Falāsifa*, "Incoherence of the Philosophers") was widely used by the schoolmen of the Latin Middle Ages, to whom it was known as the *Sufficiencia*. Nasr calls the *Shifā'* "the longest encyclopedia of knowledge ever written by one man." *Three Muslim Sages* p. 23. A complete edition of the Arabic by I. Madkour and a critical edition of the Latin by M. D'Alverny have been undertaken.

40. Waqqāshī of Toledo (d. 1095) expresses in these lines a positivism as rigorous as that of any recent logical empiricist. Mathematics and logic are, of course, the trivial science; metaphysics, the science which might be worthwhile but cannot be successfully pursued. Natural science is omitted from the dichotomy—perhaps because the poet recognizes (as did many *mutakallimūn*) that physical theory too must rest on metaphysical groundworks. Waqqāshī's position is untenable, since in itself, like any positivism, it presupposes a metaphysics. What is valid in Waqqāshī's lines is his recognition of the enormous difficulty of a finite being's formulating a meaningful metaphysical statement. Yet the history of philosophy is filled with attempts —not all of which are unsuccessful—to do just that. For the identity of the poet see Gonzalez Palencia's Spanish tr. of *Hayy Ibn Yaqzān: El Filosofo Autodidacto*, Madrid, 1934, p. 51 note

15. For an approximation of Waqqāshī's tone see Bertrand Russell's *Autobiography* vol. II.

41. Ibn Bājja's *Tadbīr al-Mutawahhid*, "The Solitary's Discipline" is Ibn Tufayl's immediate model for the prescriptive description of the life of the recluse, despite Ibn Tufayl's unwillingness to find common ground with him on the questions of practical ethics and mysticism. The treatise has been edited with Spanish translation by Miguel Asin Palacios as *El Regimen del Solitario*, Madrid, 1946, and more recently by Majid Fakhry in Ibn Bajjah (Avempace) *Opera Metaphysica*, Beirut, 1968.

42. Ibn Tufayl refers with cautious anticipation to his younger peers, among whom was Ibn Rushd.

43. Abū Nasr Fārābī (870?-950), known as "the second teacher"—in recognition of his role in the explication of Aristotle —was of Turkish background, his father being an army officer. He spent most of his life in Baghdad, but went to Aleppo in 942 at the invitation of Sayf ad-Dawla, the Shī'ī ruler of Syria. There were Christians among his teachers and students and he seems to have been in contact with a living philosophical tradition going back to the school of Alexandria. His philosophical works include a book of political aphorisms, the *Fusūl al-Madānī* ed. and tr. D. M. Dunlop, Cambridge, 1961, and "The Beliefs of the Inhabitants of the Ideal State", soon to be published with translation and commentary by R. Walzer. His logical books include paraphrases and commentaries on Aristotle as well as independent treatises, one of the best of the former being the commentary on *De Interpretatione*, ed. W. Kutsch and Stanley Marrow, Beirut, 1960. A full bibliography for Fārābī has been prepared by Nicholas Rescher: *Al-Fārābī, An Annotated Bibliography*. Pittsburgh, 1962.

44. The works referred to are Fārābī's *Al-millatu-l-Fādila*, an edition of which is soon to be published, *Al-Siyāsatu-l-Madaniyya*, ed. F. M. Najjar, Beirut, 1964, and the lost commentary on the Ethics of Aristotle. In the *Fusūl al-Madānī* ("Aphorisms of the Statesman") Fārābī argues that happiness is the logical outcome of a virtuous life, "the good which a man has gained is not taken from him by death." The "afterlife" is the intimate contact of the intellect with the divine world: ed. D. M. Dunlop, Cambridge, 1961, art. 70-1, 76. Ibn Tufayl's own eschatological views are not, as his remarks might seem to suggest, a complete rejection of Fārābī's point of view so much as an attempt to qualify and interpret, to iron out the difficulties which those views involve. See pp. 97, 131, 147, 151.

45.   Fārābī attributed prophecy to divine revelation by contact of the fulfilled human mind with the Active Intellect.   But this level is reached as well by the philosopher.   What distinguishes the prophet is his ability to find rhetoric or poetry, concrete symbolic imagery, by which the masses can be moved. Ibn Tufayl would not seem to reject the elements of this analysis; see pp. *144, 146.*   The sticking points for him are the fact that Fārābī makes prophecy dependent on imagination, a "lower" faculty in medieval thinking, since it bridged the gap between the senses and thought, and the unwillingness of Fārābī to assign the prophet a higher epistemological station than the philosophically aware.   Both these flaws are remedied in Ibn Sīnā's theory of the "sacred mind," which affords the prophet more or less superhuman status and eliminates the dependence on imagination in favor of a direct dependence on inspiration.

46.   In *Tahāfut al-Falāsifa* Ghazālī accuses the philosophers of apostasy for their doctrine of the eternity of the world and their rejection of divine knowledge of particulars and the resurrection of the flesh.   In *Fadā'ih al-Bātiniyya* ed. Badawi, Cairo, 1964, pp. 38-40, he accuses both the philosophers (i.e. neo-Platonists) and Ismā'īlīs of dualism.   In the philosophers' view, the world's eternity and the existence of a "secondary" hypostasis were implied by emanation, and the Platonic rationale for immortality did not allow for resurrection of the body—since it was the body from which immortality was the escape.   Yet, as Ibn Rushd angrily observed of Ghazālī: "From the books ascribed to him it is obvious that in metaphysics he relies on the school of the *Falāsifa*; and, of all his books this is most clearly illustrated and most unimpeachably proved by his *Mishkāt al-Anwār.*" *Tahāfut al-Tahāfut* last lines of the first discussion, ed. Bouyges p. 117, ed. Dunya p. 209.   In the *Mishkāt*, for which see my note 55 below, Ghazālī seems to accept not only emanation, but also the notions of a secondary hypostasis, and even of a "demiurge" that is not identical with God.   One should not however call Ghazālī's consistency into question too rashly.   Creation in time and emanation were not mutually exclusive for Ghazālī, for in his view time was created with the Universe.   Thus, it was not necessary for him to accept the world's eternity (which he equated with atheism) in accepting emanation.   As for secondary beings, the relevant point to the medieval radical monotheist was not their existence, but their subordination.   The philosophers may verge on dualism even for upholding causal necessity; but Ghazālī does not uphold the *independent* existence

of any finite being. Ibn Tufayl's hope is to reconcile the difficulties he finds in Ghazālī's works and arrive at a coherent picture of the truth. In so doing, he will, of course, depart from the teaching of the master, as he does from that of Ibn Sīnā, Ibn Bājja, and Fārābī.

47. *Tahāfut al-Falāsifa*, author's introduction ii *ad fin.*, and conclusion, with discussions XIX-XX. Ghazālī discusses the philosopher's doctrine of spiritual resurrection at length, and willingly grants its truth and its consistency with orthodox religious doctrine. His objections to the philosophical doctrine are based solely on the insistence of the Islamic neo-Platonists that reason is sufficient to give man his knowledge of the hereafter and their assurance that the body will not be resurrected. Bodily resurrection, he insists, is a dogma of Islam not to be trifled with: its possibility is not to be disproved by reason and its reality is assured by revelation.

48. See Ghazālī's *Mizān al-'Amal* ed. S. Dunya, Cairo, 1964, pp. 195-196: The Sūfīs and others say that to attain perfect happiness the soul must free itself from the body. How God can allow this and still preserve His promise of bodily resurrection must remain something of a mystery, but neither Ibn Tufayl nor Ghazālī, nor their great predecessor, Origen, seems to find much difficulty in believing that He can. Of the three, Ibn Tufayl would seem the most willing to part with physical resurrection: see pp. *131* ff.

49. *Al-Munqidh min ad-Dalāl* tr. Watt pp. 54 ff. See also *Ihyā' 'Ulūm ad-Dīn* passim for Ghazālī's dependence on Sūfī thinking.

50. As Ibn Rushd points out (*Tahāfut at-Tahāfut* last page, ed. Bouyges p. 587), Ghazālī says specifically that no Muslim accepts a purely spiritual resurrection, yet definitely attributes a belief in spiritual resurrection to the Sūfīs. It seems to me doubtful that Ghazālī's views on the survival of the soul, as given in *Kitāb Madnūn as-Saghīr* and *Mishkāt al-Anwār*, can be said to be significantly different from those of Fārābī. Ghazālī upheld the individuality of the disembodied soul and the intellectuality of its reward. From his remarks in discussion XX of the *Tahāfut al-Falāsifa* it would seem that Ghazālī is quite willing to accept the Islamized neo-Platonic conception of personal immortality, provided only that one further stage of Islamization is allowed: the superposition of the vivid Qur'ānic doctrine of the resurrection of the flesh. Despite Ghazālī's strong judgments against those who reject the dogma, it does not seem that the resurrec-

tion of the flesh plays a major role in the highest reaches of Ghazālī's thought, and Ibn Tufayl would appear to follow in his master's footsteps when he de-emphasizes the doctrine—letting revelation speak for it, and confining his philosophical attentions to aspects of immortality more amenable to the rationalist tradition.

51. The truth, writes Ghazālī, must be revealed in stages, according to the abilities of its recipients. See *Mizān al-'Amal* last chapter, ed. S. Dunya, pp. 405-409; cf. Ghazālī's remarks at the end of the first discussion in *Tahāfut al-Falāsifa*: some arguments have only a dialectical use. Ghazālī's caution is based less on a cynical disregard for the truth (or any incapacity to formulate a coherent system of unified truth as Ibn Rushd suggests: *Tahāfut at-Tahāfut, loc. cit.*) than on a genuine fear that the truth if known too soon by "those unfit to know it" might be misapprehended and misused. This is a fear in which Ibn Tufayl heartily concurs; see pp. *154-157.*

52. Ghazālī's verses proclaiming the eclipse of traditional faith (*taqlīd*) in first-hand religious experience and his recommendation of doubt as the catalyst by which the passion for search is unleashed are found on the last page of *Mizān al-'Amal*, ed. Dunya p. 409.

53. The receptivity to experience and the penetrating mind which will bring the self-taught man to his clear vision of the truth are, in radical monotheist philosophy, conceived to be signs of divine workmanship: since the self-taught man is taught by God, the state of natural awareness, in which he is born, may properly be considered as *the* natural religion, a religion which he himself perfects as he reaches maturity and with divine help his mind is developed.

In the Fārābian view, extrapolated from neo-Platonic Aristotelianism, the mind is raised from "potential" to "actual" to "adept", at which stage it may come into direct contact with the Active Intellect, the lowest of the disembodied "intelligences." The result is the attainment of metaphysical truth without need of the reasoning process. See Fārābī *Fī 'Aql* ed. M. Bouyges, 1938, nos. 22-37, Latin tr. Gerard of Cremona, "De Intellectu et intellecto," ed. Etienne Gilson in *Archives d'Histoire Doctrinale et Littéraire du Moyen Age*, 1929. The adept needs no teacher. His progress is attributable to the interaction of his awareness with the activating force of the Active Intellect, a dialectic which is in turn made possible by the generosity of God. In the same spirit Avicenna identified the adept as the man whose knowledge seems to come "from within himself." In reality, of course, the source of his knowledge is God. See Ibn Sīnā *Najāt* II 6 vi, tr. F. Rahman as *Avicenna's Psychology*, Oxford, 1952, pp. 35-37. Rahman *ad loc.* pp. 93 ff. noting that Aristotle's *Prior Analytics* i 34 forms the nucleus of Avicenna's argument, adds that the elaboration given the notion is "probably Avicennan." Avicenna was no doubt Ibn Tufayl's source for the notion that superior human minds need no teacher and need expend little effort in discovering the most profound metaphysical truths, but the tendency on which Avicenna's elaboration is based, the tendency to identify as divine the source of human words or thoughts too wise, too original, too uncontrolled, to be merely human is of course very old. See Homer *Odyssey* XXII 347; *Amos* iii 3-8; and the discussion of E. R. Dodds in *The Greeks and the Irrational*, Los Angeles, 1951, ch. I, cf. Philo of Byblos quoting "Zoroaster" *apud* Eusebius *Praeparatio Evangelica* I x 42a, and *op. cit.* II vi 72d. The same tendency lies at the root of the Islamic conception of the *Qur'ān* as a miracle and of Muhammad as an illiterate: The self-taught man has been taught by God. See Philo *On Flight and Finding* xxx 166; cf. Kindī's "Survey of the Works of Aristotle" ed. M. Guidi & R. Walzer in *Studi su al-Kindi*, Rome, 1940, ch. vi pp. 395 ff., discussed by Walzer in *Greek into Arabic* pp. 177-80; and Rāzī in his debate with Abū Hātim ar-Rāzī, in the ed. of Rāzī's writings by Paul Kraus, Cairo, 1939, pp. 297-303.

54. The works referred to are the *Jawāhir al-Qur'ān*; *Ma'ārif al-'Aqliyya wa-Asrār al-Ilāhiyya*; *Kitāb Madnūn as-Saghīr*; and *Kitāb al-Maqsad al-Asnā fī Sharh Asmā'i 'Llāhi'l-Husnā*.

55. Ghazālī's *Mishkāt al-Anwār* ed. A. Afifi, Cairo, 1964, tr. as *The Niche for Lights* by W. H. T. Gairdner, London, 1924 (reprinted Lahore, 1952), is a commentary on two Qur'ānic verses, XXIV 35 and 39: "God is the light of heaven and earth. The symbol of His light is a niche holding a lamp, enclosed by glass that gleams as though it were a star, fed from a blessed olive tree neither of the East nor of the West, the oil of which virtually gives light even when untouched by flame—light upon light. God leads to His light whom He will. He mints the symbols for mankind and He knows all things." "As for the faithless, their actions are like a mirage in the desert, taken by a thirsty man for water —until he reaches it and finds that it is nothing, finds God instead who settles his account, for God is swift to pay man's due; or like dark shadows on a shoreless sea, lost in wave on wave, covered by clouds, darkness upon darkness, so that if he holds out

his hand he can hardly see it. If God gives a man no light, then he will have no light." An analysis of the work will be found in W. H. T. Gairdner's article "Al-Ghazālī's *Mishkāt al-Anwār* and the Ghazālī Problem" *Der Islam* V 1914, pp. 121-53.

The interpretation Ghazālī gives these verses and an accompanying cluster of related texts and traditions is neo-Platonic— naturally enough in view of Muhammad's reliance on light imagery which a man of Ghazālī's background could only associate with emanation. The apparent inconsistency in Ghazālī's thought resultant from his difficulties in integrating much of neo-Platonic metaphysics into the Islamic world-view was observed not only by Ibn Tufayl, but also (and less charitably) by Ibn Rushd, see *Tahāfut at-Tahāfut*, last page of the First Discussion, ed. Bouyges pp. 116-7. The same difficulties have led several contemporary scholars (such as Jabre and Montgomery Watt) to cast doubt on the authenticity of the *Mishkāt*. This is not the proper place to vindicate that authenticity, or to expound the unities that underly the tensions in Ghazālī's thought, but it should be pointed out that neither Ibn Tufayl nor Ibn Rushd expresses a judgement that there might be grounds to doubt the authenticity of the work; and Ibn Tufayl, in fact, makes his more liberal reading of Ghazālī's Islamized neo-Platonism the basis of the light imagery and emanationist metaphysics that bind his book together. For Ghazali's doctrine of the *Muta'*, or 'first Hypostasis', which Ibn Tufayl graciously, but no doubt rightly, takes to be an attribute of God, see *Mishkāt* III ii 4, tr. Gairdner, pp. 171 ff., ed. Dunya, pp. 91 ff.

56. To Ghazālī blind faith in authority, complacent acceptance of dogma and ignoring of the intellectual problems of religion (*taqlīd*) was the cardinal temptation facing the potentially aware. For the masses, complacency is the natural state. For the man of ability it is a block which must be removed before the first stage of spiritual growth can be achieved. See *Munqidh* tr. Watt pp. 19, 21, 28; cf. *Mīzān al-'Amal* first and last pages. Contrast Augustine's acceptance of *auctoritas* as a positive good.

57. Those who cannot be satisfied by blind faith in situating themselves amidst the conflicting authorities of diverse religious traditions find themselves plunged into a sea from which "only a few" reach safety—for they are left without authority and must find their own way to land. The reports they bring back will be of help to those about to take the same momentous steps: See Ghazālī *Al-Munqidh min ad-Dalāl*, tr. Watt. p. 20.

58. Gauthier reads in this sentence an allusion to the miracu-

lous night journey of Muhammad to the heavens; see his French tr. p. 17 note 1. The phrase, however, is in fact an Arab proverb, meaning 'when the ordeal is over you'll be glad you did it.' The Arab traveller must press hard during the cool night hours, but his endurance will be rewarded when he sees how much ground he has covered at dawn. I am grateful to the late Samuel Stern of All Souls College, Oxford, for explaining this phrase to me.

59. "You will not find people who believe in God and the last day showing love for anyone who opposes God and His Prophet, not even for their fathers, sons, brothers, or kin. He has written faith in their hearts and has supported them with His spirit. He will bring them to gardens under which flow rivers and there they will live forever, pleasing God and He them, for they are God's side and who else but God's side will win?" *Qur'ān* LVIII 22. Ibn Tufayl applies the promise to the Aware, who are truly "of God's party."

60. Cf. Ghazālī, *Mīzān al-'Amal*, ed. Dunya, p. 195.

61. The reminder of the *Qur'ān* is more grim: "How many generations did I destroy before them, who were mightier than they and covered the earth! Did they find any refuge? There is a lesson in that for all who have a heart or ear to listen and to hear." I 36-37. The heart as the seat of understanding, not the physical organ, is meant, as Ibn Tufayl informs us p. *121*. To those "primed to understand" a tale like those of Muhammad or like that of Hayy Ibn Yaqzān will point the way, a word to the wise. For others, ignorance will be its own reward, see pp. *94* ff.

62. Ibn Tufayl lends an air of tradition to his story by attributing it to the founding fathers of Islam, the contemporaries and immediate followers of Muhammad. The sense in which the tale is traditional will prove to be metaphorical: it is meant to represent the core of truth that is guarded (and thus inevitably concealed) by the outer wrappings of traditional representation.

63. A gloss in the British Museum MS of *Hayy Ibn Yaqzān* refers the curious reader to Mas'ūdī's account of the Isle of Waqwaq, where women grow on trees. The reference may prove something less than helpful to a modern reader. Bear in mind that what we have here is a thought experiment. The object is to entertain the hypothesis that there exists a fully natural (and super-normal) human being. No parents and no society *in loco parentis* are to be assumed. For the notion of spontaneous generation cf. Aristotle *De Anima* ii 4, 415a 26; *History of Animals*:

1, 715b 25; cf. Avicenna *Najāt* II 6 i, tr. F. Rahman as *Avicenna's Psychology* London, 1952, p. 24 l. 10. Compare also the tale of Tages, the boy-god ploughed up by the Etruscans, Cicero *De Divinatione* II xxiii 50-51.

64. "True light is God. The term is applied to all else only metaphorically." This opening sentence of the *Mishkāt al-Anwār* lays the foundation for Ghazālī's notion that all reality and all realization stems from God—see *Mishkāt* ed. Afifi p. 54, tr. Gairdner pp. 100-102. Awareness particularly must stem from God: see Ghazālī's *Munqidh min ad-Dalāl* tr. Watt pp. 25-6. Ibn Tufayl accepts the notion and uses it to construct the imagined environment which will be most suited not only for the production of life, but also for the realization of a man's fullest potentials.

65. For the geographical zones and their habitability cf. Ibn Khaldūn *Muqaddima* I second prefatory discussion, tr. Franz Rosenthal, New York, 1958, pp. 93-109, and Rosenthal's copious notes *ad. loc.*

66. The perplexing claims put forward by Ibn Tufayl, as to the possibility of spontaneous generation, the temperateness of the equator and the "demonstrated" fact that the sun is not really hot do indeed require some further explanation. What Ibn Tufayl is attempting to achieve is a reconciliation of the two dominant philosophical alternatives that presented themselves to his world, materialism as represented by the "naturalists" and neo-Platonism, as taught by the *Falāsifa*. (see Ghazali *Munqidh* tr. Watt pp. 30-32 for descriptions of these two "kinds of seekers.") When these two positions have been reconciled, the main task of relating philosophy to traditional Islam, thus delineating a specifically "oriental" philosophy can be undertaken.

Ibn Tufayl attacks the preliminary problem head on: the materialists and many even of their well-meaning Platonist opponents are mistaken about optics. This simple failing in physical theory has blinded them to the fundamental metaphysical fact about the Universe, the fact of emanation. Had the errant philosophers understood that light travels by the non-physical means of radiation (cf. the Plotinian—*Enneads* II 8—optics of Ghazālī's *Kitāb Madnūn as-Saghīr*), had they seen—as Fārābī failed to see (*Fī 'Aql* ed. Bouyges no. 33)—that "receptivity" to light was based not on transparency, but on reflectivity, the whole secret of being might have been opened to them. They might, then, have seen that just as warmth must come only from what is not itself hot, by a medium which transcends the physical, so all perfections (and equilibrium is, of course, a prime perfection), all forms, and even potentials (which are no more than a special class of forms) must come from above, from a source which gives being to all that is, since it is itself overflowing with being. In short, they would have seen the sun as symbol of the Form Giver and Active Intellect (cf. *Najāt* II 6 xvi and *De Anima* iii 5) by whom all things are perfected, including men—who to the extent that they "absorb" (and redistribute) the light may be once again received to the fuller being from which they have sprung.

Living as he does in an age of optimism, and holding as he does a profound faith in the power of truth to make itself known, the transmissibility of his familiar message, Ibn Tufayl retains the hope that his self-conscious paradox will jolt the reader into recognition of a truth which he believes to be literally too manifest, too true to be expressed in simple words.

For Avicenna's "proof," see his "Treatise on Love" vii, ed. Mehren pp. 12 ff.; cf. *Najāt* II 6 xv, tr. F. Rahman, p. 67.

67. Traditionally in Islam, a young girl's nearest male relative—father, brother, or cousin—has the right of "guardian" to approve her husband. The cousin, in addition, has a "right of first refusal" of her for himself, which is still often demanded in Islamic countries.

68. *Yaqzān*, that is "wide awake," is in the more traditional version of the story the name of the human father of Hayy. The father in the philosophical version would seem to be God. Ibn Tufayl seems to be making mild fun at the expense of fundamentalists who must assign a concrete correlative to everything—be it the throne of God or the scales of justice on the Judgment Day: Even consciousness must be represented, in tradition, by a concrete analogue. To the philosopher, by way of contrast, true concreteness is approached only as commonplace reality is left behind. For Avicenna's intension by the name Hayy Ibn Yaqzān, cf. Aristotle *Prior Analytics* 38A 41.

69. Ibn Tufayl is strongly opposed to any antinomian tendencies that might be inherent in the notion of a higher truth. The superior human being accepts more obligations than his inferiors, not fewer; see pp. *145-146*, cf. pp. *136-138*. The obligations of positive religion are taken for granted by the aware, not rejected: p. *147*.

70. Islam is most emphatic in the demand that babies be nursed and not neglected. See p. *33* and note *ad loc.*

71. "Was there ever a time when man was nothing, a thing

without a name? I it was who created man from a drop of semen and to try him gave him eyes and ears. . ." Thus God speaks in the *Qur'ān* of the act of creation, LXXVI 1-2.

72.   Taking as his point of departure *Qur'ān* XV 28-29, XXXII 6-9, XXXVIII 71-72, which describe the fashioning and smoothing of man from a lump of clay, Ghazālī in the *Kitāb Madnūn as-Saghīr* interprets the "smoothing" as the establishment of proper equilibrium, the stability necessary for life and the reception of a soul. It becomes apparent on pp. 27-28 that Ibn Tufayl accepts the same interpretation (allowing Hayy's fairy-tale mother to use the words in their traditional sense) and applies it to Hayy, thus putting him in the place of Adam as the archetype of mankind.

73.   *Aslamtuhu*—I entrust him, the verb is of the same root from which *Islām*, meaning literally surrender, is derived. In *Ihyā' 'Ulūm ad-Dīn* XXXV Ghazālī designates the highest phase of faith as total trust (*tawakkul*).

74.   For the topos of the exposed or castaway infant cf. Lucretius *De Rerum Natura* V 222-232; Plutarch *Isis and Osiris* xv 357; and Hartmann von Aue (ca. 1165-1250) *Gregorius von Stein*, which forms the basis of Thomas Mann's *Holy Sinner*: cf. esp. pp. 25, 69, 98, 129 of the English translation of Mann's version.

75.   The phrase is borrowed from Muhammad's description of the resting place of the "sleepers" (identified with the seven sleepers of Ephesus.) These young men withdrew, according to the *Qur'ān*, from the society of men who worshipped anything other than the One God. They slept many years in a cave, "you might have seen the rising sun slanting off their cave on the right and going down behind them on the left when it set. . ." XVIII 16. The following verse contains the only Qur'ānic occurrence of the root of *Yaqzān*, "You might have thought them awake, but they were asleep. . ." Ibn Tufayl alludes to the story as a paradigm case of divine providence which he is eager to merge with the bounty of nature. In the "traditional" version of the Hayy Ibn Yaqzān story a mother prays for God's special providence on her child. In the philosophical version, God's "general" providence, the outflowing of his generosity, fills the role of mother. In the Qur'ānic story, reference to which Ibn Tufayl here grafts into his own traditional version, the natural and providential spheres merge. Is this not, Ibn Tufayl is asking, the true meaning of providence: the universal outpouring of God's love?

76.   In one MS a pious reader has added "It had strayed from the fold and been carried off by an eagle."

77.   Traditional religion will, of course, stoutly deny that the

act of creation has come about by itself. Only through God were man and the Universe created. The traditionally minded fail to recognize, just as do the materialists, that nothing *can* "happen by itself." The mythic version of man's origins is as inadequate an account of the almost entirely ineffable truth as is the naturalist account. Only the philosophical mystic confronts the true meaning of the creative act by his understanding of the motive (generosity) and the means (the declension of being) of emanation.

78. Avicenna's notion that equilibrium is a necessity if life is to persist is expounded at *Najāt* II 6 xv, tr. Rahman p. 67; cf. Aristotle *On Generation and Destruction* II 8; and contrast Lucretius *De Rerum Natura* I 770-781, II 583. In the *Madnūn*, as we have seen, Ghazālī ceded the point, despite the fact that certain radical occasionalists of the *Kalām* denied the need for any special prerequisites of life. Ghazālī makes the same allowance in *Tahāfut al-Falāsifa* XVII Bouyges, 2nd ed., p. 204; cf. p. 25 and my notes *ad loc.*

79. Another allusion to *Qur'ān* XV 28-29, XXXII 6-9, XXXVIII 71-72, (cf. XVII 87, XLII 52), and Ghazālī's interpretation in the *Madnūn as-Saghīr*. When man had been 'smoothed', according to Muhammad, God breathed into him of His spirit. Following Avicenna *Najāt* II 6 xii, xv, tr. Rahman pp. 56-57, 67, Ghazālī interprets the verses as assigning an emanative origin to the soul. The composition of the elements into a fitting equilibrium is, as Ibn Sīnā, Ghazālī and Ibn Tufayl agree, a necessary but insufficient condition for the existence of a soul. The soul is Platonic in its mode of existence, and a neo-Platonic origin must be assigned to it—unless the absurdity is to be accepted of identifying the soul with some merely chemical or physiological function which cannot possibly simulate its originative and arbitrational action (cf. Avicenna *Shifā'*, *Fī Nafs* I.) Support may be drawn for this from Aristotle's arguments for the immortality and external origin of the mind; but Avicenna, Ghazālī, and Ibn Tufayl apply these considerations to the soul at large, and all assign a temporal origin to the soul—despite p. *130*, where Ibn Tufayl qualifies this article of his creed.

80. The divine origin of the human soul is a fundamental dogma of neo-Platonism. Ibn Tufayl rejects the notion that the soul is identical with God, but he rejects with equal vehemence the notion that it is anything else: see pp. *127-128*. His notion, borrowed from Avicenna, is that God's being is projected forth and mirrored in creation. Thus he accepts Hallāj's emanationist inter-

pretation of *Genesis* i 26, having cleansed that reading of its in-carnationist overtones. See R. A. Nicholson *The Mystics of Islam*, London, 1963, p. 150 (first edition 1914). For an elegant statement of the neo-Platonic doctrine on the origin of the soul, see Andrew Marvell's poem "The Drop of Dew." See Plotinus *Enneads* V iv 2, vii 17; Proclus' Commentary on Plato's *Timaeus* I 360.28; cf. Cleanthes' "Hymn to Zeus." Avicenna develops the analogy of soul with light at *Najāt* II 6 xv, tr. Rahman p. 67, drawing on Philoponous' *De Anima* 196.15: see Rahman's note *ad loc.*

81. In prophecy, and to a lesser degree in the awakening of the individual human being to the truth, the purpose of creation is fulfilled, the cycle is completed and fallen being, which has been cast forth into quasi-independence, returns to its Creator, enlightened and enriched. Thus the burning glass in which the rays of divine light are focused to such intensity that other bodies are set on fire when placed before it is an apt symbol for the prophet who enlightens not only himself but others and so contributes to their return to the Fountain of their being.

82. God's word (*logos, amr*), identified with his attribute of will or wisdom by monotheists, is interposed by members of Judaeo-Christian-Islamic tradition as one of many measures to protect the divine transcendence. It serves as medium between the finite and infinite worlds for Philo, Origen, Augustine, and many others. For Muslims the word is the creative command and moral imperative, the "promise and the threat" which animate the cosmic drama. Cf. *Qur'ān* XVI 10 and the Islamic version of the neo-Platonic "Theology of Aristotle" (relevant portions of which have been published by S. M. Stern in his article "Ibn Hasdai's neo-Platonist" *Oriens* XIII-XIV 1961, pp. 58-120.) God's word of command is implicitly obeyed by the entire cosmos: Kindī "An Explanation of the Prostration of the Outermost Celestial Body and its Obedience to God" *Kindī's Philosophical Writings* ed. Abu Rida, Cairo, 1950, pp. 244-262; and Ghazālī *Ma'ārij al-Quds*, Cairo, 1927, pp. 203-205. For Ghazālī, as for Ibn Tufayl and other radical monotheist thinkers, the word plays the role of a hypostasis yet enjoys no more ontic status than an attribute. It thus represents no threat to the divine unity.

83. The three organs embryologically described here are the heart, brain (with its anterior, middle and posterior lobes) and liver. Each organ is conceived to exist for the sake of the function it performs (in accordance with Aristotle *The Parts of Animals* II 1, 646a 25 ff., IV 10, 687a 7 ff.); and the body as a whole

is deemed to be caused by—we might prefer to say "organized by"—the soul: See Aristotle *De Anima* 415b. Consciousness, which lies in the spirit (that is the soul) and to which the brain is imagined to "report," is not reduced by Ibn Tufayl to an organic function, but remains the irreducible subject of all experience. See Avicenna *Najāt* II 6 xv, tr. Rahman, pp. 64 ff. and Rahman's discussion in his introduction p. 18 and notes pp. 111-114, and 103, where numerous references are cited and a long and highly relevant passage from Philoponous' *De Anima* is translated. By assigning consciousness to an independent *I*, Ibn Tufayl shows his allegiance to the Avicennan school of thought which defended the existence of a soul as ego and argued from the role of soul as subject of experience to its status as a substance.

84.   In assigning centrality and temporal primacy to the heart, Ibn Tufayl follows Avicenna *Najāt* II 6 xv, tr. Rahman p. 66 ll. 30 ff. and Aristotle *On the Parts of Animals* iii 4, 665b - 666a, *On the Generation of Animals* ii 4, 738b, who depart, largely for scientific reasons, from Plato's *Timaeus* (which assigns the prime position to the brain).   Ibn Tufayl's motivation for the shift may well be strengthened by his rejection of sterile intellectualism, but he makes it quite clear that when he speaks of the heart in Ghazālī's sense he means not the physical organ, but the seat of the understanding: see p. *121*.

Ibn Tufayl's doctrine of the two primitive drives of attraction and rejection is based on Avicenna *Najāt* II 6 ii, tr. Rahman, p. 24 1. 4; and Aristotle *De Anima* iii 9, 432b 16. The doctrine had become a prime consideration in Stoic ethics, since values were conceived to be determined by these primitive drives; cf. p. *46* and my note *ad loc.*

The hierarchy of bodily organs is described at length by Avicenna, *Najāt* II 6 vi, tr. Rahman, pp. 37-38; cf. Fārābī *Arā' Ahlu-l-Madīnatu-l-Fādilah* "Beliefs of the Inhabitants of the Ideal State" x-xi. All members of the bodily hierarchy are subordinate to the soul, cf. p. *45*. For the relation of soul to body as one of caring for or ruling over see Aristotle *De Anima* II 4, 415; Lucretius *De Rerum Natura* III 323-416; Plotinus *Enneads* IV 8, 3.26; and of course Plato's *Republic*.

85.   The philosophers follow the materialists in paying a great deal of attention to the material and dispositional requisites of life (cf. A. I. Oparin *The Origin of Life* tr. S. Morgulis, New York, 1953, first Russian edition, 1936). Unlike their atheist colleagues however, the philosophers recognize that behind every

material disposition, as behind every other form, there lies a Cause who not only brings to fulfillment but also makes possible the realization of potential; cf. pp. *61, 73-74*; Ash'arī *Kitāb al-Luma'* ed. and tr. R. J. McCarthy in *The Theology of Al-Ash'arī,* Beirut, 1953, art. 3.

86. Traditional religion relies on the timeless emotional impact of a simple story; rational religion, on the more fallible support of apparent scientific accuracy and logical air-tightness. But beyond their differences in method, which give rise to apparently conflicting versions of the story of (man's) creation, both types of religion have fundamentally the same object: bringing men into an appropriate relationship with God, so both see fundamentally the same world: a world in which man is the creature (with whatever implications are deemed appropriate) of his Creator. It is this world which the two rival sorts of religion, speaking in their different languages, will attempt to render visible.

87. "Mothers shall nurse their children two full years for those who desire to complete their nursing. . ." *Qur'ān* II 233.

88. Hayy's mimetic ability comes naturally. Here it forms the basis for his relationship with the environment. As he develops, his mimesis will become more sophisticated, allowing him to relate to a more extended, super-sensible milieu. See pp. *105-120.*

89. Porphyry uses the specialization and differentiation of animal cries as argument for the rationality of beasts: *On Abstinence from Animal Food* III 3-4, tr. Thomas Taylor, London, 1965, pp. 110-3 (first edition London, 1823, pp. 94-8). From the limitation and stereotyped character of such signals, the opposite conclusion would seem to follow.

90. The "internal perception" does not require the presence of its object as does the external, and may "represent" to itself "intensions" which are not strictly speaking perceptible, such as harm or benefit, trend, tendency, and effect. The sheep may perceive (visually) only a blur of grey on the brink of the ridge, but instinct or experience teaches it to recognize this as a wolf and fear it as a danger. The drives by which the sheep shuns what is harmful and seeks what is beneficial are inherent in all forms of life. Thus the basis from which value judgements will arise is implanted from the outset. Cf. Avicenna *Najāt* II 6 iii, vii, tr. Rahman pp. 30, 39. See p. *46.*

91. As an animal, man is hopelessly inadequate, but the same uniqueness which now makes Hayy outlandish and inept por-

tends the discovery of his true kin. When that discovery is made even his present "deformity" will be recognized as beauty; see pp. *47, 104-105.*

92.   Awareness, discernment, self-consciousness reach a plateau at the seventh year: see Ghazālī *Munqidh* tr. Watt pp. 63-64. The notion that man's life is divided into seven-year stages is derived from Galen and goes back ultimately to the Pythagorean attempt to marshal experience by the imposition of rule and measure. Thinking of this ilk survives in Shakespeare's characterization of "the seven ages of man" and, for example, in the theories of Eric Erikson on the stages of human development. Ibn Tufayl's intention in organizing the phases of Hayy's growth according to such a scheme would seem to be to allow each phase of the human dialectic to be seen and judged worthy in its own terms before it is found wanting and transcended.

93.   To primitive man in the state of nature, generation and decay are ever present reminders of mortality. Nothing endures, all things change and die. Cf. Kindī "Essay on How to Banish Sorrow" ed. with Italian tr. H. Ritter, R. Walzer as "Uno Scritto inedito di al-Kindi" *Studi su al Kindi* II Rome, 1938. The parataxis of this with the following paragraph is carefully planned.

94.   For a similar account of man's need for clothing, see pseudo-Jāhiz *Kitāb al-'Ibār* discussed by H. A. R. Gibb in "The Argument from Design" *Goldziher Memorial Volume* I p. 157.

95.   Like Muhammad who never knew his father and lost his mother before he was seven, Hayy must face death at an early age. His grief is deep and genuine but his response is practical. His cry to his dead doe-mother is reminiscent of the ancient custom of "calling" a corpse to make sure that it is truly dead, so touchingly formalized in Catullus' poem for his dead brother.

96.   At his bourgeois, materialist stage, Hayy is incapable of assessing this new sort of difficulty: death does not respond to the prying fingers of the child; the life that has departed is not a spirit or a liquid to be trapped by a child's hands. Even for the scientist (and Hayy is about to become a scientist) life will not stand still, but slips quickly between man's fingers and is gone. For Hayy to learn this will take many years; see pp. 93 ff.

97.   Sight was the model capacity: it had a function carried out by an organ fitted with appropriate dispositions; when the organ was disabled or blocked or when the dispositions were checked by opposing forces, no functioning could take place. Life how-

ever is not a capacity and depends not on an organ, but on a system. Hayy's naive view of things is incapable of accounting for the change that has occurred; and even the materialistic conception which he will develop to account for the difference between life and death will prove to be only a partial understanding of the truth, for the material system of the body, *qua* system, that is *qua* alive, must be dependent on some organizing force that is more than merely material. Cf. the psychological portion of Avicenna's *Shifā'*, ed. F. Rahman ch. I.

98. The three body cavities, according to Plato *Timaeus* 69-71, house the "cerebral", "visceral", and passional aspects of the soul. Ibn Tufayl, as we have seen, differs with Plato in that he assigns primacy to the heart, but follows him in stressing that the soul is not of the body, but from God.

99. The ever-present heartbeat and the pounding of the heart in times of stress are taken to be evidence that the heart is the seat of the spirit—for Hayy has not yet learned (thus recapitulating the inadequacies of Stoic and Epicurean materialism) that the soul has no fixed abode. For the central location and protected position of the heart cf. pseudo-Jāhiz *Kitāb al-'Ibār* discussed in H. A. R. Gibb "The argument from design" *Goldziher Memorial Volume* I p. 157. See Lucretius *De Rerum Natura* III 137-146 for the argument; cf. Cicero *Tusculan Disputations* I ix 19.

100. Alexander of Aphrodisias knew that an organism might survive (for a short time!) without its head. Ibn Rushd writes "I myself have seen a ram with head cut off run this way and that again and again." Hayy presumably gained his knowledge on this point empirically as well. He does not seem to know, as did Alexander, that the heart too may be dispensed with for a time. Ibn Sīnā at the close of the first chapter of the psychology in the *Shifā'* offers an argument for the substantiality of the soul which depends on the conceivability of consciousness in a void in the absence of all bodily organs and of all sensory experience. The writing of *Hayy Ibn Yaqzān* seems to have been, in large measure, Ibn Tufayl's response to the challenge of Avicenna's thought experiment, a response which would construct a fuller thought experiment which would allow man to contemplate himself as truly in a vacuum as was possible; cf. pp. *103-104.*

101. Hayy's actions now are deliberate and purposive. No longer a frightened and dependent child, he recapitulates human history in his probing efforts to alleviate suffering and battle

against death. The contributions of the Arabic-speaking world to the study of anatomy and the practice of medicine are listed in George Sarton's work on the history of science.

102. To philosophers since Plato the turning toward the soul had meant a turning away from the body. Hayy's turning from the outward world to the soul is comparable to the great turning point in human history at which it was discovered that the proper study of mankind is man. Hayy does not yet know the nature of the soul. He sees it (see p. 49), in Stoic fashion, as a fiery material responsible for the acting of the body as a living percipient body. He knows its work, but not its ontic status. See the psychological portion of Avicenna's *Shifā'* ch. I, ed. F. Rahman, for a discussion of the soul as entelechy and as substance. For a recent view of the soul as entelechy (although the associations of the term are eschewed) see Edmund W. Sinnot *The Biology of Spirit*, New York, 1955.

103. For the notion that the body is the tool of the soul, see Avicenna *Najāt* II 6 xii, tr. Rahman, p. 57, based on Aristotle *De Anima* ii 4, 415b 18 ff, conflated with the idea that the soul is, like God, an intelligent workman; cf. pp. 29-30.

104. The growth of Hayy's awareness has brought him from a primitive consciousness of self to an awareness of other subjectivities, other selves; and parallel with the analogy which gives him knowledge of the existence of other sentient beings is an implicit categorical imperative which allows him to extrapolate morally from self, to other, to the universe at large. His instinctive, animal sense of his own welfare is now objectified, universalized. Value judgments are now possible, and even the sense of self and individual welfare from which the new values are extrapolated will be remolded by Hayy's transference to the universal moral sphere.

As for the raven, a similar origin for the growth of moral sentiments is assigned in the Qur'ānic version of the Cain and Abel story, only there the death involves sin and the awakening of self-judgement involves repentance: "His spirit pressed him to the killing of his brother and he killed him and so was lost. But God sent a raven that scratched at the earth to show him how to hide his brother's wretched corpse. And he said 'Misery! that I cannot be like that raven and hide the naked body of my brother.' It was then he entered the numbers of the repentant." *Qur'ān* V 33-4. Cf. Porphyry *On Abstinence from Animal Food* IV 9: the hawk "sorrows for man, mourns over his dead body and scatters earth on his eyes. . ." See also pseudo-Jāhiz *Kitāb al-*

'*Ibār* discussed in H. A. R. Gibb "The Argument from Design" *Goldziher Memorial Volume* I p. 157.

105. Hayy's search for himself finds its earliest expression in a search for his like. Is man an aberrant type or does he fit in somehow in the world in which he finds himself? The answer, in terms of Islamic neo-Platonism, is that he only half fits in. The half of Hayy that he has yet to discover belongs to another world, more real than this. Cf. pp. *36, 104, 105.*

106. Hayy's long study of his little world is meant to represent man's long involvement with the study of nature. Like the early naturalists (*physikoi*), Hayy believes that the Universe is confined within his immediate material surroundings. Primitive man, in the happy ignorance of his naive realism, is blissfully alone to discover for himself the wonders of nature. Only when he reaches an awareness of the *other* world does Hayy discover other souls and realize that throughout his silent probings into nature he was not alone but was in fact being taught by the gentlest and most retiring of teachers. Man's ignorance before the greater world beyond the world of nature is compared by Kindī, "On How to Banish Sorrow" xii, to the trepidation of an infant about to be born.

107. For the discovery of fire see Lucretius *De Rerum Natura* V 1090-1104, which, as Bailey points out in his notes *ad loc.* may be based on Democritus' lost essay on Fire; cf. Porphyry *On Abstinence from Animal Food* I 13. See also Ghazālī's remarks *Munqidh*, tr. Watt p. 79.

108. Capacity, that is potentiality, is apparent to the natural man. Neither a radical, "sense-data" empiricism nor a Megarian over-interpretation of the principle of the excluded middle is allowed to obscure this elementary given. Majid Fakhry's study *Islamic Occasionalism and its Critique by Averroes and Aquinas*, London, 1958, and Ash'arī's *Maqālāt al-Islāmiyyīn* ed. H. Ritter, Wiesbaden, 1963 (first edition, Istanbul, 1929-30) give much information on Islamic denials of potentiality. See also S. van den Bergh's notes 50.2 and 52.6 for numerous references and a brisk critique of Aristotle's compromised position on the question; cf. p. *93* and my note 164.

109. Hayy seems here to recapitulate the fire-worship of the ancients and to persevere in two of its vestiges: the Stoic belief that the matter of the soul is fire and the Aristotelian awe at the splendor of the heavens. In identifying his soul-substance with the substance of the stars, Hayy primitively anticipates his discovery of the soul's immateriality and incorruptibility; cf. pp.

100-102. For the Stoics soul is to body as God is to the world. The Stoic *deus sive natura* is "an artistically working fire going on its way to create", as Diogenes Laertius puts it, *Lives of the Philosophers* VII 156. Thus Cleanthes argues: "It is a law of Nature that all things capable of nurture and growth contain within them a supply of heat, without which their nurture and growth would not be possible: for everything of a hot, fiery nature supplies its own source of motion and activity; but that which is nourished and grows possess a definite and uniform motion. . . From this it must be inferred that this element of heat possesses in itself a vital force that pervades the whole world." *apud* Cicero *De Natura Deorum* II 23-28. See Sambursky, *Physics of the Stoics*, London, 1959, pp. 3-4, for discussion of these doctrines. Aristotle's emphasis on the fact that biological growth occurs only in set proportions (see p. 67 and note) was intended largely to show the impossibility of attributing life to fire. As Sambursky notes, *loc. cit.*, man's innate body heat was first scientifically observed by Hippocrates—see Galen *De Nat. Fac.* I ix 25, II iv 89.

110. The vital or "animal" spirit is the forerunner of the non-physical soul. It is the source of voluntary motion and sensation in animals, see e.g. Galen *On The Motion of the Muscles.*

111. The unity of a living being is organic, derived from the subordination of all the parts to a common end. By neo-Platonic standards the source of unity is the source of identity and existence; thus the "life" of the organism, that is the vital spirit, must give being to the body and must itself participate in a higher order of being than the body in order to pass along such a gift. Hayy has not yet discovered this higher order of being, but the groundwork in natural philosophy which will allow him to discover it is being laid.

112. An experimenter from the outset, Hayy uses a simple but elegant control in duplicating the work of Herophilus and Erasistratus, the third-century B.C.E. physicians who discovered (respectively) the gross anatomy and function of the nerves.

113. For the compartments of the brain (cf. pp. 29-30) and their functions: sense coordination and image representation in the forebrain, recombining imagination and intention evaluation in the midbrain, and memory-association in the rear, see Avicenna *Najāt* II 6 iii, tr. Rahman pp. 30-31.

114. As the next phrase shows, Hayy's conclusion as to the nature of death, while valid within its system of reference, is only a half truth. Hayy will not know the true nature of death until

he has learned the true nature of life and of the soul which gives life.

115. The fullest treatment of the crafts, arts, industries and sciences known and practiced in medieval Islamic society is that of Ibn Khaldūn *Muqaddima* ch. V-VI. Hayy lacks only a surrounding society to make him a full-fledged bourgeois. For a Robinson Crusoe this level of attainment might be enough; for Hayy it is a point of departure. I speak here only of the well known Robinson Crusoe (but cf. the mystic sequel: *The Farther Adventures of Robinson Crusoe* and *Serious Reflections During the Life and Surprising Adventures of Robinson Crusoe*. For the historical nexus between the thought of Defoe and that of Ibn Tufayl, see Pastore, *The Idea of Robinson Crusoe*.)

116. Hayy's "conclusion", be it observed, is *not* an inference drawn from his "survey" of reality, but a proposal for using the concepts of 'many', 'one', 'some', and 'different': Two things are really one to the extent that they are "the same as" i.e., like each other. This identification of arithmetic (same thing as) with taxonomic (same sort as) unity, a crucial premise of neo-Platonism, is Hayy's first step into metaphysics. Cf. R. G. Collingwood *Autobiography*, London, 1964, p. 40 (first edition, 1939).

117. In testing the hypothesis that species are discrete, the variation among members will not, of course, be insignificant. It was by his painstaking measurements of the range of deviation from a norm that Darwin was able to show how one species of finch might merge through a nearly continuous series of varieties into another. What is significant to Ibn Tufayl is the unity of all being, achieved here not by observation of a continuum, but by postulation of an identity in form. That identity of kind should demand arithmetic identity seems to me a most perplexing notion, but the implementation of such a notion surely does not demand irreverence toward divergent types. These too are "alike in kind." By now, we would hope, science has enough experience behind it to allow it to recognize that no divergence from expected results should be hastily dismissed as "negligible." Yet even today too much reliance is placed on "experimental error", "artifact", and other such obfuscations of anomalies that otherwise might be confronted and marshalled in a new and clearer pattern.

118. ". . .Things are called one in another sense because their substratum does not differ in kind; it does not differ in the case of things whose kind is indivisible to sense. The substratum meant is either the nearest to or farthest from the final state. For

on the one hand wine is said to be one and water is said to be one, *qua* indivisible in kind; and, on the other hand, *all* juices, e.g. oil and wine, are said to be one, and so are all things that can be melted, because the ultimate substratum of all is the same; for all of these are water or air." Aristotle *Metaphysics* Delta 6, 101a 17 ff., tr. W. D. Ross. Unity is ascribed to things whose matter is indivisible or potentially indivisible, *only in a certain sense*, as Aristotle points out. Given the interchangeability of elements, this type of unity can be extended to the whole physical world—but since this is unity only in a certain sense (or, we might say, only in a manner of speaking) it cannot form the metaphysical basis of the unity of all in all, the realization of which is the goal of Hayy's thinking. This Ibn Tufayl recognizes. It is only when matter, the basis of individuation, is abstracted away, leaving behind the forms in terms of which this unity is predicated, that absolute unity can be seen. Cf. pp. *100, 105, 124.*

119. Abstracting the essence from the matter, which is responsible for all generic particularization, Hayy now sees the arithmetic unity of all animal life: Such differences as remain, the specific differences, are due to the variation in extent of penetration by God's "light", which in turn depends on the relative adequacy or inadequacy of the recipient.

120. "Nature proceeds little by little from things lifeless to animal life in such a way that it is impossible to determine the exact line of demarcation, nor on which side an intermediate form should lie. Thus, next after lifeless things in the upward scale comes the plant, and of plants one will differ from another as to the amount of life apparent; and in a word, the whole genus of plants, while devoid of life as compared with an animal, is endowed with life as compared with other corporeal entities. Indeed as we just remarked, there is observed in plants a continuous scale of ascent towards the animal. . ." Aristotle, *History of Animals* VIII 1, 588b 4 ff. For an interpretation of one statement of the Islamic doctrine of the continuity of all forms of life, and of living and non-living being, see S. H. Nasr, *An Introduction to Islamic Cosmological Doctrines*, Cambridge, Massachusetts, 1964, pp. 89 ff.

121. The ultimate step in "uniting" all members of the natural world is the realization that the differing qualities of the elements may themselves be erased in a higher unity of the sort mentioned by Aristotle, the unity of things that are interchangeable; cf. pp. *57-59, 69*, and notes *ad loc.* Aristotle teaches the

interchangeability of the elements in *On Generation and Corruption* II 4-6, but cf. *De Caelo* III 5, where Aristotle shows that the elements cannot be reduced to one: interchangeable things are one only "in a sense." The compounding of form with matter demands particularization. For Hayy then, the unity he has seen thus far must remain equivocal until matter itself has been washed away by the mind.

122. Hayy attempts again to distill the unity of being, purify it from the residues of plurality remaining from his previous attempt. But, not knowing the non-physical world, he fails again. When he has reasoned his way to that world he will see clearly that forms are in fact imparted extrinsically, and thus the differences in behavior and appearance observable among the denizens of the natural world are indeed subsumable in a "higher unity." The external origin of all forms, even the most primitive, is a cardinal doctrine of neo-Platonism. It becomes for the Ash'arite school (see Ash'arī, *Kitāb al-Luma'* in McCarthy, *The Theology of Al-Ash'arī*, Beirut, 1953, art. 3 ff.; Ghazālī, *Kitāb Madnūn as-Saghīr* and *Ihyā' 'Ulūm ad-Dīn* XXXV) the basis of an interpretation of the notions of creation and providence which incorporates the traditional doctrines within a far larger and more sophisticated framework. It is such a doctrine which Ibn Tufayl represents.

123. Being non-organic, all these substances have no choice in their action but must follow the one course nature leaves open to them. For Ghazālī (*Tahāfut al-Falāsifa* XVII 4, Bouyges, second edition, p. 196) inanimate being is incapable of acting in its own right—a notion essential to Ibn Tufayl's radical monotheist project of "Uniting all being," since this doctrine implies the externality of all non-organic functions.

124. Hayy seeks and fails to find some form of matter that would, like Aristotle's "fifth substance", be exempt from rising and falling. Were he to succeed, he would prove to have discovered an almost immaterial material, not subject to the ordinary modes of change. Such a body, as Ibn Tufayl points out, would be simplex, thus uncreated and indestructible. For Aristotle the matter of the heavens, which neither rises nor falls but eternally revolves, satisfied this description, see *De Caelo* I 2-4, 10-12; for Hayy Ibn Yaqzān, this degree of self-sufficiency will not be found until he discovers his own spirit, and recognizes the likeness of his soul to the inviolable substances in the sky; see pp. *103-104*.

125. By the Aristotelian gravitation-levitation theory, a body

may exert either a centrifugal or a centripetal force with respect
to the center of the Universe. If these forces were essential,
reasons Ibn Tufayl, both would be found in all bodies at all
times. The argument falsely assumes that it is gravitation and
levitation which would be essential, whereas Aristotle would argue that what is essential is the capacity (in all matter) of exert-
ing one or the other of these forces. The fact that man is
uniquely and, as we might argue, essentially the laughing and crying animal does not imply that all men are always both laughing and crying. The capacity is what is essential.

By showing that gravitational forces are exerted between all
masses and dispensing with the notion of levitation, Newtonian
physics destroys the basis of Ibn Tufayl's argument. It does not,
however, succeed in finding a totally simple material substance,
for this would have *no* characteristics. Simplicity, as Ibn Tufayl
emphasizes, belongs only to the immaterial.

126.   Hayy now perceives the whole natural Universe, the only
world he has known up to now, as composed in fact of constitu-
ents from two different worlds. Without the infusion of form
from a higher unseen realm, the natural world would have no
characteristics at all, it would be prime matter, as far below being as God is above it. For the immateriality of the objects of
reason, see Avicenna *Najāt* II 6 v, ed. Rahman, p. 33.

127.   The delicate connection of souls to forms which is the
mainspring and pivot point of any system of Platonic philosophy
has now been set in place: The soul is not a physical entity, but
akin to the immortal forms, by virtue of its primitive role as
entelechy of the body. Consciousness evolves from the animal
needs of the organism and is thus legitimately grouped with the
other "functions" of a unified soul.

128.   Hayy's quest is reminiscent of the search of the pre-So-
cratics for a most primitive material, out of which all being is composed. If knowing what a thing is made of means understanding
what it is, then knowing the ultimate form of matter will afford
the ultimate explanation, open the door to an understanding of
all being. Hayy's awakening to the fact that there is no ultimate form of matter, that material being is by its very nature
perpetually qualified, allows him to see that matter itself cannot
be ultimate, that beyond it there must be some mode of being
that is at once simpler and fairer, closer to existence in an unqualified sense.

129.   For the earliest Arab philosophical thinkers, clay or mud
was paradigmatic of the most primitive matter. Thus Kindī de-

fines 'element' as the 'clay of all clay', "On the Definitions and Formulas of Things" in Kindī's *Philosophical Writings*, ed. Abu Rida, Cairo, 1950, p. 166.

130. Doubt, alienation, the loneliness of the thinker play the role in Ghazālī's *Munqidh* that sin plays in Bunyan's *Pilgrim's Progress*. Just as his awakening to the depths of his sinfulness is what starts Christian out on his quest for salvation, so the confrontation of doubt and the depths of religious despair, the fear of losing God, starts Ghazālī on his search for the foundation of religious faith. Ibn Tufayl's hero follows the same pattern; and, like Ghazālī, Hayy wrings an advantage from his setback, finding firmer footing for his metaphysics in the elementary problems on which he is thrown back.

131. If all that is requires a cause, the world too must have one. The difficulty with this most ancient argument for the existence of God is that every member of the Aristotelian Universe, at least, already *has* a cause, its natural cause. Thus, as Ghazālī is quick to point out, "the philosophers" are unable to prove the existence of God since they are unable to give any concrete meaning to their claim that God is cause of the Universe, without retracting their dogma of its eternity; see *Tahāfut al-Falāsifa* III, IV, X. "Those philosophers who came closest to the truth," Ghazālī writes, recognized the active role of God as giver of all forms, *ibid.* XVII. Bouyges, 2nd ed. p. 197, but failed to see that matter too is wholly subject to God's sway, *ibid.* p. 200; cf. *Munqidh* tr. Watt, p. 37. True to his promise (p. *18*), Ibn Tufayl attempts to reconcile the eternalism of Avicenna with the creationism of Ghazālī: What God "creates" are the forms—but matter too is form, to the extent that it has positive existence.

132. The assimilation of all "acts" to natural behavior allows Hayy mentally to reach the meaning of the words of this *hadīth qudsī*, non-Qur'ānic revelation to Muhammad, which vividly portrays not only man's dependence on his Maker (We are, as Ghazālī urges, no more than puppets on His string), but also, in a way God's need or want of man—for without particularization, the act of creation, God might see, perhaps, but never through eyes.

133. In the approved fashion of Sūfī (and more conservative) radical monotheists Ibn Tufayl broadens the sense of *Qur'ān* VIII 17 (where Muhammad attributes the victory of the Muslims at Badr not to their valor or his own but to God) into an endorsement of the doctrine that God acts through men and confirmation of the discovery Hayy has just made.

134. Cf. p. *60* and note 121 above for the relative destructibility of the elements. The fact that being as we know it cannot exist without change is made the basis of Ghazālī's creation argument for the existence of God: if the natural world is constantly subject to change and change must "come to be in time", then so must the world. Ghazālī's argument, which depends for its claim to legitimacy on an appeal from ontological to temporal finitude is found in his "letter" to the people of Jerusalem, *Ihyā' Ulūm ad-Dīn* II iii 1.1, ed. and tr. A. L. Tibawi in *The Islamic Quarterly* IX 3-4, 1965, pp. 98-99 of the English, pp. 80-81 of the Arabic, cf. my discussion in "Ghazālī's Argument from Creation" *International Journal of Middle Eastern Studies*, II 1, 2, January, April, 1971.

135. Hayy has now progressed to full-fledged and self-confident use of the syllogism. Until now his reasonings have depended mainly on propositional logic like that of the Stoics; but until now his thinking has been confined mainly to the physical world. Metaphysics demands the syllogism because only the syllogism can be categorical: propositional logic cannot quantify. Only the syllogism allows men to speak of all things in heaven and earth, of being *qua* being, without begging the question (as Stoic logic did) of whether non-physical being is real or not. Thus Hayy's first fully articulated syllogism delimits things which are bodies from things which perhaps are not.

136. Kindī bases his proof of the temporal finitude of the Universe (and thus his proof of its need for a creator) on its spatial finitude, ed. Abu Rida pp. 114 ff., 185 ff., 202, ff; the argument for a world of finite size is found in Aristotle *De Caelo* I 5. The attempt to extrapolate from spatial to temporal finitude goes back to Philoponous and is used with great sophistication by Ghazālī in *Tahāfut al-Falāsifa* I; cf. Ghazālī's teacher Juwaynī *apud* Shahrastānī *Iqdām*, ed. Guillaume, p. 5 of the English, p. 13 of the Arabic; cf. pp. *81* ff. Avicenna attempts to save the infinity of the Aristotelian Universe in the time dimension without sacrificing its finitude in space by distinguishing essentially "ordered" from essentially "simultaneous" things, see Shahrastānī *Kitāb al-Milal wan-Nihal* ed. Cureton p. 403.

137. *Sc.* the spheres.

138. The retrograde motion of the planets was the great stumbling block of all pre-Copernican systems of astronomy. Ibn Tufayl does not offer an explanation of it here, because, as he says, such things, unlike the objects of his own discourse, may be found in books, and because he recognizes with Ghazālī

(*Munqidh*, p. 36, *Tahāfut al-Falāsifa* second author's preface) and in opposition to Bellarmine, that the problems of positive science need not become a stumbling block to religion.

139. Ghazālī rejects the philosophers' conception of the cosmos as a great animal moving in obedience to God's will, *Tahāfut al-Falāsifa* XIV. The notion is a myth, a piece of poetry behind which is concealed the true relationship of creature to Creator. Hayy's awareness at this stage, then, would seem to retrace the philosophers' excursions into the uncertain realm of mythic representation.

140. Ghazālī had argued forcefully and at length in *Tahāfut al-Falāsifa* I against the doctrine of the eternity (*a parte ante*) of the world. He argues in III, IV, and X of the same work that belief in the philosophers' doctrine that the world has existed forever is tantamount to atheism. Ibn Tufayl is apparently not convinced.

For the skeptics the countervailing force of arguments was proof of man's incapacity to know the truth. Kant uses the countervailing force of creationist and anti-creationist arguments, like those promulgated by Ghazālī on the one hand and Ibn Rushd on the other, in his "first antinomy of pure reason" to delimit the sphere beyond which pure reason dare not tread. The rationalist philosophers of the middle ages had more faith perhaps in reason—pure or guided by experience—than this might allow. Ghazālī's belief was that he could prove the creation of the world and demonstrate the inconsistency of eternalism with theism; Ibn Rushd's was that he could prove the opposite. For Ibn Tufayl, what needed to be done was obvious: a meaning must be found for creation, for eternity, and for theism that would reconcile them all with the truth and with each other.

141. Eternity is not predicable of the temporal: Ghazālī defends this key premise of his *demonstratio Dei* in the "Jerusalem Letter" ed. Tibawi p. 81 of the Arabic, p. 99 of the English.

142. Aristotle disproves the possibility of "a time before time" in *Physics* VIII 1, 251b 10, in the course of proving the eternity of motion, and, by implication, of the natural world.

143. This is the penultimate step in Ghazālī's proof of God's existence, "Jerusalem Letter", ed. Tibawi, p. 80 Arabic, p. 98 English. The conclusion is the identification of God with that cause.

144. The objections raised here against creation in time are based on the first and fourth of Proclus' 18 arguments against creation, the strongest, according to Shahrastānī, apparently be-

cause they rely on conceptions of God as generous, immutable, and self-contained which, as Proclus himself points out, are intended to be more pious than those of the monotheists. Ghazālī answers the objections in the first part of the first discussion of the *Tahāfut al-Falāsifah*, but his answers seem to satisfy Ibn Tufayl little better than they did Ibn Rushd.

145. In affirming (p. 86) that the implications of creationism and eternalism are the same, Ibn Tufayl explicitly rejects one main contention of Ghazālī's *Tahāfut al-Falāsifah*, that the only valid proof of God's existence is the argument from creation and that in affirming the eternity of the world the philosophers of the Aristotelian tradition take a position which cannot be distinguished from atheism. The dependence of the world on God, Ibn Tufayl insists, may be envisioned through the notion of an act of creation in time but the real basis of the dependence is ontological, rooted in the nature of finite being itself. Thus the philosophers are *not* wrong in refusing to limit their conception of God's act to creation, in conceiving God not merely as Creator, but far more broadly, as "Author" of the Universe. Their deism is not tantamount to atheism, but is in fact the highest form of theism.

146. For the materiality of the objects of the senses see Aristotle *De Anima* II 6-12 esp. 424a 17 ff. For Avicenna's demonstration that only objects of sense can be subject to imagination see *Najāt* II 6 viii. Cf. pp. 90-91.

147. *Qur'ān* LXVII 14. God's knowledge and providence are interdependent in Islamic tradition, and either may be used as argument for the other. By recognizing these attributes of God Hayy is reaching a level comparable to that of traditional religion; see pp. 144-145.

148. The Aristotelian world was subject to constant change, but the great overriding laws of change, the laws of nature, remained always the same. Plato had taught the creation of the world (*Timaeus* 28 ff.), but no right-thinking Aristotelian could believe that Plato had affirmed a creation from nothing. Plato's seminal idea of the precipitation of finite being from the *more* real ideal became the basis of the neo-Platonic theory of emanation; his "Demiurge", the craftsman god of creation, was allegorized, and his image of the act of creation was interpreted as a *"formatio mundi"*, the forming of a world out of preexistent matter (despite his affirmation that matter, being subject to change and motion, had not the sort of being as to endure of itself.) *Formatio mundi* was a comfortable position for monotheist phi-

losophers because it preserved some notion of creation without toying with the dangerous notions of absolute being and non-being. Like all compromises, however, it was satisfying to neither extreme: for it represented neither a genuine act of creation nor a genuine eternity of the world *as it is*. For a prototype of this effort at compromise see Origen *De Principiis* I iv 4, ed. Butterworth p. 42. For evidence that Ibn Tufayl hoped to achieve such a compromise, see p. *134*, where the destruction of the world on the Day of Judgement is interpreted (like destruction of the elements) as relative, not absolute.

149. Aristotle proves the eternity of the world from the eternity of motion, which in turn is demonstrated from the ceaselessness of time. He then proceeds to demonstrate the existence of an Unmoved Mover: See *Physics* VIII.

150. Thus Ibn Tufayl explicitly parts company with Ghazālī (cf. p. 82 and notes 142-145 above), affirming not only that God's existence but also His knowledge and providence are conceivable without an act of creation *ex nihilo*. Contrast *Tahāfut al-Falāsifa* I-V, IX-XI. God transcends time as he transcends space and any attempt by men to conceive God's relation to them is, as Ghazālī should have known, bound to fail.

151. Ghazālī was wrong to have been suspicious of the philosophers' doctrine of ontological dependence just as he was wrong to have been suspicious of their doctrine of the world's eternity. There is no danger that the relative necessity of the world (as object of God's generosity) will be inflated into absolute necessity, for the world is, as Ghazālī knew, no more than the object of God's generosity and exists only as such. Its eternity is not the eternity of another god or another necessary being, but a borrowed eternity, just as its existence is a borrowed existence. Needless to say, Ghazālī would not be convinced by these reassurances.

152. Aristotle develops the notion of essential, natural, or ontological priority—that is priority not in time but in fact—through the discussions of *Categories* 12; *Metaphysics* Delta 11; *Physics* VIII 6, 260b, 19; 9, 265a 22. The *falāsifa* had become convinced that ontological priority was the true meaning of God's precedence to creation. Whether this should be considered an adequate interpretation was to become one great stumbling block of philosophical Islam; for Ghazālī was convinced that it was not, and Ibn Rushd was equally certain that any temporal interpretation was unthinkable. See *Tahāfut at-Tahāfut* I ii, ed. Bouyges p. 64 and van den Bergh's notes *ad loc.* p. 37. 2-3; cf.

Shahrastānī *Kitāb al-Iqdām fī 'Ilmi-l-Kalām* ed. A. Guillaume, p. 8.

153. *Qur'ān XXXVI* 81; cf. *Genesis* i.

154. For a classic statement of the argument from design, rivalling that of Paley in the fullness of its detail see pseudo-Jāhiz *Kitāb al-'Ibār*. Ghazālī draws many instances of the design argument (of Stoic flavor) from the *Qur'ān* in "Jerusalem Letter" 1.1, ed. Tibawi pp. 90-91 of the English, p. 80 of the Arabic.

155. *Qur'ān X* 62, *XXXIV* 3. Here again God's providence is intertwined with His knowledge: Since concern and efficacy are taken for granted, knowledge implies providence. Like the fall of a sparrow, the weight of an atom is marked by God. The line is quoted by Ghazālī, *Munqidh*, tr. Watt, p. 37; cf. Ghazālī's rejection of the philosophers' attempt to reduce divine knowledge to knowledge of universals: *Tahāfut al-Falāsifa* XIII. Ibn Tufayl accepts God's knowledge of particulars (for the particular is, after all, implied by the universal) but rejects the claim of *Tahāfut al-Falāsifa* XI that providence without creation is impossible.

156. Cf. Galen *De Usu Partium* and pseudo-Jāhiz *Kitāb al-'Ibār*.

157. Since serious monotheism began God has been held to be the source of all good and often to be goodness itself. The latter raises a serious logical problem for the theologian, as A. N. Prior points out: "We cannot have it both ways, and use a word as an abstract noun and a common noun at once. . .", "Can Religion be discussed?" *Australasian Journal of Philosophy*, 1942, reprinted in *New Essays in Philosophical Theology*, ed. Antony Flew and Alasdair Macintyre, New York, 1964. The problem is that if God's identity is no more than the goodness that we want or expect from him, if God becomes no more than his attributes, then in affirming God's existence we affirm no more than a "picture preference." Only by seeing the relationship between God and goodness to be non-analytic can the difficulty be resolved: only if evil counts against the existence of God can good be counted in its favor. For Hayy at this point God is the source of all good, and the existence of good in the world is evidence of the existence of God, a being who is good, not goodness. But cf. p. 90.

158. Having discovered the existence of God by reading the signs of His existence in His effects, Hayy invokes the Platonic axiom that like must come from like and the Aristotelian corollary that actual must precede potential. The Cause of all the

world's goodness, then, must possess all the perfections He gives it and must possess them all out of proportion to the beneficiaries of His generosity, if He is to give and they to receive His gifts. By Platonic standards of value and ontic status, God will be goodness itself. He will be identical with his attributes, His essence will be His existence, He is that He is—and in this identity of essence with existence is found the meaning of *Qur'ān* XXVIII 88, which became the banner of Sūfī monism, "All things perish except His face." The identity is not, however, at odds with Hayy's synthetic discovery of God's goodness (p. 89 and note), for it is not an identity such as will allow an ontological argument, nor does it allow the return of the objection raised by Prior. The source of good, by Platonic standards, will be the Good Itself; and, for this being alone, existence must live up to essence, but it is not possible to conclude that such a being must exist or even to ignore the problem of evil as a hindrance to belief in a being who is goodness itself. The direction of the argument is inductive, from the goodness and fullness of being to a Being who is goodness and perfection. This direction cannot be reversed. For God as the Good, cf. *Mishkāt al-Anwār*, tr. Gairdner, p. 95.

159. Ghazālī applies the Qur'ānic term *rāsikh* (III 5, IV 160) to himself (*Munqidh*, tr. Watt, pp. 55-56) at the point where the fundamental elements of the Muslim creed had become an inalienable part of his being. His crisis, like Hayy's, still lay ahead; but Islam was now "entrenched" within him, and even his crisis would be distinctively Islamic, just as Hayy's (see pp. 123-124) is the dilemma specifically of a radical monotheist. For Ghazālī's more traditional use of the term, see *Mishkāt al-Anwār*, introduction.

160. For the physical character of sound see Plato *Timaeus* 67³, Aristotle *De Anima* ii 8, 419b 19 ff., Avicenna *Najāt* II 6 ii, tr. Rahman, p. 26. If sound is physical it cannot be the medium of God's revelation: cf. Philo *Quod Deus sit Immutabilis* 83, Origen *contra Celsum* II 72, tr. Chadwick, Cambridge, 1965, p. 121, where references to Plutarch, Diogenes, Lactantius, Aulus Gellius, Clement, and Augustine are cited.

161. See p. 83 and note.

162. Like can be known only by like; and, more specifically, an immaterial being can be known only by another. To assume the contrary is to be guilty of a category error (p. 4). The soul then, that is the consciousness by which God is apprehended, must be immaterial, i.e. like God in its mode of being. Cf. Gha-

zālī *Madnūn as-Saghīr* passim, *Maʿārij al-Quds* pp. 200 ff., Avicenna, psychological parts of the *Najāt* and *Shifāʾ*.

163. Suicide is anathema to Islam as it is to all monotheist religions and to the Platonic philosophical outlook. That life is worthwhile, a thing of value in itself, is universally accepted by all these traditions. But since the worth of life is derived externally both for the monotheist and for the Platonist, a tension, a yearning away from the world, culminating in longing for death will arise in the radical phases of both these points of view. For Hayy at this point life still has its meaning—as a means to an end, a process that should run to its completion. Note well that when death itself has become a goal for him its meaning has been subtly changed. It is no longer extinction but the loss of self *in God*—which the mystic takes to be fulfillment.

164. Cf. Ghazālī *Mishkāt al-Anwār* I 2, tr. Gairdner pp. 91-93, ed. Afifi pp. 48-49, where the neo-Platonic-Aristotelian theory of the mind's self-realization through increasing awareness is set forth in some detail, the highest wisdom (or highest philosophy, in the broad sense) being identified with the word of God, the *Qurʾān*, which plays the role of the Aristotelian (and post-Aristotelian) Active Intellect, as the "Sun of Intelligence" by which all understanding is made possible.

165. The quasi-Megarian notion of impossibility, accepted here by Ibn Tufayl, implies that a future event is not possible unless it actually will take place. The doctrine is at odds with Aristotle's best insights into the nature of potentiality, since it leads to the same identification of modal with actual categories, and of possibility ultimately with necessity, against which so much of Aristotle's argumentation is directed in *Metaphysics* Theta and *De Interpretatione* 9. It is therefore rejected by Fārābī in his commentary on the latter work, ed. Wilhelm Kutsch and Stanley Marrow, Beirut, 1960, pp. 99-100, despite the fact that Aristotle himself had endorsed this strange concession to the Megarian way of thinking, *Metaphysics* Theta 4, cf. Simplicius Commentary on the *Physics* 1225.32 and the discussion of van den Bergh in his notes to the *Tahāfut at-Tahāfut* 50.4 and 52.4.

Ibn Tufayl's theological motive for accepting the doctrine here seems to be that it allows him to exempt those who are totally unaware spiritually from blame or punishment: they are to be classed not with the wicked, but with the blind.

166. Hayy's goal has now become the goal of the Sūfī, to maintain and perfect his relationship with God and thereby to

achieve salvation. His means, concentration, thus appropriately parallels the methods of the Sūfīs.

167. Equilibrium is unattainable below the sphere of the moon (cf. p. *99*). It is the instability of the natural world that renders the senses, appetites and even passions necessary in a natural body fit to be linked with a soul; for without growth, nutrition, reproduction and the like, even the limited self-sufficiency characteristic of living beings would be impossible. But such functions, to carve out a place in nature for the soul, must relate with nature, come to terms with it. It is in this that they offer the greatest challenge to the soul, for soul must recognize and use its mastery or it will become the slave of forces that were meant to be its servants and protectors. Hayy begins to see that the interests of his soul demand restriction of the needs of his body.

168. Despite his strictures against Fārābī (pp. *13-14*), Ibn Tufayl accepts the philosopher's notion that men ignorant of God will share the fate of animals, but adds that those who have known God but lost Him will not dissolve like animals but will suffer the torment of separation: this is the true meaning behind the notion of Hell. Ibn Tufayl thus allows the possibility of damnation, but he preserves the philosophical soteriology in terms of which an individual is saved by the fullness of his awareness. He follows Ghazālī in this, who likewise assigns the fate of animals to those who "never pass beyond the world of sense," *Mishkāt al-Anwār*, tr. Gairdner, pp. 93-4; cf. pp. *131, 147* and *151*.

169. Cf. Aristotle *History of Animals* VIII 1, 588b 25 ff.

170. In the universe of Aristotle the jewel-like heavens, circling eternally at the borders of the natural world, were the stepping stones to God. The order and changelessness of their motion were arguments for the existence of God; and their permanence and beauty, for Aristotle, as for all Greek thinkers in his tradition were signs of a divinity, that is a rationality, that diffused from God throughout the world. To the pagan neo-Platonist, the movers of the spheres were gods; and to the monotheist adherent of the same tradition they were angels, "intelligences", through which being and perfection declined into nature. The heavenly bodies, then, despite their dissociation from the minds with which they are linked, reflect the glory of their place in the hierarchy of being—as the first precipitates into matter of the ideal, the last outposts of the natural world about to transcend itself. In accepting these lines of thought Ibn Tufayl again

veers away from Ghazālī and his anti-eternalist campaign. For the conflict of "quintessence" with creationism, see S. Sambursky's discussion of Xenarchus, Philoponus and Simplicius in *The Physical World of Late Antiquity*, London, 1962.

171. For the relative destructibility of the elements, cf. p. 57 and note 117. For the virtual indestructibility of gold and sapphire (hyacinth) see the theory of Jābir and the Ikhwān as-Safā' elaborated by Nasr in *Islamic Cosmological Doctrines* pp. 89 ff.

172. For matter as quasi-non-being see Plotinus *Enneads* I 8. 3-4, tr. S. MacKenna, London, 1962, pp. 67-69, (first edition, 1917).

173. Hayy has now discovered that he himself is the highest form of life—that is within the natural world. The "material" which neither rises nor falls (see p. 63) is not some primitive material at all, since all matter is compounded with some specific form if it is actually to exist. It is in fact his own vital spirit, which is "so aptly blended" (see p. 27) as to have no opposite and no linear motion. Having virtually no opposite, the spirit is virtually a substance, virtually eternal. One step beyond it is the soul, which transcends all material predicates. Of the soul, once cleansed of the body and of all things physical, it is true that it will neither rise nor fall—indeed that it may be placed in space as in the thought experiment of Avicenna (*Shifā'* Psychology I) and continue to subsist and function without input or support. The dialectic of Hayy's growth has brought him to discovery of himself. His puzzlings as to his role in nature (pp. 36, 47) are now answered and the challenge of Avicenna (see p. 40 and note *ad loc.*) has been met: man has seen himself as a self-subsistent being. Now that Hayy knows himself it remains for him to discover the purpose of his being.

174. More than a vague analogy is meant by the medieval when he calls the human body a miniature of the cosmos. Like the heavenly bodies, man's corporeal nature reflects the divinity of its immaterial associate. The notion of a "perfect body" (*soma teleion*) arises in the so-called Mithras Liturgy.

175. In the case of awareness (and only of awareness) the tri-unity of subject, object, and abstract may be consistently maintained. That such unity in diversity was acceptable within the Peripatetic world was a welcome fact not only to Christian Trinitarians, but also to Platonists and radical monotheists of all traditions who hoped to account for the origin of a differentiated world in a monadic God.

176. Only materially bound beings are subject to the cate-

gories of arithmetic identity and diversity. This strange doctrine which ignores the problem of numbers and runs counter to Ghazālī's efforts to assign identities to souls with reference to their histories, or to minds with reference to their contents (*Kitāb Madnūn as-Saghīr*) relies on the fundamental equivocation (cf. p. *125*) that is the pivotal premiss of all neo-Platonism: a thing neither is nor is not itself, neither is nor is not something else. The most comprehensive effort to disentangle the elements of this paradox, provide the criteria of "sameness" and "otherness" and designate the levels at which such terms apply, is that of Proclus in the *Elements of Theology* especially chapter L. The rigor of Proclus is the natural outcome of the confrontation of Parmenides by the mentality of Socrates, cf. *Philebus* 15.

177. Total trust (*tawakkul*) is, according to Ghazālī, *Ihyā' 'Ulūm ad-Dīn* XXXV, the fruit of the highest reach of faith. The *muslim* is one who "surrenders" to God all his own concerns; he still cares (ardently), but he puts his cares in God's hands. The greatest surrender of self to God is the surrender of character: man is perfected by abandoning his character, allowing himself to be created once again in the image of God. For the notion of *imitatio Dei*, see Erich Auerbach's *Mimesis*.

178. As the French editor of *Hayy Ibn Yaqzān* delicately remarks, the introduction of sex at this point is a "*détail malencontreux, puisque notre solitaire se croit seul de son espèce*," Gauthier's French translation p. 78 note 1. What seems harder to accept than Ibn Tufayl's assumption that even when alone a man will crave sexual fulfillment, is his assumption that such cravings are to be attributed solely to the body.

179. As frequently happens in the history of thought, one man's *reductio ad absurdum* is another man's philosophy. The existentialist and the medieval philosopher are agreed that finite being without some transcendent purpose to give meaning to its existence is absurd. They differ in their perceptions of the human condition. For the existentialist, absurdity is the given. For the radical monotheist, the impossibility of the absurd is ground for undertaking the search for meaning which reaches its end in comprehension of the cosmic drama; (cf. p. *131*). For Avicenna's answer to the question of why souls were put in bodies see the passage from his "Ode on the Soul" quoted by Nasr in *Three Muslim Sages* p. 40.

180. For the radical monotheist, as for the Socratic philosopher, man's identity will be the source of his most difficult obligations. The difficulties are compounded when the traditions

are combined: Man must "know himself" as a creature in the image of God, at once a god-filled power and a fallen star, the last and best work of creation whose task it is to bridge somehow the infinite gap between God and finite being. Neither the Platonic nor the Hebraic tradition—and surely not the hybrid— leaves man without the program by which this is to be achieved. Traditional religion of the Hebraic type will find its approach to God through service, but monotheist thinkers in the Aristotelian tradition are prone to identify the "I am that I am" which is God's nature (cf. p. 90 and note 158, also Ghazālī *Mishkāt*, tr. Gairdner p. 111) with the self-sufficiency of Aristotelian first substance. In keeping with the intellectualist assumptions of *their* tradition, they posit that likeness to God is attained by knowing: *Deum colit qui novit.*

181. The loss of self and of all awareness but that of God is seen by the mystic as an essential condition of beatific awareness. The most sublime and tempered statement of the ideal of death to self (*fanā'*) and immersion in God is perhaps Augustine's recollection of his tranquil conversation, alone in Ostia with his mother and his God. "We were saying then: If to any the tumult of the flesh were hushed, hushed the images of earth, and waters, and air, hushed also the poles of heaven, and even the soul hushed to herself, and by not thinking on self surmount self, hushed all dreams and images, every tongue and sign, and all that exists only in transition—since if any could hear, all these say 'We made not ourselves, but He made us that endures forever'—if then having uttered this, they too should be hushed, having roused only our ears to Him who made them, and He alone speak, not by them but by Himself, that we may hear His word, not through any tongue of flesh, nor angel's voice, nor sound of thunder, nor in the dark riddle of a similitude, but might hear Whom in these things we love, might hear His very Self without these (as we two now strained ourselves, and in swift thought touched on that eternal Wisdom, which abideth over all)—could this be continued on, and other visions of kind far unlike be withdrawn, and this one ravish, and absorb, and wrap up its beholder amid these inward joys, so that life might be forever like that one moment of understanding which we now sighed after—were not this to enter into the joy of thy Lord?" *Confessions* IX 25; cf. Ghazālī *Munqidh*, tr. Watt, p. 61. See also Ansārī Commentary on the *Risāla Qushayriyya* Cairo 1346 A.H., p. 28; and F. Jabre "L'Extase de Plotin et le Fana de Ghazali" *Studia Islamica* VI 1956, pp. 101 ff.

182. Hayy's diet is based on reverence for the work of his

Creator; cf. Porphyry *On Abstinence From Animal Food* passim, Marinus *Life of Proclus* xii, xix; cf. Ghazālī *Ihyā' 'Ulūm ad-Dīn* XXXII ii, 1.4, Bousquet art. 137; see also pp. *115,* and for asceticism pp. *119-120, 134-135.*

183. Hayy has not yet become the enemy of his "self" (cf. p. *135*). His asceticism is not based on a policy of containment *vis-à-vis* his body, still less on any notion of mortifying the flesh; but rather, on a principle of the maximization of happiness similar to that invoked by Kindī in "On How to Banish Sorrow": Man must recognize that only the pleasures of mind—and foremost among these, the intellectual love of God, in which for the Aristotelian all other mental pleasures are subsumed—are lasting: only these are to be sought after for their own sakes.

184. Emanation could never have given rise to nature had there not been a differentiation, diversification in being as it declined toward the physical world. The "influences" of the disembodied intelligences, in neo-Platonic theory, were therefore "mediated" through the virtually immaterial matter of the spheres. Only perfections could issue from the divine Principles; matter was responsible for pluralization and the resultant falling away from self-sufficiency. Cf. e.g. Ghazālī's characterization of the philosophers' position, *Tahāfut al Falāsifa* XVII Bouyges 2nd ed. art. 8, esp. p. 198, l. 2. Ibn Tufayl accepts the philosophers' notion that capacities and incapacities are due to matter, but puts it in a better light by his emphasis on the Ash'arite (and Platonic) teaching that matter too *inasmuch as it is* is form and stems from God.

185. Cf. Aristotle *Physics* VIII 5; Ghazālī, *Tahāfut al-Falāsifa* XIV-XV.

186. Cf. Ghazālī *Munqidh,* tr. Watt p. 37; cf. pp. *29, 86-88.*

187. Ibn Tufayl has apparently forgotten his remark of p. *33* that "there were no beasts of prey on the island."

188. For the notion that all things should be allowed to achieve their divinely ordained purposes—a branch should not be broken etc.—see Ghazālī *Ihyā' 'Ulūm ad-Dīn* XXXII *Shatr* ii, *rukn* 1, *bayān* 4; cf. Plutarch: "All who reverence Osiris are prohibited from destroying a cultivated tree or blocking up a stream of water." *Isis and Osiris* 35, 365B. Since Hayy is a *fādil,* a supererogatory man, he takes on the positive obligation of tending the plants and streams, himself contributing to the natural order and beauty which a lesser man would be content not to disturb. For the acquiring of virtue by practice see Aristotle *Nicomachean Ethics* II, 1, 1103b.

189. The use of scents is ascribed by traditional Islam to

Muhammad; and, in following the custom of the Prophet, Hayy would be deemed to have fulfilled a precept of Islam. That the use of scents be ascribed to the Arab prophet need not seem precious; in a hot climate with little water, cleanliness and scent would be matters of common consideration. For Hayy, isolated in his perfect climate, observance of the custom is no matter of slavish imitation. He too has his rationale, albeit not a pragmatic one: he seems to have discovered—to have observed, almost—the relationship between cleanliness and godliness: only those with clean hands and pure hearts dare come before God—not that man's cleanliness or purity are matters of concern to God, but because only when he is pure in every way can a man hope to rise beyond himself to contact with the divine.

190. Ibn Tufayl alludes to the Muslim practice of circling the Ka'ba at Mecca, with some suggestion of the black stone it houses and the custom of jogging between Safā and Marwa during Pilgrimage. Ibn Tufayl gives an air of universal significance to the rites of *Hajj* by proposing that Hayy's fulfillment of the obligations of the pilgrim is modelled not directly on the example of Muhammad or Abraham, but on the pattern of the stars.

191. The practice of the Mawlawī dervish and other Sufis is to whirl in circles or in a dance invoking the name and attributes of God until swept into a mystic ecstasy. The rite is said to have been initiated by Rūmī, the Persian mystic and poet who founded the Mawlawī order. Its dangers are twofold: God may become an object of coercion, and thus remain no more a God; or vertigo may lead to intoxication, loss of equilibrium in that delicate balance of man's soul between divinity and nothingness.

192. The deep Platonic prejudice against the things of sense here finds its epistemological level: not merely appetite, but awareness of other—or even of self (see p. *120*)—is a blot on the purity of the experience. For the notion that sensation and imagination are impediments to intellectual activity, see Avicenna *Najāt* II 6, tr. Rahman pp. 53-54.

193. Concentration is the purest form of worship—not aimless, objectless "meditation", but the motion of the mind as it "connects" with its truest object and is engrossed and absorbed by Him. In such a framework, idolatry (no longer a practical problem of "other gods") must mean distraction, any allowing of mind or desire to wander from its rightful focus. Thus Ibn Tufayl labels distraction '*shirk*', polytheism, idolatry, the belief that there are rivals to the sovereignty of the One True God.

194. "By the olive and the fig, by Mount Sinai and the safety

of this land, I formed man at the fairest height but then reduced him to the lowest of the low. . ." *Qur'ān* XCV 1-5. Ibn Tufayl reads the Qur'ānic allusion to man's fall as symbolic of the constant fall from grace of the mystic, unable by sheer dint of his humanity to maintain his foothold in the world of God.

195. Man's obligation to struggle against the "self", i.e. the lesser, "selfish" self, in the interests of his true identity is a principal theme of Plato's *Republic* (and cf. *Phaedo* 67B, 82D), a theme which was to become progressively more strident, in later Platonic thought, with the de-politicizing of philosophy. In the personal philosophies of the post-Alexandrian Greek world, Stoic, Epicurean, or even Skeptic and Cynic, man's principal task was seen to be *self*-control, and the purpose of philosophy was to aid in its attainment. The neo-Platonic answer to the question 'how should I live?' was most forcefully expressed in the Plotinian dictum "cast away everything!" The concept of purgation, developed from the use of purifications in the Greek mysteries, attained a centrality which it has not yet lost; cf. Ghazālī, *Munqidh*, tr. Watt, p. 60, and e.g. Marinus, *Life of Proclus* xviii. Ibn Tufayl refers obliquely to the Muslim duty of Holy War in calling Hayy's struggle against himself a *jihād*, thus Sūfically interpreting the obligation in a more tolerant if not more tolerable sense than Muhammad may have intended.

196. Ghazālī, in typical Sūfī fashion, exploits the Aristotelian distinction between theory and practice in favor of the mystic approach, for philosophy in his day had become too much a matter of theory, too little a way of life. The Sūfīs, however, lived their philosophy, they joined theory and practice: see *Munqidh*, tr. Watt, p. 54; (cf. the similar complaint of Marx in the eleventh thesis on Feuerbach.) Thus in rediscovering the philosophical ideal of the interpenetration of thought and action, Hayy has become a Sūfī.

197. In keeping with the radical monotheism of their Mu'tazilite forbears, the Islamic philosophers "denied the attributes of God", that is they affirmed that all the traditional names of God designate the same one Being and denied that there was any divine power, will etc. over and above the Divine Identity. By treating the attributes of God as ontologically subordinate to His identity (*Tahāfut al-Falāsifa* VI), Ghazālī is able to remove the taint of plurality from the Islamic doctrine of divine attributes without wholly committing himself to the negative theology of Plotinus: God is an absolute unity, known to us (see the final section of the *Mishkāt*) under different aspects—*under-*

stood in various ways but never fully *comprehended.* Ibn Tufayl solves the problem through his notion that the categories of arithmetic apply only in the physical world, but not before. Hayy's human failure to discount those categories has provided the intellectual basis for his greatest blunder; see pp. *123* ff, and note 198 below.

198. Cf. pp. *108-109* and note 180. Hayy has now discovered the highest good for man—but like all good things, this good is full of dangers: The overstatement of what man is able to achieve will lead to the greatest of delusions, see pp. *4, 122-124* and notes.

199. Hayy's asceticism (see pp. *116-118*) has now become radical: it is not merely appetite or the self he battles now but the whole Universe, all that is not God, for to become like God he must become completely self-absorbed, to know God he must discover (the image of) God within himself: cf. Ghazālī *Kitāb Madnūn as-Saghīr.*

200. Traditionally Muhammad is said to have withdrawn to a cave on Mt. Hīrā' where by meditations and devotions he sought the inner awakening, which, made public, was to transform his world. The cave in our tradition, which owes more to Athens on this point than to the East, is symbol of darkness and dogmatic slumber, not of personal enlightenment but of mass ignorance and unconcern. The great awakening is the moment when a solitary individual stumbles out of the huddled darkness of the cave and away from the cave-thoughts into the blinding sunlight. Ibn Tufayl stands at a crossroads between the Muhammadan and Platonic conceptions: For him the cave is not the social womb, but the sacred solitude of a man with his Creator; yet the mission imparted is not public recognition but private enlightenment. The means remain those of Muhammad, but the end has become the end of Islamized philosophy: salvation by the intellectual approach to God.

201. Cf. *Qur'ān* V 20-21, XV 85, LXXVIII 37, verses evoking the power and majesty of God and divine judgement.

202. In *Qur'ān* LVI 6 (cf. XXV 25) it is the mountains that are "scattered into fine dust" on the Day of Judgement. Ibn Tufayl applies the imagery to the mystic's "annihilation" of self and other—for is this not, he would argue, the meaning of what will happen with the end of all in All?

203. See *Qur'ān* XL 16. In applying the Qur'ānic phrase intended by Muhammad as a designation of the awesomeness of the Judgement Day to the mystic's experience of death-to-self, Ibn Tufayl has subtly reinterpreted the whole of Islamic soteriol-

ogy: stripped of words, which can only disfigure and distort the truth, Qur'ānic judgement *is* the loss of self in god: cf. Origen *De Principiis* I vi. For the notion that God is identical with His word see Ghazālī *Ma'ārij al-Quds* pp. 200 ff. As an attribute of God, the word (here explicitly identified with revelation) is no threat to the divine unity: cf. my notes 55 and 198 to pp. *18* and *118*.

204. To the materialist the fact of consciousness is an insurmountable stumbling block—thus attempts at reduction of thought to behavior or to some mechanical reaction, to anything which it is not. Of these attempts one of the most persistent, if least satisfactory, is the attempt to reduce thought to some function of language or quasi-linguistic entity. The Stoics called thinking the speech of the soul, and Ryle attempts to dismiss thought processes and mental states as a sort of internal speech. The approach is condemned to failure from the outset, since added to all the usual paradoxes of reductionism, there is in this case the difficulty that speech or any linguistic act is essentially rational—that is what distinguishes it from mere noise or automatic behavior: The difficulties of the reductionist position become clearer when it is realized how little protection for the vital distinction between intelligence and mere behavior is afforded by these views. Ibn Tufayl, for his part, feels no qualms about describing Hayy's thoughts as the products of an internal dialogue. The thought-experiment itself resolves the otherwise eternal wrangle as to which came first, the concept or the word: In isolation the linguistic act is inconceivable but the mental act remains. With a note of triumph Ibn Tufayl points to his success: the mind has been able to follow the progress of a human being from near non-being to near the peak of human perfection without assuming the "help" of society or the intervention of language.

205. This description of the beatific vision, emphasizing its ineffability, is adapted from a *hadīth qudsī* or "sacred tradition", that is a saying of Muhammad related on the authority of God himself. Ghazālī prays for such an experience as the prophet promised on the opening page of his *Tahāfut al-Falāsifa*. The same sentence is found in I *Corinthians* ii 9, quoted by Origen *De Principiis* III 4, tr. Butterworth, p. 250, and Augustine *Confessions* IX 23: "as it is written, Eye hath not seen, nor ear heard, neither have entered into the heart of man, the things which God hath prepared for them that love him." Paul refers apparently to *Isaiah* lxiv 4: "Never, from of old has anyone heard or

heard tell of, no eye has seen a God beside you who works for those that wait for Him." The prophet forcefully affirms the unique efficacy of his God, the like of which has never been seen or heard of. By a telling shift of emphasis, Paul expresses the ineffability of the object of God's labors, the reward He is preparing for His faithful. To be sure, no one had seen it *yet*, but in a world to come—Ibn Tufayl would say a world beyond this world—all promises will be fulfilled, all pledges redeemed. The lovers of God will confront their Beloved face to face.

206. Neither the material "spirit" nor the immaterial soul— and surely not the physical heart—can form a conception of the experience of the mystic. This experience relates man to a different order of being (see p. 4) and the attempt to analyze it is the clearest possible example of a category error.

207. God is described repeatedly by the *Qur'ān* (including XXIV 35, the "Light Verse") as coining or minting symbols for the benefit of mankind. The Islamic philosophical school assigned the same function to the prophet: The prophet is a philosopher capable of conveying the truth persuasively through rhetorical language and concrete imagery. Even Ghazālī praises the *Qur'ān* for its facility in convincing the people. Ibn Tufayl follows the example of the prophets, less because of any fear that "to reveal God's secret is unbelief" (see pp. *155-156*) than because he takes the content of his teaching and theirs to be ultimately ineffable.

208. Having lost his foothold at the pinnacle of ecstasy Hayy is no longer able to be absolutely certain. He is tempted to judge the real in terms of the phenomenal. The danger inherent in attempting to express the ineffable (see p. *4*) is now made real: Just as Ghazālī warned (*Munqidh*, tr. Watt, p. 61), the overwhelming experience of contact with the divine is easily confused with incarnation or even identity with God. If the doctrine of *fanā'* must be qualified, so must that of *ittihād*. The keen mind of Ghazālī readily recognizes that the dangers of incarnationism and annihilationism are the same: No one would be so eager to lose himself if he were not hopeful of becoming God. No one would be so confident of becoming God if he were not already on the slope from pantheist to atheist to nihilist. Ghazālī navigates a tight course among these shoals, close to what he calls "the dividing edge between Islam and heresy." The essence of his solution, as outlined in the *Kitāb Madnūn as-Saghīr*, the *Mishkāt al-Anwār*, and book XXXV of the *Ihyā' 'Ulūm ad-Dīn*, is acceptance of the neo-Platonic equivocal stance on the

relationship between finite being and the ONE. Ibn Tufayl's version, with the true philosopher's genius for paradox, makes the equivocation explicit: Being neither "is" nor "is not" identical with its Source, see pp. *127-133*.

209. Through personal experience Ghazālī discovered that human reason, unaided by divine grace and mercy, will never free itself from doubt: see *Munqidh*, tr. Watt pp. 25, 55-56. In the same way, Ibn Tufayl points out, without God's help Hayy Ibn Yaqzān would have been unable to transcend the ordinary categories of human thought by which his confusion was generated. The special gratitude expressed by Ghazālī and obliquely by Ibn Tufayl, should not however be taken for fideism. It must be born in mind that for both thinkers, without God's generosity, reason itself would not exist: All awareness and all perfections come from God.

210. When Hayy sought unity in the natural world (pp. *56* ff.), he found that only matter stood in the way of the complete interchangeability of numerical and qualitative identity—thus only matter stood in the way of perfect unity. In the immaterial world such unity would seem to be easily achieved; but Hayy's supposition to that effect (on which his error is based) neglects the fact that the categories of plurality and identity themselves are dependent on matter (cf. p. *105*). This particular version of the hedge against incarnationism seems to be Ibn Tufayl's own contribution to the discussion: Ghazālī explicitly denies that physicality is the sole basis of individuation in his discussion of the mode of being of disembodied spirits in the *Kitāb Madnūn as-Saghīr*. But Aristotle argues Platonically that "all things that are many in number have matter", *Metaphysics* Lambda 8, 1074a 31; compare Avicenna *Najāt* II 6 vii, tr. Rahman, p. 38. Ibn Tufayl extrapolates from this to his own notion that both major categories of arithmetic, identity (i.e. sameness) and individuation (i.e. difference), are predicable only in the material world.

211. The bat is not blind, but rather he is applying in daylight senses which are more appropriate to darkness. The analogy was invoked originally by Aristotle by way of rendering understandable the (often legitimate) causes and (often beneficial) effects of philosophical diversity and error: "The investigation of the truth is in one way hard, in another easy. An indication of this is found in the fact that no one is able to attain the truth adequately, while, on the other hand, we do not collectively fail, but everyone says something true about the nature of things. . .

the truth seems to be like the proverbial door, which no one can
fail to hit. . .but the fact that we can have a whole truth and
not the particular part we aim at shows the difficulty of it. Perhaps too, as difficulties are of two kinds, the cause of the present
difficulty is not in the facts, but in us. For as the eyes of bats
are to the blaze of day, so is the reason in our soul to the things
which are by nature most evident of all." *Metaphysics* a 1, 993a
30 ff.

212. To the Aristotelian philosopher, not yet bedevilled by a
wholly negative epistemology, it seemed apparent that while the
definition of truth was correspondence between concept and
reality, the only workable ultimate criterion of truth was the
common consent of the many and the wise. The intuitive awareness of sound minds is the only possible judge of the validity of
axioms and thus the ultimate court for all philosophical dis-
putes. The charge is that Ibn Tufayl has violated an axiom,
an offense which might be committed, according to Peripatetic
thinking, only out of ignorance, sophistry or perversity.

213. What Ibn Tufayl is demanding is a bootstrap effort of
the mind to rise above the categories of ordinary experience.
The method of the empiricist will not allow him to perceive the
unity in being, still less the transcendence by true being of the
categories of unity and diversity. The charge is that Ibn Tufayl
has committed himself to the irrational, but what he has done in
fact is to place his intellectual powers at the service of deeper
understanding, attempted specifically to resolve the paradoxes
of the relationship between finite and infinite being through the
notion that quantification, as we know it, exists only relative to
creation and does not apply to the "world of the word."

214. "God does not go back on a threat. This most men do
not know. They know only the surface of this life and are heedless of the next." *Qur'ān* XXX 5-6.

215. The "ordinary language method" will be of no value at
all in describing the mystic experience or in relating the ultimate
metaphysical verities. Since ordinary experience extends to
neither of these, only poetry will suffice, or something like poetry,
the philosopher's effort to bend and twist words into conformity
with reality. The difficulty with ordinary language in *any* metaphysical discussion is that the word-makers have already begged
all the most relevant questions; the use of the method remains
in the fact that often words have been bent in more than one
sense at once, but Ibn Tufayl's point stands: the literal-minded
will never reach the level of philosophy.

216.   Contact, not unity, is what is promised the monotheist rational-mystic.   For the terminology of the Islamic mystics in attempting to convey the phenomenology of the experience see e.g. Hujwīrī, *Kashf al-Mahjūb*, tr. Nicholson esp. p. 180 and Ch. XXIV.

217.   Like disembodied human souls, the immaterial identities of the heavens are neither the same as nor different from their Source—again the crucial equivocation by which emanation works.   Gauthier hesitantly observes (in his French translation of the present work, p. 91, note 3 *ad loc.*) that Ibn Tufayl's treatment of intuition, the relativity of the categories of finite being, the impasse between creation and eternity are anticipations of Kant.   It would be truer to say that the work of Kant is the logical outgrowth of the débacle between the Islamic school of philosophy and Ghazālī.   Ghazālī's program of radical monotheist philosophy demands the relativity of time, space, and causality; and Ibn Tufayl's efforts to follow the master lead him to affirm the relativity even of quantity.   These are relativisms with respect to the finite world at large, rather than with respect to man, but the modern humanist shift need not obscure the direct philosophical line between the relativism of the radical monotheist and that of Leibniz or of Kant.   It cannot obscure the line between the impasse of the countervailing arguments of Ghazālī and Ibn Rushd in the *Tahāfut at-Tahāfut* on the eternity of the world and Kant's proposing these arguments as the first antinomy of pure reason.   Kant's return to intuition at the failure of reason—or rather the exposure of the pretences of rationalism —is no more than the long delayed reaction in the West to the blow Ghazālī had struck philosophy in the East.   Averroës' efforts to patch up the damaged body of philosophy were accepted in Europe in a way that they were never accepted in the Islamic world, and thus the rift that had been left by Ghazālī in philosophy (and before him by the Stoics) between the method of analysis (the method of Socrates) and the love of truth (the truth of Plato) was covered over and left to appear of itself in the natural dialectic of thought.   It appeared in the work of Hume and Kant, no longer as a demand for recognition of the sphere of faith (although it still has about it snatches of the rhetoric of Stoic and monotheist appeals to faith), but now as a thoroughly modern teaching of the inability of reason to solve the major questions of philosophy.   It was the reopening of this rift that left us our present philosophical situation: the former rationalists clinging to their faith in reason and dismissing all the

problems reason cannot solve as pseudo-problems, their former opposites exulting in the triumph of unreason and turning for guidance to faith, intuition and the irrational.

218.   Joy is the thrill of realization felt not just by man but by being at large as it fulfills itself and comes into contact with God.

219.   Being immaterial, souls, like forms and ideas, are not subject to loss and diminution when transmitted.   Love, as the conceit of the English metaphysical poets had it, does not wane but waxes when shared.   Thus the soul will not lose the marks of its divine origin on its descent to finitude, but that does not lessen the reality of the descent.   To become a finite being, soul must become dilute, it must be joined with matter to be individuated, and it must therefore become subject to limitations of time and space.   Immaterial souls will be at one with their Author, but they cannot be identical with Him; for even they are particularizations of His infinity.   To convey the paradox of at-oneness in diversity, Ibn Tufayl chooses, as the least inadequate representation, the neo-Platonic analogy of a series of mirrors reflecting the image of the sun from one to the next.   The image will be "the sun"—but only in a secondary sense, a sense that grows more remote with the increasing ontological distance from effect to cause.   Cf. Plotinus *Enneads* VI ii 22 end; Proclus *Elements of Theology* 64 corollary, and 65, ed. Dodds. p. 63; Macrobius *Commentary on the Dream of Scipio* I 14-15, quoted by Lovejoy in *The Great Chain of Being* New York, 1965, p. 63 (first ed. 1936.)

220.   Thus man's place in the Universe is pictured as that of a tiny creature spawned within the gut of some great living being —but unlike the other denizens of this nether-world, man sees his place and sees, if he is wise, the avenue of his escape—for the fact of consciousness itself is evidence that man does not belong here.

221.   Cf. "*Nishmat Kol Hayy*" (*B'rakhōt* 59b, *Ta'anīt* 6 b) and "*Yishtabakh*" of the Sabbath *Shakharit* liturgy, and Psalm 150.

For the differentiation of the Godhead into "faces," see Plotinus *Enneads* VI 7.15; for the introduction of the number 70,000, see the tradition explained by Ghazālī in the *Mishkāt al-Anwār* that God is veiled by 70,000 veils of light and darkness, tr. Gairdner pp. 77 and 157 ff.   The equivocal ontic status of finite being in the radical monotheist system was perhaps best reconciled with the "axioms of thought" and best harmonized with the categories of metaphysics by the notion of Spinoza that individuals are modes of the All.   Ibn Tufayl, trusting less in the power of language to convey the truth, chooses a metaphor in place of a model, for he fears that the inadequate concept that any words will convey will be less easily taken for a full representation of reality if, for once, it is not clothed in the deceptively abstract language of the philosopher.

222. On the traditional level, Ibn Tufayl hesitates to single out Hayy as one member of the 70,000 perhaps because it is given to no man to know whether another is saved. In terms of the true "oriental philosophy", however, the difficulty is greater as we have seen: Beyond matter there is no basis for individuation *or* unification. The immaterial soul is neither the same as nor different from the Godhead: If arithmetic categories themselves may be transcended then the dilemma of the soul's identity at once with God and with nothing but itself can be resolved. Cf. Plotinus *Enneads* VI 5.9 and the positions of Ghazālī and Ibn Rushd, *Tahāfut at-Tahāfut*, ed. Bouyges, p. 28.

223. Following Ghazālī's *Kitāb Madnūn as-Sagīr*, Ibn Tufayl affirms that the meaning of God's creation of man is the joining of body and soul; cf. p. 28. Only inasmuch as it is linked with the body is the soul subject to time, thus only its linking with the body can be called its creation. *Qua* immaterial, the soul is eternal. But the usual problems associated with the eternity of the soul are avoided—for only inasmuch as the soul is linked with matter can it be said to have a separate identity at all. *Qua* immaterial the soul is neither inside nor outside time, neither the same as nor different from the Godhead: cf. p. 127.

224. Hayy has now seen (during life) the vision promised those whom God loves. The rest of his life will be spent in blissful contemplation of that vision—and in the effort to live in accordance with the truths he has now seen.

225. Hayy now "sees" the soteriological system which he has previously known only in the abstract (see pp. 95-97 and notes *ad loc.*): Like the prime experience of the mystic (see pp. 7-9) Hayy's experience now is far more vivid, his participation far more real than when he merely reasoned (in Mu'tazilite fashion) about what *ought* to be the case. This vividness, this sense of participation, and above all the ineffability of the reality he now sees are what account for the departure of the mind from abstract and general categories to the fleshed out world not only of the visionary, but also—be it remembered—of the *Qur'ān*.

226. Hayy is now a witness of the entire cosmic drama: Creation, resurrection, and revelation, all stand before him—the disembodied souls of the aware, the shrouded minds of the damned,

the simultaneous outflow and return of the breath of life, the force of emanation that pervades and powers the Universe (see p. *17* and note 75), God's "raising up" of man and man's fall, and the moment of comprehension that gives meaning to the whole: All is summed up in an atomic insight in which all symbols are stripped away, all veils removed, the whole truth taken in at once in all its loveliness.

227.   Having tasted once of the Truth, Hayy has become a full-time seeker, prepared to devote *all* his energies to the perfection of his "intercourse with the sublime" (cf. pp. *4, 19*). He has thus become vitally aware of the rivalry for his attentions of two very tempting ways of life—as expressed in these words attributed to Muhammad—and has made his choice between them.   For a fine and relevant discussion of the historical and spiritual origins of the life of the religious, see Jacob Burckhardt, *The Age of Constantine the Great*, tr. Moses Hadas, London, 1949, pp. 323 ff. (second German edition, 1880).

228.   For the ontological interconnectedness of all things, see Arthur Lovejoy *The Great Chain of Being*, Cambridge, Massachusetts, 1936.

229.   The sense in which this world mirrors a world more real is double edged: As a less than adequate copy, a shadow world, a puppet show of false representations, the world is a sorry mockery of the paradigms from which its design is taken.   Yet, in the world, that design can still be seen.   The divine idea is still reflected, however muddily, in the lowest level of concrete being.   Thus even in the lowest level shines a truth, a reality which comes direct from God.   If so, reasons the neo-Platonist, the world cannot ever be utterly destroyed.   If it is a bad copy, it remains a copy nonetheless, and will exist as long as its eternal paradigm continues to fill it with being; cf. Proclus' second and fifteenth arguments for the eternity of the world.   The arguments apply, as Proclus argues, to eternity *a parte ante* as well as *a parte post*. Thus Ibn Tufayl does not fully accept creation *ex nihilo*, but rather favors *formatio mundi*, see pp. 83 ff. and notes *ad loc.*

230.   Cf. pp. *97, 116*.   Despite his realization that his fulfillment depended on his ability to become like the heavenly bodies (pp. *113* ff.), Hayy now sees that his one over-riding concern, attainment of constant contact with God, precludes all physical involvement.   His progress thus again recapitulates that of human society—for despite the warnings of the prophets and of Jesus that ashes and dust do not make a fast, that purity of mind counts for more than outward acts, traditions of extreme asceti-

cism early gained a firm foothold in Judaism and Christianity. And despite the stern warning attributed to Muhammad—"no monkery in Islam!"—the Sūfī tradition embodied elements that might well have passed for monkery in any other religion.

231. Cf. *Phaedo* 61, 64, 67, 80. I can do nothing to justify the paradoxical notion that the aim and end of the philosophical life is the love of death. The most beautiful and most dangerous expression of the idea is in Keats' "Ode to a Nightingale"—to prepare for death is one thing, to fall into romantic love with it, confuse it with peace or truth or fulfillment is another. To the Platonist, however, death is a consummation, the return of being to its own, thus Hayy's longing for death comes at the climax of his career, but is not the substance of his life or its motive force: As he learned in his earliest reflections, (p. 93 and note 163) the soul would not leave the body until no further use could be derived from it as a tool—that is, the tool of the soul's salvation and return.

232. Unlike Hayy, the common people gain their vision of the truth not by choice or insight but by force of rhetoric and social pressure. For the role of myth in religion, see Fārābī *Arā' Ahlu-l-madīnatu-l-Fādila* and R. Walzer "Al-Fārābī's Theory of Prophecy and Divination", *Greek Into Arabic* Oxford, 1963, ch. 12; cf. e.g. R. B. Braithwaite's Eddington Memorial Lecture "An Empiricist's View of the Nature of Religious Belief", Cambridge, 1955, reprinted in *The Existence of God* ed. John Hick pp. 229 ff., esp. pp. 244-249.

233. The names of these two men, who represent for Ibn Tufayl opposite poles of the sphere of human religious involvement, are taken, as he says (p. 20) from a work of Avicenna's; cf. Henri Corbin *Avicenna and the Visionary Recital* pp. 223 ff. So is the name Hayy Ibn Yaqzān: see Corbin *op. cit.* pp. 123 ff. In keeping with his belief that symbols may change while realities remain the same, Ibn Tufayl has completely restructured the situations by which he hopes to restate the Avicennan "oriental philosophy" in the light of the thought of Ghazālī—leaving only the names the same, as markers of the underlying continuity.

234. In Stoic fashion, classical Islam presupposed that if there was a God (and there was) then He might be expected to reveal to mankind what actions were imperative, prohibited, recommended, disapproved of, and neuter. Like *halakhic* Judaism and the Christianity of the monks, traditional Islam was, from the point of view of its adherents, fundamentally an elaborate system of ordinances directing human life at every level of ac-

tivity with laws whose moral and intellectual authority was the ultimate Source of all goodness and all truth. The wise son, according to the Passover Haggadah, on being told the history of Pesach, asks not for more details or an explanation, but rather "what are the laws and ordinances" commanded in regard to the Pesach. His attitude is typical of all three monotheist religions at their traditional levels: To the traditional monotheist, as to the two young men by whom Ibn Tufayl represents him, what was primary was action befitting awareness of the constant presence of God. The further question of the meaning of the Law or the true nature of the Lawgiver was a secondary matter, reserved for specialists; cf. pp. *145-146*.

235. Salāmān is probably right in guarding his thoughts. Not all men are as resolute morally or intrepid intellectually as Hayy Ibn Yaqzān, (see p. *147*), and an ordinary man would only be confused by the diversity of possible opinions and baffled among the countervailing arguments of opposing forces: See Ghazālī *Munqidh*, tr. Watt, p. 20; cf. pp. *18-20, 155*. The Law would not include admonitions to stay within society alongside exhortations to solitude unless there were different sorts of people and different sorts of life best suited to them (see p. *153* and note 280). Society and social institutions are well designed, in Ibn Tufayl's view, to restrain independent thought (see p. *155*), and its functioning in this worthwhile purpose should not be resisted by the philosopher, for exile is in any case the most independent course.

236. Cf. p. *117* and my note 195.

237. *Sharī'a*, the term normally applied by Muslims to the Islamic revealed law, is used here in a generic sense, to refer to what Ibn Tufayl's "thinly veiled" (p. *156*) allegory presumes would be the scriptural law which gives any established (i.e. traditional) religion its positive content.

238. On the philosopher's need for isolation, see *Republic* VI 496, and cf. *Theaetetus* 174C.

239. Salāmān may seem superstitious in fearing *waswās*, the promptings of the devil, but in keeping with Ibn Tufayl's remark that it was independent thought Salāmān most feared (see note 235) and his description (p. *136*) of Salāmān as a Godfearing and righteous man, it would appear that Salāmān's "Devil" is less a moral tempter than an intellectual deceiver. If Salāmān is afflicted with the philosopher's love of paradox or propensity to wander from the most vital objects of his quest—as Hayy Ibn Yaqzān is not—he may well feel safer within the confines of a

tradition—and within the walls of a society which upholds the traditional ways of thought.

240. The well established ascetic pattern of the devotee giving up all he has to search for Truth was followed not only by Buddha but also—in his own way—by Ghazālī: see *Munqidh*, tr. Watt, p. 59.

241. Cf. p. *144* and my note 249.

242. For the life of trust (*tawakkul*) see Ghazali *Ihyā' 'Ulūm ad-Dīn* XXXV ii. Hayy lives naturally the life which a civilized man can achieve only by a conscious break with his whole background and environment—a break the results of which may be even more dangerous than continued existence within the social womb; see note 177.

243. A heavy woolen cloak was the familiar badge of the Sūfī and is thought by many to have given the Muslim followers of "the way" their distinctive name, from the Arabic *sūf* meaning wool. Hujwīrī, the Sūfī theorist, devotes the fourth chapter of his *Kashf al-Mahjūb* to the patched garment of the Sūfī, and advises his readers (tr. R.A. Nicholson, London, 1967, p. 56; first ed. 1911) to secure a copy of his book on the subject. Hujwīrī is at pains to point out that clothes do not make the man: it is the spark inside the man that makes him a Sūfī, not external behavior (p. 47); the real Sūfī does not care what he wears or what he is called (p. 48)—a rose by any other name would smell as sweet. Cf. Plutarch *Isis and Osiris* 3, 352C: "having a beard and wearing a coarse cloak does not make philosophers. . ." A fact obvious but easily forgotten.

244. Hayy recognizes now in no uncertain terms the reality of the difference between God and man—awareness of the Truth implies humility in the face of something far better, purer and more beautiful than man can conceive, a Being whom it is man's task to emulate, not to become: contrast pp. *123* ff.

245. Unlike Hayy, Asāl has sought enlightenment through the spoken and written word. Like the Sūfīs he has apprenticed himself to foreign sages. Like the *falāsifah* he has delved into foreign tongues. The truth has eluded him. Words are no more than veils between a man and God, concrete representations in which the Truth, manifest to those with the strength to seek but ineffable even by them, is disguised and hidden from prying eyes.

246. Like Barth's protagonist in *Giles Goat-Boy*, Hayy undergoes his first experience of remorse as a direct result of his first contact with another human being. Social contact would

seem to be a necessary condition of sin. But unlike Barth, Ibn Tufayl does not imply that man outside human society is exempt from moral categories; on the contrary, Hayy's obligations when alone are greater than any society could dare to impose on men. But only involvement with another (fallible, finite) subject can cause the sort of compromise of principle over which Hayy now feels guilt. For the assumption that human ties are an impediment to the aspirant after truth, cf. Ghazālī *Munqidh*, tr. Watt, p. 60.

247. Despite the fact that human contact will distract him from his station and may even pose a threat to the purity he has attained, Hayy feels a need which will not be put off to communicate with his fellow man. He rationalizes this feeling in terms of his familiar motive of curiosity, but his eagerness to meet and get to know another member of his species obviously goes deeper; cf. pp. *47, 105.*

248. Absāl preserves the literal notion of reward, the true meaning of which Hayy has discovered. Despite his relative independence of mind, he remains bound within the confines of tradition: reality for him remains obscured by symbol. Thus he knows of God "by name"—and so presumes to teach Hayy, who has "met" Him. He has yet to learn the lesson of Ghazālī (*Munqidh*, tr. Watt, pp. 39-42) to judge ideas not by their source but by their content.

249. Cf. p. *129* and note 221. The names Absāl praises correspond (see pp. *89, 138, 141, 144*) to the attributes Hayy has independently discovered. Only revelation can tell man the names of God, but that personal revelation which comes through the mind is sufficient to inform us of His attributes—and of His essence: see pp. *88-90.*

250. Cf. pp. *7-9.*

251. Cf. pp. *16, 22, 28-29,* and notes *ad loc.*

252. See *Qur'ān* L 36; cf. p. *20.*

253. *Qur'ān* II 36, 264, 375 promises that those who follow God's guidance, spend their wealth in behalf of God's cause, and do so with a good grace, will be divinely rewarded and will know neither fear nor sorrow. Traditionally in Islam the promise has been interpreted to apply to ascetics and the latter part particularly to saints, the "friends" of God.

254. That is, he wished to make him his *Imām*. Absāl has not yet purged his religion of the need for human authority. To the extent of his imperfection, he never will; see p. *154.*

255. From the Muslim point of view the pre-Islamic period of

Arab history forms a barbarous age of ignorance (*jāhiliyya*), a prehistory filled with heroic legends of moral excess and spiritual deficiency. The coming of Islam brought not only national unification and spiritual rationalization, but also far-sweeping legal and moral changes which were seen by the Muslims as the birth of civilization in their part of the world. For the pre-Islamic age, see Ignaz Goldziher's analysis of the sources in *Muslim Studies* (*Muhammedanische Studien*, Halle, 1889-1890) tr. S. M. Stern London, 1967. Ibn Tufayl, in his pseudo-abstract philosophical style refers obliquely to the benefits of Islam (or any religion?) as a civilizing influence—benefits which are at best negative, since man's highest attainments will be reached not through society, but either outside it or in spite of it (cf. p. *154*).

256. For the specific instances of Qur'ānic imagery with which fundamentalist Islam associated concrete entities—the throne, the scales, the "narrow path", etc. see A. J. Wensinck *The Muslim Creed.*

257. Having seen for himself the truth of all that the Prophet conveyed in symbols, Hayy has no difficulty in complying with the requirement that all Muslims give testimony (*shahāda*) of their faith not only in God but in his prophet. Ibn Tufayl consciously leaves his Muslim reader wondering whether Hayy has not been a Muslim all along—and indeed a better Muslim than most—despite his ignorance of the tradition of revelation and his consequent inability to pledge fealty to it.

258. Cf. notes 234, 237 to pp. *136* and *137*. Ibn Tufayl's attitude toward religious obligations is an ambivalent one: He has no quarrel with traditional Islam and surely not with the precedent of the Prophet (*Sunna*), but he refuses to believe that divine ordinances are either necessary or sufficient to the perfection of the supererogatory man. They are not necessary because such a man will discover and obey the truly binding laws himself. They are not sufficient because the supererogatory man will discover further obligations which ultimately absorb his whole life and being. Yet Ibn Tufayl is no antinomian, as page *147* shows: Hayy's quasi-anarchist musings as to why mankind at large is not like himself (at once exempt from law and subject to a more stringent, inner law) can arise only in naivete.

259. For the five pillars of Islam, (1) the confession of faith in God and His prophet Muhammad, (2) the ordained daily devotions, (3) the welfare tax, (4) the fast of Ramadān, and (5) the Pilgrimage to Mecca, see e.g. Ghazālī *Ayyuha 'l-Walad* ed. T. Sabbagh, Beirut, 1959, p. 13. Hayy has already independ-

ently discovered analogues of all five of these fundaments of Islamic faith and practice.

260. To the supererogatory man the most difficult obligations come naturally and seem as pressing as the most minimal demands of morals: one more reason why such a man might be best dissociated from society, for society's sake as well as his own.

261. The nomadic and agricultural character of the life of ancient Israel and the early Christian prejudice against the things of the world in general and the codes of law in particular prevented the full development of commercial law in the Torah or the Gospels—although for both religions the field came into prominence later as the needs for it grew and the legal systems were expanded. In Islam, by contrast, where the earliest environment was commercial (so much so that the language of commerce strongly influenced the rhetoric of the *Qur'ān*) and the fullest efflorescence was urban, the development of commercial law was early and sustained. Ibn Tufayl finds such regulation necessary but (see p. *10*) distasteful—and far beneath the level of involvement of the *fāḍil*, the supererogatory man.

262. According to *Qur'ān* XXV 46, cf. VII 178, the damned "have eyes but do not see, ears but do not hear, hearts yet do not understand. They are like sheep only more astray." Ghazālī interprets the verse as a lesson in Fārābian eschatology: men who do not know the mystic's vision are like beasts in that they do not rise to the heights of which a man is capable; they are worse in that they do not live up to their potential: "for beasts are not given the wings on which to fly to that unseen world." See *Mishkāt al-Anwār* tr. after Gairdner p. 94.

Ibn Tufayl assigns the fate of animals to men only if they have never known God. Those who have known and lost Him suffer the pain of separation, a true Hell, more Islamic than the Platonism of Fārābī might allow, yet a Hell that is reached by a failing Fārābī would recognize as damning: failure of moral and intellectual nerve; (cf. pp. *97*, *131*, *151*). Ibn Tufayl softens the blow with the reminder that the function of organized religion is to firm the resolve of the people. As Matthew Arnold wrote, religion is necessary because "moral rules apprehended as ideas first, and then rigorously followed as laws, are, and must be, for the sage only. The mass of mankind have neither force of intellect enough to apprehend them clearly as ideas, nor force of character enough to follow them strictly as laws." "On Marcus Aurelius" reprinted in Appendix II of *The Stoic and Epicurean Philosophers* ed. W. J. Oates, New York, 1940, pp. 593-594. It is presumably because the majority still insists on proving this principle true that even today new or heterodox ideas and socio-moral schemes take shelter behind quasi-religious movements which provide their adherents with an intellectual authority and moral discipline they would otherwise lack, thus forming a counter-orthodoxy of their own.

263. A Sūfī-like body is meant. The Sūfīs err if they suppose that their rules or their order can give them anything of what can only be found by struggling alone, mind, body, and soul, with God.

264. Human factionalism is nothing in the eyes of the One Truth: Muhammad is traditionally believed to have said "My people will divide into 73 different sects, and only one of them will be saved." The Qurʾānic characterization (XXIII 55, XXX 31) of "every faction delighted with its own" is interpreted by Ghazālī along with this tradition as referring to the problem of intellectual diversity (on the second page of his *Munqidh*; cf. Ashʿarī's introduction to the *Maqālāt-al-Islāmiyyīn*.) The question of how men can differ when there is but one truth is as much a problem for the rationalist as for those who place their faith in revelation. The answer suggested by Ibn Tufayl is that men's preoccupation with the things of the senses has prevented them from penetrating the confusing array of symbolic representations with which they are presented and thus left them unable to discern the naked truth.

265. Cf. *Qurʾān* XXV 43 ff. and Ghazālī's discussion of it *Mishkāt*, tr. Gairdner, p. 159. To the radical monotheist the notion of a man without some god is virtually inconceivable; the courage he receives from God and the devotion he returns seem to him to be misattributed and misapplied by the godless; he can only assume that the values and principles in terms of which a man orients his life (cf. pp. *152-153*) are his gods. It was, perhaps, because Nietzsche feared this might be true that he so abhorred objective value systems, "the ghosts of God." Ibn Tufayl again identifies distraction (this time hedonic) with polytheism, idolatry (*shirk*), cf. p. *116* and note 193.

266. Cf. *Qurʾān* CII 1-2.

267. With Muhammad (and under similar circumstances of personal rejection), Hayy Ibn Yaqzān now sees that no human power, but only grace can give man the truth; see Ghazālī, *Munqidh*, tr. Watt, p. 25; see also Marinus, *Life of Proclus*, xxii. But bear in mind that both for the Platonist and the radical monotheist alike human powers *are* grace.

268.   Cf. *Qur'ān* LXXXIII 14.

269.   "As for the faithless, whether you warn them or not it will make no difference, they still will have no faith. God has sealed their hearts, and shrouded their eyes and ears. Theirs will be an awesome punishment." *Qur'ān* II 6-7, cf. XLVII 18, quoted by Ghazālī, *Munqidh*, tr. Watt, p. 63.

270.   "There is no punishment in Hell more painful than being veiled from God. . . And in Paradise there is no pleasure more perfect than not being veiled." Sarī *apud* Hujwīrī, *Kashf al-Mahjūb* (literally, "The Mystery Unveiled"), tr. after R. A. Nicholson, p. 111. cf. Ghazālī, *Ma'ārij al-Quds*, Cairo, 1927, pp. 167 ff. See also p. *131*. Cf. Fārābī *al-Madīnatu-l-Fādila*, Beirut, 1959, p. 118.

271.   Ghazālī warns at length of the dangers of becoming actively involved in religion for self-deceptively worldly reasons. *Bidāyat al-Hidāya*, tr. Montgomery Watt in *The Faith and Practice of Al-Ghazali*, London, 1963 as "The Beginning of Guidance," pp. 86-90. He recognizes such temptations in himself *Munqidh* tr. Watt p. 56, and assesses the prevalence of such attitudes among his colleagues as one of the major social problems of his day, *ibid.*, pp. 71, 83-85.

272.   "God made a covenant with those who received the Book: 'You must expound it to mankind and not hide it from them'—but they flung it away, sold it for a bad price, and evil is all they got in return." *Qur'ān* III 184.

273.   The lamp spoken of in the Qur'ānic "Light Verse" is found "in houses which God has allowed to be raised up and there let His name be spoken and His praise be offered morning and evening by men whom business and selling do not distract from the thought of God and prayer, and charity—who fear a day when hearts and eyes will be turned inwards." *Qur'ān* XXIV 36-37.

274.   "Whoever desires the hereafter, bends his efforts to it and is faithful will find his efforts welcome to God." *Qur'ān* XVII 20.

275.   Cf. *Qur'ān* LXXIX 37-39.

276.   Ghazālī assigns the lowest level of religiosity, "the husk of the husk," to those whose profession of faith goes no further than lip-service. Their hypocrisy will "save their necks" from human punishment, since man cannot "look inside his fellows' hearts" to determine the sincerity of their faith; but it cannot, of course, bring them happiness in this world or save them from divine punishment in the next. *Ihyā' 'Ulūm ad-Dīn* XXXV I ii.

277.   For *Qur'ān* XXIV 40, the "darkness verse" and Ghazālī's discussion of it (*Mishkāt al-Anwār* epilogue), see note 55 above.

278. In the context of the Darkness Verse, Ibn Tufayl interprets *Qur'ān* XIX 72, God's promise of hellfire for all mankind, only the just and Godfearing being saved from it, as applying to the present life of darkness and confusion, and warning of the danger for all men of perpetual isolation from God if they choose their pleasures and their ways unwisely.

279. The notion of the completeness of scripture is a dogma characteristic of the fundamentalist approach to revelation, expressing the emphasis of traditional religion on obedience, for it seems to imply that faith, like works, is a matter of will—scripture is a positive fact, not to be tampered with by the mind of man: the best interpretation is *no* interpretation (see note 283). Hayy's endorsement of this dogma must be viewed in light of his "*kitman*" (see note 282); and Ibn Tufayl's enunciation of it must be qualified by Ghazālī's doctrine that for the élite an allegorical interpretation is necessary where a literal one is impossible and his assertion that for fear of misleading the masses Muhammad did not reveal all he knew. For the wise, at least, some scope remains for the exercise of intelligence.

280. As Ghazālī points out, one man's medicine is another man's poison, *Munqidh*, tr. Watt, p. 29. Hayy does not reject the image of the truth conveyed by traditional religion, nor does he scorn the discipline by which traditional religion controls men's violent tendencies. But he does recognize that such concrete imagery would only be an impediment to his own higher understanding and he cannot discover in himself the need for the crude discipline of the cave. He does not abandon the law but lives it freely, and ranges beyond its demands. He does not forsake revelation, but sees within it meanings which human language can convey only stutteringly. In apologizing for his failure, in refuting the Bātiniyya, to present a complete history and systematic refutation of the movement, Ghazālī points out that much of what the movement teaches is true, and remarks politely that there is a man for every task: *Fadā'ih al-Bātiniyya* ed. Badawy, Cairo, 1964, pp. 9 and 47. Hayy likewise has no wish to offend the common people, but must decline to stay among them.

281. Thus the *Qur'ān*, of the rout of the unbelievers: "If the faithless fight with you they turn and run. They find no one to help or save them. This was God's way before and you will never find a change in the ways of God." XLVIII 23, cf. XXXV 41-2. Muhammad's words of encouragement were to become the motto of the fundamentalist Salafiyyah movement: see "Our Nation's Past and Present and the Cure of its Ills" in *Al-'Urwatu-l-Wuthqā*, "The Firm Bond" by Jamāl ad-Dīn al-Afghānī and

Muhammad Abduh, Cairo, 1957, p. 13 (first published in journal form, Paris 1884). The same words were to express for Ibn Rushd the theological basis of his rejection of the notions of divine caprice in general and temporal creation in particular, see *Tahāfut at-Tahāfut*, ed. Bouyges, p. 523. With his usual facility, Ibn Tufayl reads the passage as a manifesto of his own attitude of qualified pluralism and toleration: God has never demanded that men surpass their abilities, he will not do so at present. The *Qur'ān*-supported notion that God will not impose an impossible task is Mu'tazilite; Ash'arī maintained that God may do so if He will.

282. The obligation of self-defense by concealment of one's true convictions and even dissimulation for the sake of preserving human knowledge of the truth is well established in practice and recognized in theory by the non-conformists of the Islamic east. For a comparison of this practice with that of the inhabitants of Communist countries, see Czeslaw Milosz, *The Captive Mind*, New York, 1951, ch. 3.

283. For the duty of *balkafa*, humble and unquestioning acceptance of the theological given *bilā kayf*, 'not asking the reason why,' see Wensinck, *Muslim Creed*, London, 1965, pp. 86, 116, 190, 207, 238. The champion of this "knownothing" position, Ahmad Ibn Hanbal (d. 855), apparently hoped that the establishment of positive dogmas particularly on the difficult problems of anthropomorphism would deaden the (perverse) urge to raise such problems. Philosophical perversity, however, was not so easily killed; and, as Wensinck points out, p. 207, Ibn Hanbal's dogmatism was ultimately replaced by a doctrine of divine transcendence such as that of Ghazālī and Ibn Tufayl. Ibn Tufayl preserves dogmatism, however, as sufficient (and often necessary) for the masses—in keeping with Ghazālī's elitist stratification of the faithful *Ihyā' 'Ulūm ad-Dīn*, XXXV 1.

284. To traditional Islam, as to any traditional religion, innovation (*bid'a*) is the mark of heresy. Ibn Tufayl has somewhat greater confidence in his hero's capacity to think for himself than the point of view of, say, Salāmān would allow: just one more reason for leaving him outside the walls of civilization. Ibn Tufayl is as confident of Hayy's abilities as he is despairing of the intellectual powers of most men, thus his double standard on the question of independent thought—As Ghazālī had warned, for the common mentality religious speculation will create only confusion; the unwary navigator in the dangerous sea of monotheism will most likely capsize if he attempts to go it alone. He will become easy prey to heretical scavengers unless somehow his

thoughts are salvaged by the suasions of *kalām*; cf. *Ihyā' 'Ulūm ad-Dīn*, XXXV 1; *Munqidh* p. 2.

285. "Once blind faith has been left behind there is no hope of going back to it. For one essential characteristic of naive belief is that the believer not know that his belief is naive. When he finds out, his faith is shattered, and it cannot be patched up or pasted together, but must be melted down and remade." Ghazālī, speaking of his own awakening, *Munqidh*, ed. Jabre, p. 15, tr. Watt, p. 27. E. R. Dodds quotes from this passage at the head of Ch. VII of *The Greeks and the Irrational*, Berkeley, 1964, where he speaks of aspects of Plato's role in the awakening of Western thought.

286. Ibn Tufayl alludes to the vivid description of the Judgement Day in the opening verses of *Qur'ān* LVI. "Those who run in the forefront," he interprets to be the "supererogatory" men, whose works and faith surpass the bare minimum demanded of the masses. Cf. Origen: "Some will take the lead and hasten with swifter speed to the highest goal, others will follow them at a close interval, while others will be left far behind; and so the process will go on through the innumerable ranks of those who are making progress and becoming reconciled to God from their state of enmity, until it reaches even to the last enemy, who is called death, in order that he, too, may be destroyed and remain an enemy no longer." *De Principiis* III vi 6, tr. Butterworth, pp. 251-252. For an introduction to the preliminary obligations of the supererogatory Muslim, that is his duties that go beyond the call of duty, see Ghazālī, *Bidāyat al-Hidāya*, "The Beginning of Guidance", tr. Watt in *The Faith and Practice of Al-Ghazali*.

287. Ghazālī too had found it necessary quietly to withdraw from a harried and much scrutinized life. He discovered, much against his will, that he was in grave danger of becoming a hypocrite and a time-server unless he removed himself from the stage of his students' demands and the arena of emulation with his colleagues long enough to examine himself and his life and thinking in solitude with his conscience and his God; see *Munqidh*, tr. Watt, pp. 56-59. For Hayy the danger is perhaps less visible, but equally grave: If he stays among men—even for the service of the illusory ideal of saving them (the ultimate temptation)—he will become one of them. He will become involved in human concerns, lose the purity of his experience; ultimately, he will become subject to doubt and delusion, like the rest. For ordinary men, all this may be necessary, but for Hayy Ibn Yaqzān, a higher course has been marked out.

288. The error spoken of would seem to be that of identifying

the self with the Godhead, which, as Ibn Tufayl indicates, is the main threat to the mystic enterprise.   See pp. *4-5, 129.*

289.   Turning from his friend and disciple to the wider circle of his peers in understanding, Ibn Tufayl pleads one final time for recognition of the fact that what he has learned is ultimately ineffable—the task of reason is to argue and to name and finally to point toward the course on which the individual must set out for himself, a course which leads where his guide can no longer take him.

Notes to the Introduction

CHAPTER I—THE LIFE OF IBN TUFAYL

(Pages 3-6)

1. For the life of Ibn Tufayl see Léon Gauthier, *Ibn Tufayl, sa vie, ses œuvres.* Paris, 1909. The reports quoted will be found in R. Dozy ed. *The History of the Almohades* by 'Abdu-l-Wāhid al-Marrākushī, Leiden, 1881. pp. 169-75.

CHAPTER II—EDUCATIONAL PHILOSOPHY

(Pages 7-22)

2. pp. *33-4.* In this and in all subsequent references, pages numbered in italics refer to the pagination of the standard Arabic text of *Hayy Ibn Yaqzān* edited by Léon Gauthier, Beirut, 1936. The translation is keyed for reference to Gauthier.

3. p. *34.* For the higher phases of Hayy's mimesis see pp. *105-6.*

4. cf. Aristotle *Physics* I 1, 184b10.

5. cf. Wolfgang Kohler *The Mentality of Apes* p. 22.

6. p. *34.*

7. p. *35.*

8. pp. *36-7.*

9. p. *38.*

10. pp. *39-44.*

11. pp. *45-8.*

12. p. *54.*

13. p. *48.*

14. pp. *47-50.*

15. p. *53.*

16. pp. *78, 80.*

17. pp. *56-72.*

18. p. *64.*

19. p. *72.*

20. pp. *72* ff.

239

21. pp. 75-7.
22. p. *80*.
23. pp. *81-83*.
24. pp. *90 ff*.
25. *loc. cit.*
26. pp. *105-106*.
27. p. *135*.
28. For Dewey's philosophy of education, see, for example, *The Child and the Curriculum*. Chicago, 1902; and the essays collected in *Education Today*. New York, 1940. For Dewey's conception of the relationship of education and society see *The School and Society*; *Democracy and Education*; and *The Public and its Problems*. For his educational philosophy in general see Paul Schilpp, ed., *The Philosophy of John Dewey*, New York, 1939; and Joseph Ratner, ed., *Intelligence in the Modern World, John Dewey's Philosophy*, New York, 1939.
29. See, for example, Ratner, pp. 606-14.
30. *loc. cit.*
31. pp. *75, 78, 48, 46*.
32. pp. *147-148*.
33. *Emile*, pp. 6-7.
34. *Ibid.*, p. 5.
35. *Ibid.*, pp. 172 ff.
36. *Ibid.*, p. 5.
37. *loc. cit.*
38. pp. *127-130*.
39. pp. *27-29*, cf. p. *130*, and Ghazālī *K. Madnūn as-Saghīr*.
40. pp. *73-74*.
41. pp. *88-89*.
42. p. *25*.
43. For Ibn Tufayl's characterization of Islam as a phase of the likening of man to God see p. *106*.
44. Tor Andrae *Muhammad, The Man and his Faith*, tr. Theophil Menzil, New York, 1960, p. 62 (first German edition, Göttingen, 1932).
45. *Deuteronomy* xi 26.

CHAPTER III—RELIGIOUS PHILOSOPHY

(Pages 23-51)

46. p. *4*.
47. *Aristotle a complete exposition of his works and thought*, New York, 1953, pp. 175-82 (first edition, London, 1923).

48. *A Preface to Morals,* New York, 1929, pp. 23-30.
49. *Ibid.* p. 26, quoting from Whitehead's Lowell Lectures, 1925, reprinted as *Science and the Modern World.*
50. *loc. cit.*
51. See F. C. Copleston's 1948 BBC debate with Bertrand Russell on the existence of God, reprinted in *The Existence of God* ed. John Hick, New York, 1964, pp. 167-91, n.b. p. 186.
52. "Nirvana," poem by Florence Jeanne Goodman, in *Four Lyric Poets,* Los Angeles, 1967.
53. cf. W. F. R. Hardie "The Final Good in Aristotle's Ethics" *Philosophy* XL (1965) pp. 277-95, reprinted in *Aristotle a collection of critical essays* ed. J. M. E. Moravcsik, Garden City, New York, 1967, pp. 297-322.
54. "Mystery and Meaning" in *Discerning the Signs of the Times,* New York, 1949, pp. 152-173.
55. p. *15.*
56. pp. *127-34.*
57. p. *134.*
58. p. *5.*
59. p. *7.*
60. p. *9.*
61. pp. *55-90.*
62. p. *1.*
63. pp. *4-5.*
64. p. *7.*
65. p. *153.*
66. pp. *108-120.*
67. pp. *3-4.*
68. p. *20.*
69. p. *7.*
70. p. *11.*
71. pp. *14-5.*
72. *Ibn Tufayl, sa vie, ses œuvres,* pp. 59 ff.
73. See translation, note 1.
74. Quoted in Corbin, *Avicenna and the Visionary Recital,* New York, 1960, p. 17. (first French edition, Paris, 1954).
75. p. *12.*
76. pp. *5-6.*
77. *Avicenna and the Visionary Recital,* p. 39.
78. pp. *10-11.*
79. p. *15.*
80. pp. *3, 132.*
81. p. *137.*

82. p. *10*.
83. p. *11*.
84. pp. *126-7*.
85. "The Philosophical Significance of Ibn Tufayl's *Haiy Ibn Yaqzān*", *Islamic Culture*, XXII, #1, p. 66.
86. "The Principal Subject of Ibn Tufayl's Hayy Ibn Yaqzān", *Journal of Near Eastern Studies*, XV, pp. 40-46.
87. p. *144*.
88. p. *145*.
89. p. *11*.
90. Gauthier, *Ibn Tufayl, sa vie, ses œuvres*, p. 7. The Almohades, it must be remembered, had curtailed the power of the Malikite conservatives and founded their own theological claims upon the doctrine of monotheism, *tawhīd*, from which they took their name. This doctrine, of course, had been given one of its loftiest statements by Ghazālī, who had himself recognized affinities between the "true" philosophers and the highest level of monotheism. Ibn Tufayl treats these affinities as conclusive evidence of the ultimate identity of the truths of reason *and* revelation with the "inner meaning" of scripture. Thus while Ibn Tufayl recognizes certain dangers in speaking openly of his subject, one could hardly claim that the *immediate* environment in which he worked was hostile to his philosophical enterprise.
91. See Ch. I above.
92. pp. *145-6*.
93. p. *16*.
94. pp. *139-41*.
95. pp. *145-7*.
96. p. *14*.
97. pp. *146-8*.
98. See Ibn Khaldun *Muqaddimah* tr. Franz Rosenthal, New York, 1958, e.g. vol. I p. 79 and vol. II p. 417 *inter alia*. This widespread Islamic justification of rule is traced to Ibn Mas'ūd (7th century) by Rosenthal in his introduction lxxiv note 99. It is found also in the *Mishnah, Pirke Avoth* III 2, "R. Chanina, the Vice-High-Priest, said, 'Pray for the welfare of the government, since but for the fear thereof men would swallow each other alive.'" (tr. J. H. Hertz, p. 47).

CHAPTER IV—MAN AND SOCIETY

(Pages 52-91)

99. *A Discourse on the Origin of Inequality*, tr. G. D. H. Cole, New York, 1950 (first French edition, 1754). p. 191.

100. Ibid., p. 193.
101. sc. in Chapter II above.
102. p. *4.*
103. p. *45.*
104. pp. *127-30.*
105. pp. *28-9.*
106. p. *146.*
107. pp. *78-80.*
108. pp. *76-7.*
109. *Lord of the Flies*, New York, 1959, p. 27.
110. pp. *23* and *27.*
111. pp. *102-3.*
112. pp. *20-24.*
113. pp. *33-38.*
114. pp. *31-32.*
115. pp. *37-38.*
116. pp. *53-54.*
117. *Emile*, pp. 147-149.
118. pp. *39-45.*
119. *Lord of the Flies*, p. 7.
120. *Ibid.*, p. 8.
121. *Ibid.*, p. 5.
122. *Ibid.*, p. 8.
123. *Ibid.*, p. 45.
124. *Ibid.*, p. 12.
125. *The Captive Mind*, tr. Jane Zielonko, New York, 1951, pp. 25-26.
126. *Lord of the Flies*, p. 85.
127. p. *107.*
128. See *De Anima* II 3, 414 b, Avicenna *Najāt* II 6 i-iii.
129. *Metaphysics* IX 3, 1047.
130. pp. *93-4.*
131. p. *48.*
132. p. *50.*
133. p. *45.*
134. p. *34.*
135. p. *107.*
136. p. *35.*
137. p. *47.*
138. *Lord of the Flies*, pp. 8, 10.
139. *Ibid.*, p. 84.
140. *Ibid.*, p. 34.
141. *Ibid.*, p. 10.

142. *Ibid.*, p. 105.
143. *Ibid.*, p. 19.
144. *Ibid.*, pp. 72-76.
145. *Ibid.*, p. 17.
146. *Ibid.*, p. 43.
147. *Ibid.*, p. 46.
148. *Ibid.*, pp. 16-17.
149. *Ibid.*, pp. 26-27.
150. *Ibid.*, p. 37.
151. *Ibid.*, p. 51.
152. *Ibid.*, p. 15.
153. *Ibid.*, p. 33-34.
154. *Ibid.*, pp. 72-77.
155. *Ibid.*, pp. 127-132.
156. *Ibid.*, p. 82.
157. *Ibid.*, pp. 134-135.
158. *Ibid.*, pp. 140-141.
159. pp. *30-31.*
160. *Timaeus*, 44, 69-70.
161. *Lord of the Flies*, notes p. 189.
162. *Muqaddimah*, tr. Franz Rosenthal, New York, 1958, vol. I, pp. 253-254.
163. *Civilization and Its Discontents*, tr. James Strachey, New York, 1961, p. 58.
164. *Ibid.*, p. 59.
165. loc. cit.
166. *Civilization and Its Discontents*, p. 92. This disturbing last page was last revised by Freud in 1931 as he watched with mounting anxiety the ominous rise of Nazi power in Germany.
167. *Lord of the Flies*, pp. 56-57.
168. loc. cit.
169. *Lord of the Flies*, p. 11; cf. p. 33.
170. *Ibid.*, pp. 161-167.
171. *Ibid.*, notes p. 189.
172. *Ibid.*, pp. 24, 167.
173. p. *137.*
174. *Lord of the Flies*, p. 54.
175. *A New View of Society*, p. 1.
176. *Walden Two*, p. 196.
177. *Ibid.*, p. 223.
178. *Ibid.*, pp. 8, 30, 208-209.
179. *Ibid.*, p. 23.
180. *Ibid.*, p. 78.

181. *Ibid.*, p. 45.
182. *Ibid.*, pp. 25-26.
183. *Ibid.*, p. 46.
184. *Ibid.*, p. 29.
185. *Ibid.*, p. 48.
186. *Ibid.*, pp. 144-145.
187. *Ibid.*, p. 155.
188. *Ibid.*, pp. 97-98, 107-108.
189. *Ibid.*, p. 8.
190. *Ibid.*, p. 104.
191. *Ibid.*, p. 226.
192. *Ibid.*, p. 104.
193. *loc. cit.*
194. *loc. cit.*, pp. 296-297.
195. *Walden Two*, p. 296.
196. *Ibid.*, p. 6.
197. *Ibid.*, p. 9.
198. *Ibid.*, p. 76.
199. *Ibid.*, p. 54.
200. *Ibid.*, p. 73.
201. *Ibid.*, pp. 61-62.
202. *The Rebel*, New York, 1951.
203. *Walden* Two, p. 101.
204. *Ibid.*, p. 88.
205. *Ibid.*, pp. 96-97, 142.
206. *Ibid.*, p. 102.
207. *Ibid.*, pp. 88-92.
208. *Ibid.*, p. 160.
209. *loc. cit.*
210. *Walden Two*, p. 131.
211. *Ibid.*, p. 82.
212. *Thus Spoke Zarathustra*, tr. R. J. Hollingdale, Baltimore, 1961, p. 46.
213. *Walden Two*, p. 151.
214. *Ibid.*, p. 159.
215. *Ibid.*, pp. 225-256.
216. pp. *10-11.*
217. p. *4.*
218. *Walden Two*, p. 223.
219. *Walden; or Life in the Woods*, New York, 1950, p. 180, (first edition, 1854).
220. *Ibid.*, p. 88.
221. *Ibid.* pp. 158-159.

222. *Ibid.*, p. 88.
223. p. 48.
224. p. 4.
225. *Walden*, p. 159.
226. pp. 48-9.
227. *Walden*, p. 127.
228. *Ibid.*, p. 119.
229. *Ibid.*, pp. 51, 71, 77, 90, 79, 122.
230. *Ibid.*, pp. 93-94.
231. *Ibid.*, p. 19.
232. *Ecclesiastes* iii 2.